Contemporary
British Fiction

Contemporary British Fiction

Edited by Richard J. Lane,
Rod Mengham and Philip Tew

polity

First published in 2003 by Polity Press in association with Blackwell
Publishers Ltd, a Blackwell Publishing Company.

Editorial office:
Polity Press
65 Bridge Street
Cambridge CB2 1UR, UK

Marketing and production:
Blackwell Publishers Ltd
108 Cowley Road
Oxford OX4 1JF, UK

Published in the USA by:
Blackwell Publishers Inc.
350 Main Street
Malden MA 02148, USA

A catalogue record for this book is available from the British Library.

Library of Congress Cataloging-in-Publication Data

Contemporary British fiction / edited by Richard Lane, Rod Mengham,
and Philip Tew.
      p. cm.
Includes bibliographical references and index.
   ISBN 0–7456–2866–4 (acid-free paper)—ISBN 0–7456–2867–2
(pbk. : acid-free paper)
   1. English fiction—20th century—History and criticism. I. Lane, Richard, J.,
1966– II. Mengham, Rod, 1953– III. Tew, Philip.
PR881.C66 2003
823'.91409—dc21
                                                          2002008388

Typeset in 10.5 on 12 pt Sabon
by Kolam Information Services Pvt. Ltd, Pondicherry, India
Printed in Great Britain by MPG Books Ltd, Bodmin, Cornwall

This book is printed on acid-free paper.

Contents

Contributors

Stephen Baker   is the author of *The Fiction of Postmodernity* (Edinburgh University Press, 2000), and was Course Director on the MA in Postmodernism and Postcolonialism at South Bank University until 2002. He has published widely on Salman Rushdie, and is currently writing his first novel.

Tamás Bényei   is Reader at the Department of British Studies, University of Debrecen, Hungary. He has published articles on a number of postwar and contemporary British novelists (including Fowles, Powell, Golding, Nye, Ishiguro, Rushdie, Ballard, Martin Amis, and Chatwin) as well as on Latin American, American and Hungarian literature and literary theory. He has written three books in Hungarian. His *Acts of Attention: Figure and Narrative in Postwar British Fiction* was published by Peter Lang in 1999.

John Brannigan   teaches English at College Dublin University. He is the author of *New Historicism and Cultural Materialism* (Macmillan, 1998), *Brendan Behan: Cultural Nationalism and the Revisionist Writer* (Four Courts, 2002), *Literature, Culture and Society in England, 1945–1965* (forthcoming Edwin Mellen, 2002), and *Orwell to the Present: Literature in England, 1945–2000* (forthcoming Palgrave, 2003). He is currently working on a book-length study of the novels of Pat Barker.

Brad Buchanan   has completed his PhD in English at Stanford University and has recently taken up a position at the California State University at Sacramento. He has published articles on Samuel Beckett, Christine Brooke-Rose and Aldous Huxley, and is working on a book manuscript based on his dissertation entitled: *Oedipus Against Freud: Myth and the Critique of Humanism in Modern British Literature*.

James Diedrick is the Howard L. McGregor Professor of the Humanities at Albion College, Michigan, USA, where he teaches courses on nineteenth- and twentieth-century British literature. He is the author of *Understanding Martin Amis* (Columbia, SC: University of South Carolina Press, 1995) and essays on Amis, Ian McEwan, Charlotte Brontë, Charles Dickens, George Eliot and John Ruskin. He is also manager of the Martin Amis Web, an independent web site containing criticism, interviews and a selection of Amis's essays (*http://martinamis.albion.edu*).

Robert Eaglestone works on contemporary and twentieth-century literature, literary theory and philosophy. His publications include *Ethical Criticism: Reading after Levinas* (Edinburgh University Press, 1997), *Doing English* (Routledge, 2000), *Postmodernism and Holocaust Denial* (Cambridge: Icon Press, 2001) and articles on Beckett, ethics, contemporary European philosophy, science, the Holocaust, archaeology and historiography. He is currently working on a book called *The Holocaust and the Postmodern*. He is a literature advisor to the British Council and is the series editor of *Routledge Critical Thinkers*.

Liorah Anne Golomb is an independent scholar with a doctorate in Drama from the University of Toronto. She has written on several contemporary American and English playwrights, including Shepard, O'Neill, Pinter, Churchill, Hare, Barker and Peter Barnes, and has published articles on the work of Barnes and Hare in *Essays in Theatre/Etudes théâtrales* and *Modern Drama*. She is currently working on a book about the plays of Peter Barnes.

Dominic Head is Professor of English at Brunel University. He is the author of *The Modernist Short Story* (CUP, 1992), *Nadine Gordimer* (CUP, 1994), *J. M. Coetzee* (CUP, 1997) and *The Cambridge Introduction to Modern British Fiction, 1950–2000* (CUP, 2002). He is currently writing a book on Ian McEwan.

Anthony Ilona has taught a range of subjects in the field of postcolonial studies at Queen Mary College, University of London, and the University of Sussex. He is former managing editor of the literary journal *Wasafiri* and is currently preparing a monograph in the field of his special interest, Caribbean literature.

Richard J. Lane is Senior Lecturer in English at South Bank University, London, and Honorary Reader in British and Post-colonial Studies at the University of Debrecen, Hungary. He is also co-director of the London Network for Modern Fiction Studies and is the editor of *The Malcolm Lowry Review*. Publications include *Jean Baudrillard* (Routledge, 2000), *Mrs. Dalloway: Literary Masterpieces* (Gale Group, 2001) and *Beckett and Philosophy* (ed.) (Palgrave, 2002). Forthcoming books include *Reading Walter Benjamin* (Manchester University Press, 2003) and *Contemporary British Fiction: An Introductory Study* (co-author, Continuum).

Rod Mengham is a Senior Lecturer in the English Faculty at Cambridge University, where he is also Curator of Works of Art at Jesus College. He is the author of books on Charles Dickens, Emily Brontë and Henry Green, as well as of *The Descent of Language* (Bloomsbury, 1993). He has edited collections of essays on contemporary fiction, violence and avant-garde art, and the fiction of the 1940s. He is also editor of the Equipage series of poetry pamphlets, and his own poems have been published under the title *Unsung: New and Selected Poems* (Folio/Salt, 1996; 2nd edn., 2001). He is currently working on *Modern Literature: An Introduction* for Polity, and on *Upward Spiral: Edward Upward and the Politics of Writing* for OUP.

Kim Middleton Meyer is currently a doctoral candidate in English at the University of Notre Dame and an instructor at Washington College, Maryland, USA. She is the author of the article 'Tan'talizing Others: Multicultural Anxiety and the New Orientalism' ed. Jim Collins, in *High-Pop: Making Culture into Entertainment* (Blackwells, 2002).

Drew Milne is the Judith E. Wilson Lecturer in Drama and Poetry, Faculty of English, University of Cambridge. He co-edited *Marxist Literary Theory* with Terry Eagleton and edits the journal *Parataxis: Modernism and Modern Writing*. His books of poetry include: *Bench Marks* (Alfred David Editions, 1998), *The Damage: New and Selected Poems* (Salt Publishing) and *Mars Disarmed* (The Figures, Great Barrington, 2002).

Philip Tew is MA Course Director in the School of English, University of Central England in Birmingham, and honorary Reader in English and Aesthetics at Debrecen University, Hungary. His publications include *B. S. Johnson: A Critical Reading* (Manchester University Press, 2001), 'Reconsidering Literary Interpretation' in *After Postmodernism: An Introduction to Critical Realism* (Athlone, 2001), and a chapter on Beckett and Habermas in *Beckett and*

Philosophy (St Martin's Press, 2002). He is joint Director of the London Network for Modern Fiction Studies and an editorial advisor for *HJEAS: The Hungarian Journal for English and American Studies* and *The Malcolm Lowry Review.*

Mark Wormald   is Director of Studies and Fellow in English at Pembroke College, Cambridge. His essay on Salman Rushdie and Jeanette Winterson appeared in *An Introduction to Contemporary Fiction: International writing in English since 1970*, ed. Rod Mengham (Polity, 1999), and his edition of *The Pickwick Papers* was published by Penguin in 2000.

General Introduction:
Contemporary British Fiction

Rod Mengham

It is one of the central paradoxes of contemporary British fiction that much of it – much of the best of it – is concerned with other times and other places. During the last thirty years, the period covered by the essays in this book, the contemporary has been linked to a sense of endless change, to the rapid turnover of novelties, to the commodification of artistic experiment; attitudes to the past have been influenced by marketing, by a consumer demand for the *retro*, by an investment in history reproducible as style. British fiction has reflected this behaviour as mechanically as any other art form, but it has also recovered a quite different sense of direction, an alternative vocation, which is that of the historical novel. Perhaps rather surprisingly, the history of Britain and of the peoples inhabiting it, the temporal and spatial relationships that determine the margins of Britishness, have all been questioned and amended by the more ambitious fictional projects of a time in which the scale of history itself has been revised. The millennial shadow set a formal limit on an era whose own history had been dominated by political narratives that were either exhausted or under threat. Fiction concerned itself with the attempt to understand the individual's relationship to these narratives, with the extent to which individual experience confirmed or denied their meanings.

The fiction of Graham Swift and A. L. Kennedy, as read by Tamás Bényei and Philip Tew respectively, revolves constantly around the issues of historical meaning. Swift's writing construes the formation of the subject in terms of a process of malformation, of damage incurred by the failure to negotiate the gap between the movement of history and the rhythms of ordinary lives. Failing to participate, to share in the collective agency that gives a pattern and meaning to events, the subject experiences the public world in terms of submission to control, more often than not of an economic variety, limiting human relationships to the scope of business agreements (as in Swift's novel *The Sweet Shop Owner*). For A. L. Kennedy, the separation of public and private does not protect individuals from the vicissitudes of history, but renders them invisible, without presence or effect in the world of social meanings; the characters in her stories arrive at an awareness that Bényei ascribes to the protagonist of Swift's *Shuttlecock*, a numbing realization of the emptiness of existence, of their utter dislocation from any means of interpreting their own lives and making them cohere. This rerouting of significance, away from the characters that provide a focus for reading, is made even more striking by appearing in narratives that take the form of a quest, as many of Kennedy's do. The suspicion that meaning follows a trajectory quite different from that being traced by the characters themselves is endemic to Kennedy's fiction; it is also an organizing characteristic of the elaborate compositions of Kazuo Ishiguro, explored in this volume by Mark Wormald.

Ishiguro concentrates on British history only rarely, but in his writing he probes patiently the action of memory that has both private and public dimensions. Personal memory intersects obliquely but powerfully with some of the most turbulent currents of twentieth-century politics; Wormald considers the centrality of artists in Ishiguro's fictional world, figures whose work neighbours on moments of ideological crisis, sometimes encapsulating an historical episode, sometimes contributing to the form it takes. The history recorded by this fiction is mediated by distance, revised by a sensibility that is always in the process of selecting, framing, rearranging. This editing is exemplified in the points of view of several of Ishiguro's protagonists, but its manipulations and displacements are kept at a suitable distance, made the objects of enquiry in a narrative structure that engages its readers in a critique of the artistic imagination.

The relations between author, reader and character are controlled very subtly in Ishiguro's prose – their situations are parallel but demarcated by rational contemplation. This is far from being the case in Iain Sinclair's fiction, where all three are drawn inexorably into the same energy field. For Sinclair, history assails the present, but the pressure it exerts is always felt in particular places. Writing provides a means of investigating the constructions that have been placed, literally and metaphorically, on the urban landscape of past and present London. The most influential and widely disseminated versions of that history are rarely the most valuable or revealing, and the unequal relationship between truth and power in the fashioning of rival versions is what motivates the urgency and momentum of Sinclair's investigations. His fiction searches for, and discloses, the hidden potency of ignored or suppressed or displaced accounts of what has determined the present contours of urban life; it takes the form of a quest, a project of decoding, in which every clue brings closer the realization that the past has scripted the present. The author's purpose is to sustain the work already begun by others, to articulate a collaborative project that echoes with reminders of other texts.

Will Self's predominantly urban enquiries cover much of the same ground, physically and conceptually. In 'The North London Book of the Dead' (1996) and *How the Dead Live* (2000), the dead live side by side with the living, in a different part of London. Self's enthusiastically literal rendering of the idea that the past and the present are mutually permeating gives a peculiar immediacy to the historical dimension by mapping it onto physical space. The extension of the conceit is typical of a writer for whom the secret structures of contemporary culture must be teased into view by a method of literary estrangement. As Liorah Golomb shows, this can be achieved by the use of shock tactics like Kafka's, or by slowly acclimatizing the reader to a radically revised view of commonly held values and relationships. Fiction is a laboratory in which various experiments with consciousness are conducted with great deliberateness and precision.

For both Self and Sinclair, London lives are shadowed by an alternative order of experience. It requires literary cunning to decipher the relevant connections in Self's fiction, while in Sinclair's work, the debt owed to history triggers anxiety in author, character and reader alike. The presence of the past is registered through an encounter with revenants, for whom writing functions almost as a form of invocation. According to John Brannigan, commenting on Pat Barker's work, this textual equivalent of the experience of *déjà vu* is a structural principle of much twentieth-century writing; 'haunting', he says, 'is a constituent element of modernity.' Barker's fascination with the visitation of doubles should be seen as a reflection of the century's preoccupation with dissociated sensibility, with the dividing and fragmenting of selves conditioned by the disciplinary structures of modern society. The haunted self embodies a project of denial: it suggests how the construction of civic identity involves the repression of certain aspects of the self, the disavowal of memories that will nonetheless reassert themselves. These are ghosts that can never be exorcized or ignored, since the alternative to being haunted is to deny the history of one's own being. Both Barker and Swift allow their work to be haunted by the memory of historical upheavals; for Barker, the First World War, for Swift, the Second. History figures in both *oeuvres* largely as trauma that needs to be acknowledged and worked through.

The use of psychological models to account for the pattern and significance of historical events is particularly well suited to the structure of the post-nineteenth-century novel, resulting in the especially compelling fictions of crisis and trauma that characterize the work of Barker, Swift, Ishiguro and Caryl Phillips. An alternative template, in which the organizing tensions of the writing are still primarily psychological in their mode of operation, comes from the cultural historical version of Oedipal conflict. The theory of the anxiety of influence, whereby contemporary writers work always in the shadow of, and with the ambition of superseding, their most influential forebears, is used by James Diedrick to examine the novels of Martin Amis. In Amis's case, the usually symbolic relationship with a literary father-figure is inescapably literal, and family rivalry is partly what lies behind the younger Amis's inclination towards the comedy of the grotesque, as opposed to Kingsley Amis's preference for the techniques of comic romance. According to Diedrick, every aspect of Amis's writing shows the far-reaching effects of this conflict. But despite its intensity, the complex ritual of dependence, antagonism and succession at the centre of Amis's work is far from being unique. Steve Baker has identified a similar dynamic operating in the career of Salman Rushdie, and in fact his essay begins with a reminder of the competitive nature of the relationship between Rushdie and Amis: friends whose every interaction seems to stem from and return to professional rivalry. Their brief dialogue provides an anecdotal index for the pervasiveness of this concept of literary and cultural history as a 'field of endless competitive conflict'.

For both Rushdie and Angela Carter, writing proceeds by contradiction: through conflict with, and revision of, the cultural dominants. Rushdie shares with Amis a tendency to combat the power of charismatic forefathers, but he also shares with Carter the impulse to challenge traditional forms and methods of narration. While the two male authors seem locked into desperate struggle with other male antagonists, Carter's revisionism has a much less aggressive focus, although its scope is potentially extremely wide; as Robert Eaglestone explains, 'she reworks and repatterns the culture of (mainly) the European past in all its forms'. If there is a mêlée of styles and motifs and mythographic traditions in Carter's work, its eclecticism is suggestive of a freely ranging authorial imagination that is less restricted than the narratorial points of view in Rushdie's fiction, which returns repeatedly to the problem of adjudicating between radically different cultural traditions. If Carter's resources are all European, she can draw on them more variously than Rushdie's author-surrogates, who must concentrate to a degree on the points of overlap between European and Eastern cultures, and specifically between English, Indian and Pakistani variants.

Rushdie's work epitomizes the issues of cultural hybridity, which have had a decisive importance in British fiction in the two decades since publication of *Midnight's Children* in 1981. It is the largest single preoccupation of the essays in this volume, affecting several which have been placed in different categories, according to their proportional emphases. Although the sections into which this book is divided are valuable for organization and useful for identifying certain key themes, they should not be regarded as an attempt at a final categorization of the authors or texts concerned. In almost every case, individual chapters could easily have been included in more than one of the chosen sections. The position in which we have left each chapter is intended to alert the reader to issues central both to the understanding of the individual works and to the ways in which they have helped to compose a post-1979 sensibility. Jeanette Winterson's novels form a crossing-place for different strains in the British cultural tradition, unsettling the familiar patterns of disempowerment by mixing male and female stereotypes and reconfiguring the historical landscapes of class and religion. They achieve this through a blend of fantasy and realism, implicating history in the procedures of fiction, and vice versa. Their objective is summarized by Kim Middleton Meyer as an attempt to generate a culturally hybridized identity: 'each novel grapples with the task of narrating multiplicity'.

For Hanif Kureishi, Caryl Phillips and Zadie Smith, multiple identities could only ever be ambiguated in the British context by an awareness of the history of immigration, which gives a special urgency to their examinations of the grounds for cultural hybridity. Kureishi's personal experience of life in the Pakistani immigrant community has sharpened his focus on the parameters of national identity. Tony Ilona argues that Kureishi presses against both essentialist and relationist conceptions of nationality: against the assertion of a set of traits that are counted as intrinsically British, as well as against the assumption that an ensemble of differences from Britishness will mark it out by default. His novels and screenplays work to unfix the conventional proofs of belonging, and hence the criteria of inclusion and exclusion.

Brad Buchanan's essay on Caryl Phillips historicizes the evolution of hybridity as a social category. He points out that the reasons hybridity was regarded as catastrophic in the eighteenth and nineteenth centuries are identical to the advantages it offers now as a means of destabilizing racial hierarchies. However, he is also cautious about the degree to which hybridity could ever be realized in practice, and sees its allure chiefly in terms of its marketability as an aspiration. For post-colonial societies emerging from the historical domination of British values, the project of grafting an emergent national culture onto the residue of empire may be little more than an aesthetic gesturing, a distraction from the underlying process of Americanization.

Dominic Head develops the analysis in his discussion of Zadie Smith. He periodizes the changing fortunes of the notion of multiculturalism according to the altered conditions of successive generations of migrants. What was once figured as an imperilled, defensive position does not correspond to the situation of a younger generation for whom the dislocating of culture from geography has not been a defining issue. If multiculturalism once meant creeping assimilation, a form of gradual homogenization in which the pressure came from one direction only, it can now be grasped as an opportunity to activate the contradictions in British culture as a whole. Fiction provides a model for the coincidence of traditions, for the mutual adaptation of different points of view; the construction of narrative in which various characters share in what Head refers to as 'the joint construction of their history' allows the reader to imagine the grounds for a genuinely polyvocal culture.

The risk, of course, is that fiction will provide a merely spectacular version of purposeful dissidence. Drew Milne considers the likelihood of this outcome in his essay comparing the fictional languages of James Kelman and Irvine Welsh. The latter's work is in danger of commodifying protest against social conditions in a way that actually obscures the necessity for political analysis. Kelman's scrupulous attention to the spoken language of a particular locale (Glasgow) ties the justification of protest down to a specific historical moment in a specific place. The friction between spoken and written, which theory is so fond of generalizing, needs historical content in order to serve any purpose that could not be achieved equally well by other discourses and other media. That content will mean different things to different audiences, particularly Scottish and English; Kelman's work makes it impossible to posit an universal subject at the point of reception of the work; his readers are unavoidably the products of the specific histories that the business of reading his texts will evoke.

In this connection, it is no coincidence that at least four of the essays in this volume include either explicit or implicit references to Walter Benjamin's meditation on the relations between text and audience in his essay 'The Storyteller'. Richard Lane uses Benjamin's distinction between the situations of storyteller and novelist to explore the organizing tensions of Jim Crace's work. The storyteller operates from within a knowable community, speaking on its behalf and addressing it in familiar terms; the novelist works in isolation, cut off from his audience, and the exchange between them is conducted in silence. Contemporary British fiction, in its most ambitious varieties, re-engages with history in a way that amalgamates the methods and modes of address of both novelist and storyteller. It draws on the resources of literary modernism, on the technical experiments developed by a tradition of writing from the margins of the dominant culture, but uses them to present an array of different constituencies, to bring together in one place fragments of the history of various communities, and to give them voice; it is this articulation of a 'participative generation of history', as Dominic Head describes it, which is the 'narrative lifeblood of all post-colonial futures'.

Part I

Myth and History

Part I
Introduction

After 1979 Britain seemed tentatively aware that a new phase of history might well have begun, which if acknowledged, separated it from the earlier post-war period. A new generation of writers, responding to their literary antecedents, developed a newly focused literary consciousness. This was not simply a matter of reflecting historical events or trends. In politics, the reality and myth of Margaret Thatcher and an attendant concept of history were dominant. The themes of myth and history long considered by literature acquired a currency in the public sphere. Novelists responded to both the contemporaneous political domain and their literary predecessors. The place of history in our everyday lives, its literary recovery and the question of its status recur in a variety of contemporary British fictional texts.

The following chapters consider what might be regarded as a new phase of the historical novel. The writers selected are part of a wider literary commitment to reworking the past as fiction. The novels and other texts featured in this section consider the creation of myth within a perspective framed almost entirely by recognizable everyday events.

Jim Crace's fiction is typical in this respect. In *Quarantine* the culturally resonant contexts of Christ's experience in the desert are stripped of religious significance and made prosaic. In another work, *Signals of Distress*, Crace creates a setting where slavery and its trade in human life serve as a moral backdrop to a very human story of sexual desire and temptation. The effect of Crace's almost lyrical prose is determined both by his use of repetition and by his constant undermining of the parabolic force of narrative. History in contemporary fiction reaches for an extended sense of its interpretative possibilities (in myth, and in the placing of signification or meaning), drawing themes from the present, such as sexual orientation and gender that Pat Barker, for example, makes central to the social reading of war and its effects in the *Regeneration* trilogy.

Graham Swift addresses the act of reading history when Thatcher's state appears to distort the communal values prized by an older generation. For many of this new generation of writers the perceived crisis of values in the present, so publicly declared by successive Conservative administrations, helped define their need for retrieving the human, the domestic and social patterns of the past. *Waterland* meanders through a social history of family intrigue and illicit sexuality in an attempt to search for some sense of personal identity in a world of flux, as fluid, protean and elusive as the water and eels flowing through the fens of its settings.

Iain Sinclair weaves a mythopoetic account of the rhythms of modern urban life to reveal that the present is integrated into our sense of an almost magical, often turbulent past. Crime, politics, struggle and the mundane lives of ordinary people converge in an incantatory and yet elusive cartography of urban existence. In buildings, hidden links are suggested, a mapping of a symbolic order of history. There is something innately transitional in this sense of history. As Bergson reminds us in *Creative Evolution*: 'Change is far more radical than we are at first inclined to suppose.'[1] So is history in the eyes of these novelists. Throughout contemporary fiction the adjacency of past and present becomes an aesthetic dynamic, a motive force for narrative, self-identifications and cultural models in a changing society. History is both interrogated and becomes interrogative.

Note

1   Henri Bergson, *Creative Evolution*, trans. Arthur Mitchell, (London: Macmillan, 1954), p. 1.

1 Pat Barker's *Regeneration* Trilogy: History and the Hauntological Imagination

John Brannigan

> Only the conscious horror of destruction creates the correct relation-
> ship with the dead: unity with them because we, like them, are the
> victims of the same condition and the same disappointed hope.
>
> Theodor Adorno and Max Horkheimer, *Dialectic of Enlightenment*

In a footnote to his essay 'The Uncanny', Freud offers an anecdote of
his own encounter with the deceptive elision of the real and the
imagined, of the living and the dead, which might illustrate the
experience of the uncanny:

> I was sitting alone in my *wagon-lit* compartment when a more than
> usually violent jolt of the train swung back the door of the adjoining
> washing-cabinet, and an elderly gentleman in a dressing-gown and a
> travelling cap came in. I assumed that in leaving the washing-cabinet,
> which lay between the two compartments, he had taken the wrong
> direction and come into my compartment by mistake. Jumping up with
> the intention of putting him right, I at once realized to my dismay that
> the intruder was nothing but my own reflection in the looking-glass
> on the open door. I can still recollect that I thoroughly disliked his
> appearance.[1]

Freud insists that this incident did not *frighten* him, but served merely
to register his failure to recognize his own image. The anecdote is
offered in the context of a distinction between 'primitive' beliefs in the
return of the dead, or the power to translate thoughts and wishes into

reality, and the 'modern' incredulity to such superstition and myth. Freud's lack of fear, confronted with the ghostly reflection of himself, certifies his modernity, his rational distrust of 'animistic beliefs'. There is some room for doubt in Freud's mind, however. Is it not possible, he asks, that his dislike of his double 'was a vestigial trace of the archaic reaction which feels the "double" to be something uncanny?'

Freud's concern is that the archaic might seep into the modern, that the boundaries between primitive superstition and modern rationality are more permeable than he imagines. He insists that 'anyone who has completely and finally rid himself of animistic beliefs will be insensible to this type of the uncanny', and yet, for a moment, disoriented by the jolt of the train, perhaps, Freud too has *seen* the fiction of another being, 'an elderly gentleman'. The 'double', experienced as a kind of ghostly apparition, threatens to undermine the teleological distinction between superstition and rationality, primitive and civilized, reality and fiction, and so, as Avery Gordon argues, it is inevitable that Freud 'simply refutes the reality of haunting by treating it as a matter of lingering superstition'.[2] The primitive belief in the 'uncanny' or ghostly appearance of the double, for Freud then, is the anachronistic trace of a different mode of knowing, a different way of seeing the world, which he experiences, if only briefly.

Freud's anecdote recounts an experience which recurs consistently in the novels of Pat Barker. Barker's characters, from *Union Street* (1982) to *Border Crossing* (2001), frequently see themselves in others, mistake their own image for others, encounter the ghosts of past lives, experience visions of ghostly visitations, and are haunted by the uncanny doubling of time and space. In the *Regeneration* trilogy (1991–5), in particular, these experiences of the uncanny occur in the context of a confrontation between the modern rationalism of psychoanalysis and the disorienting, traumatizing effects of war. *Regeneration* (1991) constructs a fictional account of the treatment of the poet, Siegfried Sassoon, by the anthropologist and psychoanalyst, W. H. R. Rivers. Sassoon is sent to Rivers to be 'cured', because of his supposedly irrational protest against the war. Rivers is certain that Sassoon's protest is a great deal more rational than the war, but it is nevertheless his duty to restore Sassoon to psychological fitness so that he can return to the front. *The Eye in the Door* (1993) takes up the story of a fictional patient of Rivers, Billy Prior, who develops a dangerous split in his psychic life, which magnifies Freud's experience of his 'double' to 'Jekyll and Hyde' proportions. The final volume of the trilogy, *The Ghost Road* (1995), shifts between Prior's account of his fateful return to the war in France, and Rivers's own psychological crisis, as he wrestles with his own demons and ghosts. Barker's historiographic trilogy, I will argue in this essay, examines figures of psychic disturbance – doubling, hallucinations, ghosts – as signs of crisis in scientific (or more accurately psychoanalytic) modes of knowledge. Moreover, Barker's novels suggest that haunting – or what I will call here the hauntological, the logic of haunted being – is a constituent element of modernity.

Like Freud, Rivers seems certain that the ghosts who haunt his patients are not 'real', but he is nevertheless compelled to acknowledge that his patients are haunted. Haunting, in this sense, as Gordon argues, 'describes how that which appears to be not there is often a seething presence, acting on and often meddling with taken-for-granted realities'.[3] Sassoon in *Regeneration* sees corpses lying all around the streets of London,[4] and in Craiglockhart hospital he wakes to find the ghosts of dead soldiers in his room.[5] Burns, another of Rivers's patients in the same novel, continually relives the smells and tastes of finding his nose and mouth filled with the decomposing flesh of a German corpse.[6] So, too, in *The Ghost Road*, Wansbeck is visited in hospital by the ghost of the German prisoner he murdered, who becomes, visibly and olfactorily, more and more decomposed with every visit.[7] Prior in *The Eye in the Door* becomes his own ghost, by splitting into two opposing personalities, one of whom, as Prior's demonic alter ego, commits the betrayals and deceptions which the 'real' Prior finds unpalatable. Prior's demon even visits Rivers, where he demonstrates, by his oblivion to pain, that he has a physiological reality distinct from his double.[8] Rivers is left in no doubt of the 'reality' of Prior's demonic other, which is to say that he knows that Prior is not just pretending, but lives, remembers, feels and thinks differently from his alter ego. These examples from the novels are all manifestations of things which are verifiably 'not there', and yet which exercise a disturbing, sometimes dangerous, effect on Rivers's patients.

Rivers responds to these ghostly manifestations with an impressive array of psychoanalytic and rational explanations. Sassoon's ghosts are simple – his guilt for being absent from the front takes the form of hallucinated images of his dead comrades come to beckon him to return. Wansbeck's apparitions perform the same function, in exercising his feelings of guilt and regret. In both these cases, ghosts appear as the visible forms of feelings which both Sassoon and Wansbeck think they should have, or indeed desire to have. Burns is a more difficult case, and Rivers entertains the simple notion that Burns's experience of finding his mouth and nostrils filled with rotting human flesh might just be so disgusting and vile to warrant his traumatic recurrences of nausea, and the 'complete disintegration of personality' which such recurrences have produced. However, when Burns begins to put his experience into perspective, the first stage of recovery, Rivers finds that 'his own sense of the horror of the event seemed actually to have increased'.[9] A persistent theme of the trilogy is the effect that the war is having on Rivers, as the psychoanalyst who must encounter and make sense of the horrific experiences of his patients. Burns, like Sassoon, Prior, and others, serve to transform Rivers's sense of himself, and his conception of the war, science, psychology and modernity.

Prior's demonic double is, for Rivers, an all too transparent manifestation of the dissociation of self required under the disciplinary structures of modern society. Prior works for the intelligence services of the Ministry for Munitions, and finds himself tasked with destroying a group of anti-war protestors with whom he is already familiar from childhood friendships. While Prior works subtly to help the protestors, his demonic alter ego carries out the acts of subterfuge required to ensure their destruction. Rivers suggests, in other words, that Prior is generating his own monster, precisely to conduct the tasks he finds himself unable to do. Thus, his alter ego appears as a kind of exaggerated parody of an arch-villain, the self-conscious product of Prior's imagination, whom Prior even describes as his 'Hyde' figure.

Prior experiences the 'uncanny' effect of an alienated self, the substance of Freud's anecdote, in a violent, magnified form. But *The Eye in the Door* seems at the same time to represent continually the scene which Freud describes. When Prior is 'puzzled by something unfamiliar' in his office, he realizes 'that the change was in himself'.[10] Later, when his train enters a tunnel, Prior 'turned to face his doubled reflection in the window and thought he didn't like himself very much'.[11] And again, on a boat, Prior sees himself going up to a man and tapping him on the shoulder, 'and the face that turned towards him . . . was his own'.[12] Like Freud, Prior *sees* himself as an other, as an alien self, and constantly encounters himself as a stranger. Rivers finds that Prior invents this dissociated self, or rather, hypnotizes himself into a dissociated state, in order to escape from traumatic situations. The originary childhood scene, which Rivers helps Prior to remember, is of domestic violence, in which the child Prior was torn between obedience to and fear of his father and empathy with and fear for his mother. In order to resolve the conflict, Prior would sit on the staircase and hypnotize himself into the reflection on the glass of a barometer.[13] Prior's invented other is thus a kind of psychic safety valve, which enables him to cope with conflicting demands or situations.

Here again, Rivers solves the mysterious appearance of a psychic double, or a troublesome ghost, with skilful rational examination. Prior turns out not to have a monstrous alter ego, after all, just a rather mischievous coping mechanism. Prior is cured of his split personality and, in *The Ghost Road*, is sufficiently stable to return to the front line, where, with tragic but inevitable irony, he joins the ranks of the dead in one last senseless assault. Rivers, in the same novel, is forced to confront his own ghosts. He can explain the ghosts of his patients away, but his own return to haunt him. In *Regeneration*, in order to assuage Sassoon's anxieties about confessing to seeing apparitions, Rivers confesses to his own encounter with ghosts on an anthropological mission in the Melanesian islands. At a wake, at which the mourners await the sound of the spirits coming in canoes to collect the soul of the dead, Rivers hears not the paddles, which he has been told he might hear, but instead a sudden gust of 'whistling sounds':

> Nobody was making those sounds, and yet we all heard them. You see, the *rational* explanation for that is that we'd allowed ourselves to be dragged into an experience of mass hypnosis, and I don't for a moment deny that that's possible. But what we'd been told to expect was the swish of paddles. Nobody'd said anything about whistling. That doesn't mean there *isn't* a rational explanation. Only I don't think that particular rational explanation fits all the facts.[14]

In *The Ghost Road*, Rivers becomes obsessed by this scene, and the events surrounding it, and the novel concludes with Rivers being visited in hospital by the 'not in any way ghostly' apparition of Njiru, the witch doctor in Melanesia.[15] Rivers must distinguish between the irrational visions and healthy realities of his patients constantly and unequivocally. Yet his own experiences of the hauntological in Melanesia defy his attempts at rational explanation, and serve to disturb the stability of his distinctions between appearance and reality, illness and sanity, superstition and reason. If he must deal with the effects of his patients' haunted memories routinely, Rivers cannot finally dismiss the reality of ghosts either.

Barker's trilogy represents the crisis for modern rationality principally through conflicting modes of visibility and vocality. Rivers's patients suffer from a variety of speech impediments and hallucinations, which it is his duty to observe and cure. Rivers must teach his patients to see or to speak again, by encouraging them to put their repressed experiences into perspective, and to recover absent, traumatic memories through introspection. As Anne Whitehead argues, *Regeneration* shifts from 'a series of ghost stories, in which Rivers's patients are haunted by their pasts and by the recent dead, to a detective story', in which Rivers must uncover the missing fragments of memory which will enable his patients to see or speak clearly again.[16] In this sense, Rivers is cast as the agent of salvation for his patients, the medium through which they will achieve sanity and perspective. But, he is also perceived, chiefly in his treatments of Prior and Sassoon, as an agent of social discipline.

Regeneration begins with Sassoon being sent to Rivers for 'speaking out' against the war, and for seeing corpses in the streets of central London. Rivers 'can't pretend to be neutral', and must induce Sassoon to change his view.[17] Rivers concedes that Sassoon's protest against the war is far from irrational and, through his increasing despair at the severity of some of his patients' mental traumas, comes to share Sassoon's belief that '*Nothing justifies this*'.[18] Rivers can explain away Sassoon's visions of corpses and ghosts. They are simply the return of his repressed feelings of horror and guilt. But Sassoon's protest provokes a crisis for Rivers in his conception of the function of psychoanalysis. Towards the end of *Regeneration*, Rivers has a nightmare, which fuses his recent experiences of observing Dr Yealland using electric shocks to 'cure' a patient's silence with his own influence on Sassoon's decision to return to the front. When he analyses the nightmare, he comes to recognize that both he and Yealland 'were both in the business of controlling people', and, more disturbingly, in silencing them:

> Just as Yealland silenced the unconscious protest of *his* patients by removing the paralysis, the deafness, the blindness, the muteness that stood between them and the war, so, in an infinitely more gentle way, *he* silenced *his* patients; for the stammerings, the nightmares, the tremors, the memory lapses, of officers were just as much unwitting protest as the grosser maladies of the men.[19]

The image of an open mouth recurs throughout Barker's trilogy (and indeed many of her other novels), but has particular significance in *Regeneration* for notions of protest and control. Rivers's nightmare revolves around 'the tortured mouth' of Yealland's patient, and figures his treatment of Sassoon as 'uncomfortably like an oral rape'.[20] Rivers thus reconsiders his relationship with Sassoon, who has 'spoken out', and with Prior, who has been unable to speak, as a form of domination rather than healing. His methods may be 'infinitely more gentle' than Yealland's, but he has still functioned effectively as an instrument of control and authority over his patients.

If *Regeneration* is a novel about violence and protest, figured through tropes of speech and silence, *The Eye in the Door*, as its title suggests, is a novel about visibility as a mode of knowing. The novel's dominant image is the panopticon, the ideal architectural technology for correctional surveillance, which Foucault studies as a model of modern authority and control.[21] The panopticon prison appears just briefly in the novel, when Prior visits an old friend who is incarcerated for plotting to kill Lloyd George.[22] In the prison, Prior is disturbed by the 'eye' hole in the cell door, particularly as it reminds him of his traumatic experience of finding nothing of his dead comrade but an eyeball in a trench in France. The recovered eyeball (which Prior thinks of as a 'gob-stopper', thus prompting him to 'stop' his 'gob', to become silent) is the source of Prior's psychological breakdown in *Regeneration*. In *The Eye in the Door*, the 'eye' replaces the 'mouth' as the instrument of control and resistance.

Panopticism pervades the novel as a mode of social control. Prior is aware of the scrutinizing gaze of others from the beginning of the novel, when he considers self-consciously how he must look to passing strangers.[23] His suspicion that he is watched intensifies considerably in the prison, and thereafter the novel shows Prior encountering his own uncanny image repeatedly as the object of scrutiny. This develops into his extreme dissociated state, in which he lapses out of consciousness for hours at a time, during which his double conducts the tasks to which Prior remains blind. In this schema, Rivers is just one 'eye' in the surveillance net in which Prior is caught, observed and monitored constantly, not least by his demonic double. Rivers, as a psychoanalyst, must subject Prior to observation and objectification, and so becomes part of the disciplinary apparatus which defines and controls Prior.

The trouble for Rivers is that Prior is capable of subjecting *him* to the same objective gaze. Rivers reveals to Prior during one of their sessions that he has no visual memory after the age of five, which is too tempting a 'blind spot' in Rivers's psyche for Prior to leave unexamined. Rivers and Prior change places, and Prior probes Rivers's memory of a childhood experience in which something so terrible happened that his mind 'suppressed not just the *one* memory, but the capacity to remember things visually at all'.[24] Prior's diagnosis is emphatic, and troubles Rivers afterwards: '*Whatever it was, you blinded yourself so you wouldn't have to go on seeing it... You put your mind's eye out.*'[25] Rivers is sufficiently self-conscious to realize that he has his own psychological problems and repressed memories, but that he might be the victim of what Prior suggests was a monstrous rape or beating when he was five shocks and disturbs the analyst. The realization that his own lack of visual memory may conceal as dark a repressed past as he has encountered in his patients triggers a crisis of authority in Rivers, and, in the final novel of the trilogy, he is immersed in his own anamnetic efforts to trace the source of his ghosts. Rivers, in one sense, becomes his own patient in *The Ghost Road*, as haunted by spectres as Prior or Sassoon. Here, his own divisions are especially manifest, since his rational self – what he calls the 'epicritic' mind – must analyse and exorcize the demons of his emotional self – what he calls the 'protopathic'. This division between the epicritic and the protopathic occupies much of Rivers's thinking throughout the trilogy, but it becomes especially significant in the final volume, in which it appears to take the form of a split personality. Rivers in *The Ghost Road*, then, is both the capable analyst, who unravels his patients' anxieties and repressions, and the haunted, frightened patient, vulnerable to his own nightmares and hallucinations.

Neither Rivers's ghostly visions nor his paralytic stammer undermine his authority as a psychoanalyst. In fact, Rivers's vulnerability appears to earn him greater credit with Prior. The return of Rivers's spectres and repressed memories illustrates instead the inseparability of the epicritic and the protopathic or, to put it another way, it shows that the rational is thoroughly infiltrated by the irrational. This is an argument which Michel de Certeau makes in relation to haunting more generally:

> There is an 'uncanniness' about this past that a present occupant has expelled (or thinks it has) in an effort to take its place. The dead haunt the living … [Any] autonomous order is founded upon what it eliminates; it produces a 'residue' condemned to be forgotten. But what was excluded re-infiltrates the place of its origin – now the present's 'clean' place. It resurfaces, it troubles, it turns the present's feeling of being 'at home' into an illusion – this 'wild', this 'obscene', this 'filth', this 'resistance' of 'superstition' – within the walls of the residence, and, behind the back of the owner (the *ego*), or over its objections, it inscribes there the law of the other.[26]

De Certeau here counters Freud's notion that the modern rational mind can 'rid himself' of primitive beliefs in the ghostly and the uncanny, and argues that the present is perpetually haunted by the dead. In psychoanalytic terms, de Certeau seems to be addressing the return of the repressed, but he is also implicitly critiquing the conceit of psychoanalysis that it can make the ghosts go away. If, as de Certeau argues, haunting is the figurative return of the 'residue' or excluded others of the past to the 'present occupants', then the attempt to exorcize these ghosts is merely an attempt to prolong the repression of voices of protest or difference. Rivers recognizes that this might be the case when he worries about whether he has, in 'curing' his patients, merely silenced their intuitive expressions of protest.

The return of the dead to haunt the living, whether in the form of ghostly apparitions or uncanny experiences, functions to unsettle the conceit of the present. This appears to be an important recognition in Barker's trilogy. The teleological narratives of historical progress, cultural superiority and technological prowess, which underpinned notions of European civilization, and which ultimately led to the 'Great War', produced the most savage, regressive and irrational conflict the world had yet known. The dead lying on the battlefields of France are material testimony to the gaps and contradictions in such narratives, and hence, they are witnessed by Rivers's patients in the trilogy as the spectres haunting Europe. The uncanny experiences represented in the *Regeneration* trilogy, then, are disturbing not just in their meanings for scientific and psychoanalytic claims to knowledge, but also in their implications for the chrono-and geo-politics of modernity.

Barker represents this crisis in European modernity through tropes of displacement and temporal disjunction. Throughout the trilogy, everywhere – the hospital corridors of Craiglockhart, the landings of a prison, the hollows of an urban waste-land, the labyrinthine streets of a city – comes to resemble the topographical features of the trench or no-man's land. The streets of London and the fields around Craiglockhart seem to resemble the battlefields of France, so that Rivers's patients sometimes behave, mentally and physiologically, as if they are still at the front. They listen for the whine of incoming shells, and see the corpses of their comrades lying all around them. Rivers experiences his own version of this, when his memories of life with a 'primitive' tribe in Melanesia become confused with his waking life in England. Here, the geographical 'otherness' of Melanesia refuses to remain in its place – it continually appears to haunt and disrupt Rivers's sense of 'home'.

Time, too, is continually disrupted in Barker's trilogy. The very notion of anamnesis, as Freud explained it in 'Beyond the Pleasure Principle', involves a radical disturbance in the patient's sense of time: 'He is obliged to *repeat* the repressed material as a contemporary experience instead of, as the physician would prefer to see, *remembering* it as something belonging to the past.'[27] Rivers's patients are, for the most part, stuck in time, in reliving one particular moment of experience or trauma, which continues to exercise a grip on their consciousness. The effect of the severe disjunction of time undergone by the war veterans, Middleton and Woods explain, is that they 'find that the ordinary realism of memory is no longer adequate and must re-imagine the space-time of the past'.[28] Both Owen and Sassoon, when they share their experiences of the war, project their visions either back or forward in time, for example:

> [*Owen*:] 'Sometimes when you're alone, in the trenches, I mean, at night you get the sense of something *ancient*. As if the trenches had always been there. You know one trench we held, it had skulls in the side. You looked back along and...Like mushrooms. And do you know, it was actually *easier* to believe they were men from Marlborough's army than to to to think they'd been alive two years ago. It's as if all other wars had somehow...distilled themselves into this war, and that makes it something you...almost can't challenge.'
>
> [...]
>
> [*Sassoon*:] 'I had a similar experience. Well, I don't know whether it is similar. I was going up with the rations one night and I saw the limbers against the skyline, and the flares going up. What you see every night. Only I seemed to be seeing it from the future. A hundred years from now they'll still be ploughing up skulls. And I seemed to be in that time and looking back. I think I saw our ghosts.'[29]

Owen's experience of the war is filtered through its historical resonances, through notions of cyclical recurrence and repetition, while Sassoon sees the war through the postmodern lens of the future anterior.[30] For both, it is necessary to see the present through images of its otherness, of its double, or, more pertinently, of its ghostly resemblances through time. What is not possible is for Owen and Sassoon to see their own time in its modernity, to see the present as a homogenous self-present identity. Instead, they, like other characters in the novel, such as Burns, who can only find solace in a medieval moat, or Manning's soldiers billeted in a graveyard, achieve some understanding of their situation only by radically dislocating their 'place' in historical chronology. To situate themselves, it is necessary, in other words, to conceive of the radical heterogeneity – the hauntedness – of their own time.

In Barker's *Regeneration* trilogy, then, history is experienced always as untimely, as anachronistic. It is not just that her characters fail to grasp the significance of the events of their own time, but rather that time itself seems to become profoundly discontinuous and unstable. The war repeats the time of other wars, churns up the dead of other centuries, and refuses to be contained in its present time. For Barker's characters, to use Paul Fussell's terms, 'war detaches itself from its normal location in chronology and its accepted set of causes and effects to become Great in another sense – all encompassing, all-pervading, both internal and external at once, the essential condition of consciousness in the twentieth century'.[31] This is experienced in the trilogy as a chronic disturbance in the function of memory.

Rivers's patients suffer either from amnesia or anamnesia, too little or too much memory. Both amnesia and anamnesia are forms of representation (especially after Freud), open to psychoanalytic inter-pretation, and marking out by presence or absence the reappearance of the past in the present. It becomes apparent to Rivers that the memory crises of his patients are not just indications of psychological failure – not just the signs of mental disorder – but instead are registering a more general, social and cultural, crisis. Memory appears, in the words of Richard Terdiman, as 'a problem, as a site and source of cultural disquiet'.[32] It emerges as the involuntary coun-ter-narrative of modernity, bearing witness to that which modernity forgets or fails to see. But memory functions not just as the *repetition* of the past, not just as a kind of video replay of the event, but rather, as Derrida indicates, as the deferred past. The recovered memory of the past is, for Derrida, 'the *supplementary delay* . . . the reconstitution of meaning through deferral, after a mole-like progression, after the subterranean toil of an impression':

> This impression has left behind a laborious trace which has never been *perceived*, whose meaning has never been lived in the present, i.e. has never been lived consciously. The postscript which constitutes the past present as such is not satisfied . . . with reawakening or revealing the present past in its truth. It produces the present past.[33]

Not surprisingly, Derrida describes this eruption of the past into present consciousness in ghostly or hauntological terms – trace, delay, deferral, the present past. The past as such is a perpetual palimpsest, continually rewritten, and in continual dialogue with its present enunciation. Derrida's conception of the time of memory is structured by absence, in which the possibility of the past revealing its truth is endlessly deferred. In this sense, as Jean-Luc Nancy argues, to represent the past 'is not to re-present some past or present presence. It is to trace the otherness of existence within its own present and presence.'[34]

Barker's trilogy concludes on this theme of the encounter with the 'otherness of existence'. Rivers envisions his cultural other, the Melanesian witch doctor, Njiru, dancing an invocation to the gods to 'go down and depart'. The dance repeats a scene he has witnessed often in Melanesia, but appears now dislocated from its normal time and place, in Rivers's hospital ward. Njiru sees the 'end of men', and his dance is performed for the *mate*, the living dead. Rivers now belongs, the scene implies, to the land of the living dead, like all his patients. Just as the final scene signifies the dramatic return of Rivers's powers of visualization, it indicates too a traumatic shift in historical consciousness, from one in which time unfolded progressively towards healing, to one in which time is structured around loss, absence and otherness. History, after the Great War, Barker's trilogy suggests, is continually haunted by the memory of loss, and is constantly striving to regenerate the past.

Notes

1   Sigmund Freud, 'The Uncanny', *The Penguin Freud Library: Volume 14 – Art and Literature*, ed. Albert Dickson (London: Penguin, 1985), p. 371.
2   Avery F. Gordon, *Ghostly Matters: Haunting and the Sociological Imagination* (Minneapolis, MN, USA: University of Minnesota Press, 1997), p. 53.
3   Ibid., p. 8.
4   Pat Barker, *Regeneration* (London: Penguin, 1992), p. 12.
5   Ibid., p. 188.
6   Ibid., p. 19.
7   Pat Barker, *The Ghost Road* (London: Penguin, 1996), p. 26.
8   Pat Barker, *The Eye in the Door* (London: Penguin, 1994), p. 242.
9   Barker, *Regeneration*, p. 184.
10 Barker, *The Eye in the Door*, p. 44.
11 Ibid., p. 88.
12 Ibid., p. 185.
13 Ibid., p. 248.
14 Barker, *Regeneration*, p. 188. Original emphases.
15 Barker, *The Ghost Road*, p. 276.
16 Anne Whitehead, 'Open to Suggestion: Hypnosis and History in Pat Barker's *Regeneration*', *Modern Fiction Studies*, Vol. 44, No. 3 (Fall 1998), 688.
17 Barker, *Regeneration*, p. 15.
18 Ibid., p. 180.
19 Ibid., p. 238. Original emphases.
20 Ibid., p. 236.

21 Michel Foucault, *Discipline and Punish: The Birth of the Prison* (1975), trans. A. M. Sheridan Smith (London: Penguin, 1979). See also Jeremy Bentham, *The Panopticon Writings*, ed. Miran Božovič (London: Verso, 1995).
22 Barker, *The Eye in the Door*, p. 29.
23 Ibid., p. 3.
24 Ibid., p. 137.
25 Ibid., pp. 140–1.
26 Michel de Certeau, *Heterologies: Discourse on the Other*, trans. Brian Massumi (Manchester: Manchester University Press, 1986), pp. 3–4.
27 Sigmund Freud, 'Beyond the Pleasure Principle', *The Penguin Freud Library: Volume 11 – On Metapsychology: The Theory of Psychoanalysis*, ed. Angela Richards (London: Penguin, 1991), p. 288.
28 Peter Middleton and Tim Woods, *Literatures of Memory: History, time and space in postwar writing* (Manchester: Manchester University Press, 2000), p. 88.
29 Barker, *Regeneration*, pp. 83–4. Original emphases.
30 Jean-François Lyotard argues that the future anterior is the defining tense of the postmodern. See *The Postmodern Condition: A Report on Knowledge*, trans. Geoff Bennington and Brian Massumi (Manchester: Manchester University Press, 1984), p. 81.
31 Paul Fussell, *The Great War and Modern Memory* (Oxford: Oxford University Press, 1975), p. 321.
32 Richard Terdiman, *Present Past: Modernity and the Memory Crisis* (Ithaca, NY: Cornell University Press, 1993), p. vii.
33 Jacques Derrida, 'Freud and the Scene of Writing', *Writing and Difference*, trans. Alan Bass (London: Routledge, 1978), p. 214.
34 Jean-Luc Nancy, 'Finite History', *The States of 'Theory': History, Art and Critical Discourse*, ed. David Carroll (Stanford, CA: Stanford University Press, 1990), p. 165.

Primary texts

Union Street (London: Virago, 1982)
Blow Your House Down (London: Virago, 1984)
The Century's Daughter (Liza's England) (London: Virago, 1986)
The Man Who Wasn't There (London: Virago, 1989)
Regeneration (London: Viking, 1991)
The Eye in the Door (London: Viking, 1993)
The Ghost Road (London: Viking, 1995)
Another World (London: Viking, 1998)
Border Crossing (London: Viking, 2001)

Selected critical texts

Sigmund Freud, 'The Uncanny' (1919), *The Penguin Freud Library: Volume 14 – Art and Literature*, ed. Albert Dickson (London: Penguin, 1985)

Paul Fussell, *The Great War and Modern Memory* (Oxford: Oxford University Press, 1975)

Avery F. Gordon, *Ghostly Matters: Haunting and the Sociological Imagination* (Minneapolis, MN: University of Minnesota Press, 1997)

Catherine Lanone, 'Scattering the Seed of Abraham: The Motif of Sacrifice in Pat Barker's *Regeneration* and *The Ghost Road* ', *Literature and Theology*, Vol. 13, No. 3 (September 1999), 259–68.

Peter Middleton and Tim Woods, *Literatures of Memory: History, time and space in postwar writing* (Manchester: Manchester University Press, 2000)

Richard Terdiman, *Present Past: Modernity and the Memory Crisis* (Ithaca, NY: Cornell University Press, 1993).

Anne Whitehead, 'Open to Suggestion: Hypnosis and History in Pat Barker's *Regeneration*', *Modern Fiction Studies*, Vol. 44, No. 3 (Fall 1998), 674–94.

2 The Fiction of Jim Crace: Narrative and Recovery

Richard J. Lane

Nowhere in Jim Crace's *oeuvre* is the human body so remorselessly dissected in all of its rotting glory, as in his novel *Being Dead*. In the novel, the body outlasts its temporary living narratives and meanings, offering – eventually – putrefaction as the final signifier or emission. What is left, when all is said and done, is a stain and a smell. Emissions are invariably enframed by other stories in Crace, and *Being Dead* is no exception – the dead have only just managed to rest and they are instantly disturbed: by insects, microbes, the wind and the rain, by other people. Life may quickly be reduced to a puddle, the bodies becoming what in some medical and other circles are called 'leakers', but the reduction does *not* represent some kind of literary nihilism. Unlike one of the many famous phrases from Samuel Beckett's *Trilogy*, 'I can't go on, I'll go on', the subject in Crace is constantly reduced to stasis, to nothingness, while the narrative continues: the narrative can't go on, but it does go on. Not only does narrative continue, it continues reinvigorated by the various protagonists' pratfalls, their lurching and leaping from the sublime to the ridiculous. Somewhat controversially in *Quarantine*, one of these protagonists is portrayed as Christ; in *The Gift of Stones*, the protagonist is a storyteller; in *Signals of Distress*, the protagonist is a humanist, someone who thinks he cares, but is revealed to be a pompous prig out of touch with the world he wants to save. Why save a world which has already moved on? These protagonists all suffer in a sense an ontological and epistemological displacement from the world: they are in the world, but do not live according to its rules; they think they understand the world, but they are using the wrong interpretative parameters. They see through a glass, darkly. The world has always moved on, and in the fracturing between character and world, there is much laughter: huge, stomach-churning bursts of laughter, countered by a redemptive/narrative force that may, or may not, be a result of that laughter. Who laughs? Is it Crace? Is it the reader? Is the laughter nihilistic? Any hint of nihilism in Crace appears to undergo transformation; nihilism becomes affirmation.

This chapter will explore the mysteries of such a literary–alchemical transformation by focusing upon three of Crace's novels: *The Gift of Stones* (1988), *Quarantine* (1997) and *Being Dead* (1999). These novels examine loss, which is also explored by Crace elsewhere, for example, the loss of the 'authentic' marketplace in *Arcadia* or the loss of naiveté or foolish innocence in *Signals of Distress*. The three novels studied here are also particularly 'crystalline', to borrow a phrase from Iris Murdoch (as Frank Kermode reminds us): 'Crace's way is closer to what Iris Murdoch distinguishes as "crystalline" construction, the end of the fiction spectrum where the novel is most like a poem, most turned in on itself, most closely wrought for the sake of art and internal cohesion – the other pole being the social or even, at the extreme, journalistic...'[1] Such 'turning within' or self-reflexivity will not be examined here as a marker of postmodernity; rather, it is seen as part of a tension generated by the themes of individualism and societal transformation/revolution.

The Gift of Stones

Never trust a storyteller, because even his wildest fantasies will ultimately be surpassed by reality, and then all the magic of the story is lost as life goes remarkably plodding on. The paradigm shift in *The Gift of Stones* is that of (what else?) technology: from stone to bronze. The bulk of the novel is spent in the world of stone, seen through the eyes of the storyteller and his daughter, the divided narration being one more device to alert us to the necessary duplicity that charges and enhances the tall tale. Walter Benjamin theorizes two groups of storyteller: '...people imagine the storyteller as someone who has come from afar. But they enjoy no less listening to the man who has stayed at home, making an honest living, and who knows the local tales and traditions.'[2] Benjamin imagines the exemplary groups as being 'tribes', the one embodied by the farmer and the other by the sailor. He argues: 'The actual extension of the realm of storytelling in its full historical breadth is inconceivable without the most intimate interpenetration of these two archaic types.'[3] The storyteller in *The Gift of*

Stones is both inside and outside of his community: incapable of becoming a stone-worker because of his amputation, but still part of a stone-working family and environment, he is also a wanderer, an explorer of remote places, inspired as a child by the sight of a sailing ship that he attempts to follow along the coast: 'My ship threw up an arc of its own phlegm as it dipped and bounced before the wind. I bounced and dipped myself. We were a pair. At times the ship sank out of sight, lost in the trenches of the water. More often it was I who dropped from sight.'[4] As the storyteller chases the ship, two realities are formed: that of greeting the sailors as they land on a beach, and that of the ship disappearing from view, lost on the horizon. The loss of the ship does not negate the first reality, and it leads to something new, something far beyond the world of the stone-workers: a different environment of soft red sandstone and a woman in a hut with a child.

Benjamin theorizes the storyteller in relation to the novel: 'The earliest symptom of a process whose end is the decline of storytelling is the rise of the novel at the beginning of modern times.'[5] The novel initially emerges from a new societal relationship with the world, eventually negating storytelling itself; as Benjamin says, the novel neither comes from the oral tradition nor feeds anything back into it.[6] The opposition is simple: the storyteller derives material from the community and involves the community in a shared experience when completing the circuit by speaking; the novelist, in contrast, sits in a profound solipsistic silence: 'The birthplace of the novel is the solitary individual ... To write a novel means to carry the incommensurable to extremes in the representation of human life. In the midst of life's fullness, and through the representation of this fullness, the novel gives evidence of the profound perplexity of the living.'[7] In *The Gift of Stones*, Crace manages to connect Benjamin's two narrative circuits: the oral and the written; in fact these circuits interlock throughout the novel in a sequenced chiasmus. The storyteller's daughter embodies the detachment of modernity, the increasingly suspicious, questioning perspective: 'Beware of father's tongue'. (p. 9) The daughter enjoys her father's stories, but foregrounds their embroidered, rhetorical nature; she sifts and sorts through them as if she were looking for the sharpest stone, the one that will cut through all untruths, all mysteries: 'I – his daughter and his only child – took his most frequent, detailed repetition as the truth. It was less fantastic than his other tales and his expression, in its narration, lacked the usual mannerisms of the story-teller, the floating eyebrow, the single, restless hand, the dramatic contours of the voice.' (pp. 1–2) The storyteller's daughter realizes that there are limits to knowledge, that even in the shifting paradigm from stone to bronze, technology temporarily silences the fantastic: all is possible, for a while, when a new technology is born.

The relationship between the two narrators in *The Gift of Stones* is crucial: it is not a blood relationship as such, although stories bind them; rather the relationship is about the *repetition* of stories. One of the criteria for ascertaining the truth of the storyteller's narratives in the first place, for his daughter, is the number of times he repeats a particular version: 'I – his daughter and his only child – took his most frequent, detailed repetition as the truth.' (p. 1) The daughter's statement is virtually a signature, suggesting that she is plying the same trade: she is not, strictly speaking the storyteller's daughter, and she confuses extra detail with the truth, a criteria of performativity over factuality. The signature is a recognition and a warning: a statement of kinship, but not quite what the reader understands by the term. The daughter, narrator or novelist, mediates the storyteller's stories, partly by placing them in quotation marks. This simple act is one of repetition and difference, losing the immediacy (of performance and the social circuit) that Benjamin laments, but also complicating the temporality of narrative (the past is brought into the present, repeated in the present, and repeated as versions, rather than absolutely factual accounts of events). The result is a temporal montage effect where there is a '. . . copresence of different times'.[8]

One argument differentiating the English novel from the epic or the French romance (in both cases) concerns a temporal and spatial shift from distance and heroic scale to the 'here and now' of bourgeois immediacy. Even in the case of, say *Robinson Crusoe*, the *other* is experienced, interpreted and so on, through the rhythms and practices of mercantilism, profit and loss, conservation and gain. The English novel functions therefore as an exquisitely controlled *differentia* of time and space, whereby the narrator constructs a temporal montage to override all other visions, or, to put it another way, subsumes the other via the controlled *differentia*. In the case of *The Gift of Stones*, the past is as alien as the future, narrated in effect from the cusp of the two, from the perspective of narrator rather than storyteller. While the novel could be said to be about the shift from the stone age to the bronze age, this chronological and technological progression does not explain or exhaust the art of novel-writing itself. The *differentia* is a crystalline structure, its rotational symmetry competing with strong, teleological narrative forces.

Quarantine

As Tyndale narrates the scene in his great English translation of 1526: 'And immediatly the sprete drave hym into a wilderness: and he was there in the wilderness xl. days, and was tempted off Satan, and was with wylde beestes. And the angels ministred unto him.'[9] It is tempting to think of *Quarantine* as another version of this narrative, where the 'wylde beestes' are the human beings who recreate a thoroughly rotten society in the wilderness, and Crace's Christ is a poor carpenter forced to suffer ignominy at arms' length. Such a notion of versioning means that the slightest sliver of redemption in the text enables some kind of authorial recuperation by the Christian community of close-readers. A whole host of issues arises with the latter reading, that Crace has explored elsewhere: that the secular versioning is overtaken by a Christian interpretation; that the text is out of control and, in its plethora of meanings, enriches a secular notion of the redemptive power of narrative; that the act of engaging with the wilderness narrative from the New Testament cannot be a one-way process, the wilderness narrative affecting the author almost as profoundly as the author affects the narrative, and so on. Questions of authorial intentions and meanings will not be explored here; rather, the issue of a literary redemptive 'force' will continue to be of concern.

The trader Musa soon begins to control the lives of the people in the wilderness, yet he cannot quite grasp who it is saved him from his fever – he cannot yet name his saviour. 'Whose words were those, Be well again? Who haunted him? Whose throbbing voice was that? He concentrated hard. And, yes, there was a half-remembered figure now. A face within his fever. A peasant face. A robber's face.' (p. 37) The unnamed man can take on multiple identities while the named are merely human beings; eventually Jesus becomes 'Gally' to be visited or hounded from above his part of the cliff. In turn, Jesus decides that he is being pestered by Satan: 'So Jesus was in little doubt that, should the devil choose, he could easily appear as Musa on the precipice. [...] He could invade his soul and jostle for a perch inside his heart as truly and as tangibly as a raiding jackdaw could invade an open nest and jostle out its chirping innocents with its black wings. That was the drama and the cruel romance of Jesus's theology.' (p. 149) The hallucinatory quality of the quarantine begins to provide a rationalistic account of metaphysical experience (such as the profound physiological changes that affect the mind), yet the sliver of redemption is still there, constantly undermining rationalism in the absurd misidentification of people and things (such as the wilderness being property or dreams affecting reality) and the rational versus the spiritual. A type of misidentification also occurs with Jesus's use of language:

> He had taught himself at home to recognize a few words in written Greek script, more words than anyone else in his family. He could read and write his own name, and the name of God. He could roughly translate the inscription on the local temple stone which promised death to gentiles if they strayed into the inner court. He knew the meaning of TI.CAES.DIVI, the truncated Latin on the tribute coins. It designated Tiberius to be an Emperor and God. A blasphemy, the priest had said. The priest had little sympathy for Rome, although when it came to collecting tithes he much preferred their silver blasphemies to the copper ones. (p. 134)

Once more, the paragraph moves from the sublime to the ridiculous, from language as a naming of self in relation to God, through translation, the construction of new, false gods, to language, finally, as a debased currency. There are obviously a number of language theories embedded in this section of the novel: language is linked to power and communication, such as the Jewish interdictions literally written on stone tablets in the Temple; to the physicality of language (e.g., patterns, shapes, and the allusions to the *wearing* of language as a separate entity, e.g., *tefillin/phylacteries*); also to the dissemination and decay of language through imperialism, travel, overspending, wear and tear. Jesus resists learning too much language (the rote repetition of words divorced from their evocative shapes and sounds) but is versed in translation. Language functions not as a mere communication device of, or for human desires, but as a mysterious spiritual entity in its own right, permeated in its presence and absence by God. This 'other conception of language' as Benjamin puts it, '... knows no means, no object, and no addressee of communication. It means: *in the name, the mental being of man communicates itself to God.*'[10] Further, such a conception of language is non-instrumental, as Bolz and Van Reijen argue: 'This naming should not be confused with an organizing activity undertaken with a view to instrumental action; it is a matter of communicating a spiritual nature through language.'[11] The portrayal of Jesus thus withholds judgement, since he appears to engage with language in both instrumental and non-instrumental ways: for communication with spirit, but also communication with the world; in a pure act of naming, but one that is also contaminated by economies of debasement and accumulation. He is outside of Musa's economy, but not totally separate from it; Jesus's position on the margins forces an engagement with and an interpretation of whatever these evil beings/spirits might be; but most of all, this marginal, liminal position forces a continual engagement or production of essentially human history.

Naming is followed by narrative in *Quarantine* – the narratives of, and generated by, the mill-game: 'This was how bad boys avoided temple lessons, hiding in the medlar trees, and playing on the millboard for prizes of dried grapes, with sacrilegious forfeits for the ones that lost... And this was how old men killed time until the time killed them, sitting with their backs arched in the shade, above a mill-game board, waiting for their girls to serve a meal or for the moon to send them home.' (p. 136) Jesus realizes that the game can also be interpreted parabolically: it generates a potential sermon for him, a discourse that functions quite differently from pure, spiritual naming; now language functions through words being sutured together, in sequences that have teleological force and pedagogical meaning. The image of a randomly lost or won game (even though gaming may or may not relate to 'skill') constructing symbolic signification is slightly absurd – it is another shift from the sublime to the ridiculous and back again. The image also appears to offer another theory of language: this time, that of the later Wittgenstein, of the *Philosophical Investigations*, where language-games are used to counter earlier theories of abstracted rules and signification; with language-games, meaning is embedded inextricably in, generated by, the event, such a notion being an extremely long way from the belief in a divine *naming*. The world of the *Investigations* is Musa's: carrying the performative *word* with him as living proof of Jesus's resurrection that may, ultimately be nothing but '...disturbances of wind, and shadows shaking in the breeze'. (p. 241) There are a number of ironies in Musa's adoption and 'acceptance', via fraudulent or hyperbolic narrative, of the spirituality of Jesus and the dissemination of the latter as 'truth': that biblical narratives are thus built on tunneled, labyrinthine ground, rather than solid, factual rock, and that the fraudulent/hyperbolic versioning of events becomes, in turn, contaminated by the redemptive (or it becomes an unwitting vehicle for the redemptive). Keeping with the Wittgenstein analogue, for the moment, we are no longer dealing with the opposition between an abstracted system of higher or 'pure' meaning versus the secular world of language-games and performative truths, but rather the expression of the former through the latter. Another way of putting this is to argue that rather than the misrecognition of Musa – as looking '...like some king-prophet come down from the hills, like Moses...' (p. 240) – being a rationalist undermining of spirit, it is more powerfully an intertwining of the rational with the spiritual. The labyrinthine 'origins' of the Jesus narratives adds to a sense of mystery, with laughter, with absurdity, even with Musa's corrupt aims; but the labyrinth only accumulates, rather than subtracts from a sense of wonder. Also, Musa occupies (as do all the characters in *Quarantine*), structurally speaking, a place in the narrative called by Propp a *function*. One of the fundamental Proppian principles of narrative, as Hawkes summarizes it, is that: 'Functions of characters serve as stable, constant elements in a tale, independently of how and by whom they are fulfilled. They constitute the fundamental components of a tale.'[12] Musa's positioning as a 'prophet', as a Moses figure, fulfils, however absurdly or ridiculously, his function in the syntagmatic sense of structural repetition. Clearly, at the level of parody, Musa as a character is a critique of misrecognition via the syntagmatic positioning or fulfilment of the requirements of another text: say, the Old Testament. But there is still the ghostly effect of the structural fulfillment even as it is undermined. This binding of one text to another is quite literally uncontrollable, and however hard the rationalist narrative works, it is constantly being subverted by the unremitting nature of textual binding, a displacement of intention and meaning. *Quarantine* thus functions unwittingly in an allegorical sense; the novel could be thought of as an allegory *about* textual relations, about the economy of biblical narrative. Frank Kermode calls allegory '...the patristic way of dealing with inexhaustible hermeneutic potential'.[13] Yet, contra this sense of agency, *Quarantine* is embedded in an automatic allegorization; put differently, allegory functions like an autonomous machine. The so-called 'concealment' of knowledge within biblical narrative[14] would appear to be in opposition to Crace's *revealing* text; however, allegory takes what appears to be literally obvious or manifest and manages to obscure it in the moment of 'clarification'. Parody, in *Quarantine*, rather than clarifying in humorous ways the interpretive bonds between Old and New Testaments, turns into a parabolic force.

Being Dead

Crace just won't let the dead rest; their stories are charted in a dialectical movement that ignores the meaning of the commonly used euphemism or phrase 'passed away', so suggestive of gentle closure or negation. Further, Crace ignores the etiquette of 'good' or 'polite' speech to wrench euphemistic language aside like some skin torn or ripped from the body to reveal its underlying guts. Reading *Being Dead* is analogous to witnessing a skilful surgeon performing an operation, or, better (worse?) still, watching a visual recording of one's own session under the surgeon's knife. *Being Dead* is a series of post-mortems, not all of them in human control: 'The flies lined up like fishermen along the banks of the bodies' open wounds. They settled mainly on Celice... Her hair was matted with wet blood and the syrup of her brain. One cheek was flattened by the pounding impact of the granite. Two teeth were cracked, longways. Her facial artery... had been torn in two.' (p. 38) In the foreground is the fact that the novel form itself is an *autopsy*, with the latter's contradictory claims of truth, insight, and record or narrative: the body is sliced open to find the cause of death, in the descriptive process keeping the body alive. Temporality is complex, the narrative being once more a *differentia* where there is a struggle between past meaning (life before death), and post-mortem meaning (the meaning(s) assigned to the life/ lives after death). Embedded within the latter is the possibility that the stain of life can easily be washed away, that death is a fact of life, so to speak, that the universe has long learnt to cope with the event that humanity has so much trouble with. As a dialectical account of death, the novel is less a necropsy, and more a suspension of closure; rituals compete to own or take control of the decomposing bodies:

> It is, of course, a pity that the police dogs ever caught the scent of human carrion and led their poking masters to the dunes to clear away the corpses for 'proper burial', so that the dead could be less splendid in a grave. The dunes could have disposed of Joseph and Celice themselves. They didn't need help. The earth is practised in the craft of burial. It gathers round. It embraces and adopts the dead. Joseph and Celice would have turned to landscape, given time. (p. 207)

Ritual, be it a Christian burial or some other mode, is an intervention in time; the earth may work unremittingly to dissolve all forms into one vast landscape or 'timescape', but humanity's need to intervene, to redirect dissolution through spiritual transition or even rebirth, is driven in part by the negation of the forces of nature. Ironically, given the protagonists, scientific beliefs, the efficacy of natural wear and tear, or, more precisely, consumption of the bodies, is a more fitting process. With suicide, interpretative 'sense' becomes harder for a scientist to construct; Celice's colleague, the Academic Mentor of the Natural Science Faculty, takes his life in the middle of its self-satisfactions: 'Celice should not have been so shocked or taken it so personally. The Mentor's suicide was not a judgement on the world, on life, on her. It might have been nothing more than chemistry and genes. He was disposed to it, perhaps. This was his programmed death. [...] The Mentor's suicide, she could persuade herself, was neo-Darwinist.' (p. 63) The discourses of chance, myth and spirituality that enframe this pre-programmed event jar with the scientific world view; Celice must make sense of myth to make sense of death, but the interconnections are strangely playful, both factual and full of errors, connecting through a blurring of fact and fiction rather than a complete clarification of their relationships. Finally, myth allows Celice to re-imagine, re-narrate death: '...this was wisdom widely honest in a way that Celice found comforting. As she imagined it, there was no hose-pipe and no car. There was just the Mentor on his back, awaiting her, the wispy canopy of pines, the deadly buttons on the ground, a ladder leading to his underworld and hers, and everlasting sin.' (pp. 65–6)

Death, in *Being Dead*, interrupts life in multiple ways, making a mockery of all human systems, all human desires and deeds; the protagonists of the novel are murdered *in flagrante delicto*, doubly exposed to the elements, through sex and violence, they appear ridiculous, absurd and messy. Their leaking bodies are a continuation of Joseph's premature ejaculation in a play on the notion of premature death: the latter is almost always so, for human beings. In life, young people often discuss the 'best way to die'; *Being Dead* suggests the hierarchy and choice implicit in the question may not be quite so readily available. Systems making sense of death proliferate even in a secular world; genetics replaces spiritual destiny, but both suggest a lack of control, even if there is a fantasy that one day death may be endlessly deferred. The subject of death, beyond media visions of catastrophe and tragedy, becomes taboo as the symbolic gives way to the semiotic (e.g., genetic *code*); only Woody Allen appears to keep the subject of death continually alive in the West, through neurosis and laughter. Such introspective investigation may in fact be the best survival strategy, as Jung suggests: 'If the demand for self-knowledge is willed by fate and is refused, this negative attitude may end in real death.'[15] Jean Baudrillard argues that the modern, semiotic, irreversible concept of death derives from notions of the machine, with its binary logic of functionality, or on/off states of existence; the 'reality' is of course far more complex:

> The subject's identity is continually falling apart, falling into God's forgetting. But this death is not at all biological. At one pole, biochemistry, asexual protozoa are not affected by death, they divide and

branch out (nor is the genetic code, for its part, ever affected by death: it is transmitted unchanged beyond individual fates). At the other, symbolic, pole, death and nothingness no longer exist, since in the symbolic, life and death are reversible.[16]

If scientific thinking believes that death can be overcome, then the actual deaths that occur must be explained away, as accidents, unsolved biological problems or even as malevolence: '...death as unacceptable and insoluble, the Accident as persecution, as the absurd and spiteful resistance of a matter or a nature that *will not* abide by the "objective" laws with which we have pursued it'.[17] Death, ultimately within modernity, is *annoying*. In Crace's novel this is embodied by the protagonist's daughter, interrupted, disturbed and irritated by her parent's rapid and unexpected swerve from their slow-lane pursuit of dullness. In her dreams, Syl becomes haunted by spectacular deaths, stereotypes or televisual endings: 'In one dream they'd been driving when they died and the car had left the road, hovered in mid-air, burst into flames. Freeze-frame. A death by Hollywood.' (p. 103) But what annoys Syl most of all, once she wakes from her prescient dreams of 'death and nudity', is that her own life is dragged into the past, prior relationships are re-established as if they had never been disengaged from, and roles are reversed: death is now akin to teenage irresponsibility.

Narrative and Recovery

Benjamin once wrote that 'The enslavement of language in prattle is joined by the enslavement of things in folly almost as its inevitable consequence.'[18] Such a perspective (early on in Benjamin's *oeuvre*) leaves no room for the creative possibilities of narrative, based as it is upon one overriding tale: that of the Fall. In Crace's work, narrative is recovery, regardless of the ridiculousness of the particular loss. Such a position is deeply subversive, with Crace appearing to debate and debunk world-systems, appearing to leave the teleology of the material or natural world in place, meanwhile dancing with delight through the possibilities of writing, or, the continual reinvigoration of the contemporary British novel. Other critical approaches will place Crace differently: read as a postmodernist, his debunking man-oeuvres are part of a playful suspension of certainties, of overly fixed/fixated humanist values; read as a realist, his abstracted worlds are in fact allegories of contemporary society, endlessly applicable and critical. But the attention here is upon the aesthetic act as a redemptive force; while Crace explores, parodies and ridicules the holding on to the symbolic in a 'semiotic' world, his aesthetic is a recoding of the semiotic via the symbolic: narrative becomes efficacious in a way that it should no longer be, but continually *is* in his literary production.

Notes

1   Frank Kermode, 'Into the Wilderness', review of *Quarantine*, *New York Times*, 12 April 1998, late edition.
2   Walter Benjamin, 'The Storyteller: Reflections On The Works Of Nikolai Leskov' in *Illuminations*, trans. Harry Zohn (London: Jonathan Cape, 1970), p. 84.
3   Ibid., pp. 84–5.
4   Ibid., p. 38.
5   Ibid., p. 87.
6   Ibid., p. 87.
7   Ibid., p. 87.
8   Andrew Benjamin, *Present Hope: Philosophy, Architecture, Judaism* (London: Routledge, 1997), p. 49.
9   *The New Testament*, translated by William Tyndale; text of the Worms edition of 1526, ed. W. R. Cooper (London: The British Library, 2000); The Gospell off. S.Marke, p. 72.
10 Walter Benjamin, 'On Language as Such and on the Language of Man' in *Walter Benjamin: Selected Writings, Volume 1, 1913–1926*, eds, Marcus Bullock and Michael W. Jennings, trans. Rodney Livingstone (Cambridge, MA & London: Belknap/Harvard University Press, 1997), p. 65.
11 Norbert Bolz and Willem Van Reijen, *Walter Benjamin*, trans. Laimdota Mazzarins (New Jersey: Humanities Press, 1996), p. 22.
12 Terence Hawkes, *Structuralism and Semiotics* (London: Methuen, 1986), p. 68.
13 Frank Kermode, *The Genesis of Secrecy: On The Interpretation of Narrative* (Cambridge, MA & London: Harvard University Press, 1979), p. 44.
14 Ibid., p. 44.
15 C. G. Jung, *Mysterium Coniunctionis* trans. R. F. C. Hull (Princeton: Princeton University Press, 1989), p. 474.
16 Jean Baudrillard, *Symbolic Exchange and Death*, trans. Iain Hamilton Grant, (London: Sage, 1998) p. 159; see also Richard J. Lane, *Jean Baudrillard* (London: Routledge, 2000), pp. 58–61.
17 Baudrillard, *Symbolic Exchange and Death*, pp. 161–2.
18 Benjamin, 'On Language as Such and on the Language of Man,' p. 72.

Primary texts

Introduction 6 – Stories by New Writers (London: Faber & Faber, 1977)
Continent (London: Heinemann, 1986)
The Gift of Stones (London: Secker & Warburg, 1988)
Arcadia (London: Jonathan Cape, 1992)
Signals of Distress (London: Viking, 1994)
The Slow Digestions of the Night (London: Penguin, 1995)
Quarantine (London: Viking, 1997)
Being Dead (London: Viking, 1999)
The Devil's Larder (London: Viking, 2001)

Selected critical texts

Jean Baudrillard, *Symbolic Exchange and Death*, trans. Iain Hamilton Grant (London: Sage, 1998), p. 159
Walter Benjamin, 'On Language as Such and on the Language of Man', in *Walter Benjamin: Selected Writings, Volume 1, 1913–1926*, eds, Marcus Bullock and Michael W. Jennings, trans. Rodney Livingstone (Cambridge, MA & London: Belknap/Harvard University Press, 1997)
Judy Cooke, *Jim Crace* (Contemporary Writers pamphlet) (London: Book Trust in conjunction with the British Council, 1992)
Frank Kermode, 'Into the Wilderness', review of *Quarantine*, *New York Times*, 12 April 1998, late edition

3 The Novels of Graham Swift: Family Photos

Tamás Bényei

Critical readings of Graham Swift's novels tend to belong to one of two categories. The first, taking its cue from Linda Hutcheon, concentrates almost exclusively on Swift's 1983 *Waterland* which was almost instantly and enthusiastically canonized as a major example of what Hutcheon called 'historiographic metafiction'. These, usually highly theoretical, interpretations of *Waterland* read the novel as a postmodern text that dutifully interrogates and subverts many of the traditional conceptual patterns and dichotomies we take for granted in thinking about history, self-reflexively and self-consciously exposing the ideological, narrative and rhetorical assumptions behind historicist discourse, painstakingly exploring the ambiguities in the meanings of the word 'history', and, of course, questioning the meta-narratives that determine the substructure of narrative patterns. All these things *Waterland* accomplishes with considerable originality and complexity. Nevertheless, many interpretations[1] make this novel seem like a text with a clear theoretical and political agenda; although emphasizing the fallible enunciating position of the narrator as a subject of history, they tend to rely for their insights on certain of Crick's theoretical statements taken out of a context in which such theoretical statements are embedded ironically.

The second category of significant criticism[2] tackles Swift's *oeuvre* in its entirety, identifying the dominant narrative mode of the fiction as one of mourning and/or melancholia, inscribing the melancholic narrative personae into the broader cultural pathologies of nation, empire or age.[3] Although it has been adopted only by two of Swift's best interpreters, this style of questioning deserves to be treated as a different approach, as it represents a major dilemma in the reception of Swift (and a large number of other postmodern British writers, from Ishiguro to McEwan and Barnes): these writers' novels, for all their postmodern strategies, can be interpreted at one level within the tradition of the psychological novel by virtue of the psychological and ethical relevance of the speech situation that they present.

Of course, these two styles of reading Swift are not irreconcilable, and are equally problematic if left unexplored. Both read Swift's texts as extended explorations of the basic situation grounding all of his novels, the ways in which the individual is affected by and responds to the vicissitudes of twentieth-century history, becoming as in *Last Orders* 'A small man at big history.' (p. 90). The 'historiographic metafictional' reading starts from above, coming to the subject's inscription into history from the level of theoretical statement, whereas the 'melancholy' kind of reading starts with the pathological voice of the narrator, qualifying in advance the relevance of any theoretical statement as bearing the mark of the enunciative situation of narrating. It is natural that the latter kind of reading, inevitably in the case of Swift, lends itself more to a discussion of the ethical dimensions of the narratives.

Any survey, however brief, of Swift's work as a whole is more likely to profit from the second style of reading; in Swift's textual world, all theoretical or generalizing statements, indeed all abstractions, are shown to be inextricably bound to the particular situation in which they are uttered. The passage from the concrete to the abstract is invariably fraught with disjunctions, so that abstractions always return into the fictional world as strange alien presences that do little apart from defining the immediate world of the characters as somehow deprived, pervaded by absence in its inability to be amenable to abstraction. Given the nature of Swift's interests, the abstraction that enters the world of the novels is usually history. Swift's excellent first novel, *The Sweet Shop Owner*, is in this sense, as in many others, the foundation of his textual world – as one defined and damaged or crippled by a rupture between everyday experience and the abstraction of history. History in this novel appears repeatedly as a conspicuously alien, abstract *word*, that has nothing to do with the everyday experience of day-to-day living, and is therefore unable to acquire any real referential value in the world of the novel. There is a radical disjunction between the word and the situations into which it repeatedly intrudes, and the sense of alienation is further increased by the use of capitals and quotation marks (e.g. p. 59). The most typical example of this incommensurability is the embarrassing conversation between Willy Chapman and his daughter's boyfriend who is a history graduate: 'History –' offers Chapman, 'Now I've always been fascinated by history' (p. 179). The conversation inevitably peters out at this point, not only because Chapman never reads the newspapers he is selling (apart from the headlines) but also because the word is totally meaningless in his world, something he cannot connect meaningfully with his own experience. (In Swift's second novel, *Shuttlecock*, 'history' as a meaningless abstraction is replaced by 'Nature'; the verbal world of *Waterland* is dominated by the narrator's allegorizing impulse that tends to transform almost anything into an abstract, even metaphysical concept, as is testified by the ubiquity of capitalized words like 'Curiosity' and the 'Here and Now' – the latter particularly absurd in its attempt to allegorize the irreducible singularity of traumatic events.)

Here I will consider in detail what are arguably Swift's four most successful novels – *The Sweet Shop Owner, Shuttlecock, Waterland, Last Orders* – with occasional references to two other texts – *Out of This World, Ever After* – to indicate how the essential rupture between ordinary individual experience and what is referred to as history is subsumed in, or is a privileged example of, the more general rupture between the individual psyche and experience in general. This rupture organizes the world of the novels in two ways: at the level of language, in the attempts of the narrator/protagonists to make sense of their experience, and at the level of narrative organization and temporality. Many readers have noted the large number of recurrent motifs in Swift's fiction (these include the experience of the Second World War, the oppressive presence of a heroic soldier figure, usually the father, the ubiquity of mental hospitals, prosthetic limbs, certain types of family conflicts, the psychological and anthropological concern with storytelling and with images, the ethical quandary involved in the contrast between the desire to know and the pain that this knowledge might bring, etc.); for all the similarities and recurrent elements, each of Swift's novels uses a unique basic terrain or condition,[4] the experiential life-world of landscape and community that provides the immediate environment of the individual, and a set of tropes, unobtrusively arising out of the setting.

The Sweet Shop Owner presents the deliberately, self-consciously ordinary, untheorized world of South London suburbia: the novel explores in a Heideggerian way the experiential world of the subject in terms of its physical and figurative relationship with objects, the tangible things of the world. The novel, indeed, starts down below, dealing with the most basic interactions between man and thing, subject and object (using, working, owning), to such an effect that even the simple, primary act of touching things becomes increasingly resonant. When he first meets his would-be wife, Willy is working in a print-works, and his labour involves the marking of his body: 'you had to roll up your sleeves and get your fingers covered in ink or machine grease' (p. 24). After he is installed in the shop that is bought for him by his emotionally damaged wife in exchange for excising love from their relationship, what used to be the dirt of labour is merely the dirt of money: 'the grime of loose change came off on your hands, you were really intact. Nothing touches you, you touch nothing' (p. 44; the sentence becomes the most frequently recurring refrain in the novel, cf. pp. 45, 46, 146, 175). The chief irony of Willy's relationship with objects, indicated by the adjective 'intact' and spelt out in the refrain, is that he loses his ability to touch them precisely when he becomes the owner of a shop full of things that are all his. Willy, just like his wife Irene (she collects useless items, like porcelain, that keep their value [p. 148], yet 'she seemed to be renouncing all contact with things' [p. 182]) and his daughter Dorothy, quite literally loses touch. Objects cannot be touched, cannot be really owned because they are disembodied, used as mediating signs between individuals (it cannot be an accident that Irene's reckless ravisher, Hancock, is an estate agent). It seems that an item of property is derealized, dematerialized and therefore untouchable inasmuch as it ceases to function as an object with use value. The paradox, first spelt out by the drill sergeant referring to the soldiers' kit, but later generalized into another refrain-like sequence, indicates the difference between owning and belonging: 'What you 'ave don't belong to you' (pp. 58, 74, 79).

But this is not all. The interchanges between individuals are carried out by means of objects: every human relationship becomes, or is revealed as, a business transaction. The opening chapters, describing the relationship between Willy and all the other people around him (his wife and employees), are full of references to exchange, bargain, deal, investment, return, terms of agreement, reward, bribe, forfeit, price (even smiles are likened to coins [pp. 29, 30]), and, of course, to the possibility of another, non-economic kind of object-mediated relationship, that of presenting a gift – which, given the nature of Chapman's relationships, is revealed as simply another kind of payment. What makes the novel successful, however, is the fact that the transformation of intersubjectivity into business transactions is not simply a wistfully allegorical comment on the reification and commodification of human relationships, but can also be read in psychological and ethical terms.

The transformation of intersubjectivity into terms of business agreements and economic exchange infects in a metonymic way the subjects who all begin to turn into objects (puppet, dummy, statue, toy and machine are the major tropes, primarily connected to Chapman, but also unobtrusively deployed to refer to Irene and Dorothy as well). The structure of the most frequent refrain[5] ('Nothing touches you, you touch nothing') suggests chiasmus as the dominant structuring figure of this metamorphosis and of the entire narrative. The founding contrast of the chiasmus is the one between man and thing, where man, enclosed in his/her ephemeral existence, is oppressed by the ironical physical endurance of objects: 'the objects in the room loomed triumphantly' (p. 55); 'See, things remain' (p. 218). The chiasmic process, itself a kind of economic exchange on the level of rhetoric, involves the increasing 'thingness' of the human participants: throughout the text, this process is signalled by the metaphor of stiffening – Chapman's stiff leg is a physical sign of his infection. The parallel reverse metamorphic process, however (the economy of the chiasmus would suggest something like 'the humanization of objects'), is extremely ironical: before sitting down to die in his armchair, Chapman roams his house to initiate some dialogue with the objects in it, inspecting its 'silent contents', perhaps 'to summon life from those unmoving objects'. 'Perhaps he was already sitting, motionless himself, in the armchair where he'd decided he would sit, and it was only some shadow of himself, touching but not touching these frozen items of stock, who drifted now – out of his daughter's room – onto the landing at the top of the stairs' (p. 220). Things cannot be touched, not only because they are derealized, disembodied as a result of their reduction to exchange value, but also because there is no one to touch them, since men have also become like objects in their lifeless immobility: 'The garden beckoned, as things do which cannot be touched' (p. 222). Things do not become human or humanized – nothing could be further from the novel than any version of the pathetic fallacy – or if they do, it is only, as the pervasive museum imagery of the closing pages suggests, with the death of their owner, by becoming memorials. However, even this word begins to float, severed both from the speaking subject and from its purported referent: it has got nothing to do either with them or with us. 'Memorials. They don't matter. They don't belong to us. They are only things we leave behind so we can vanish safely' (p. 221). Chapman's death is thus the logical culmination of this process, a kind of mimicry seeking endurance in the extinguishing of the moving self: 'Be still, look at the things that are fixed' (p. 222). The self stiffens, turns into an object, whereas the stiff, hard surfaces of the world's objects become elusive and begin to melt as soon as one tries to touch them (such melting objects are referred to by Chapman repeatedly as 'landmarks', see pp. 24, 29, 60, 194), just as the other begins to melt away the moment one attempts to hold on to her (metaphors of melting or crumbling refer primarily to Irene's passive, immobile body: Chapman repeatedly feels that 'Her body might dissolve if he touched her', see p. 72, also pp. 41, 99, 127).

The chiasmic process of transaction is not simply or not only an economic but also a psychological allegory. Transactions are deadening, mutually stiffening in the novel because what is primarily transferred is the experience of trauma, something beyond language; since it cannot be articulated either by Irene or by any of the other members of her family who are partly responsible for the rape, it becomes a transferential object transferred in the course of everyday transactions to her husband Willy Chapman and their daughter Dorothy, who also inherits the chiasmic refrain (p. 146), each intercourse within the family a stand-in for the essential transaction. The result is a condition of intangibility and inability to touch, a sense of being cut (wounded), cut off from the world of objects and others, and also cut off in the sense of existing in a stiffened temporality cut up into discrete moments that refuse to coalesce or be synthesized in a living continuum. The narrative strategy of the novel expresses this traumatized temporality on the micro level, in the numerous insertions into the text (dominated by free indirect speech or internal monologue) of one-sentence 'descriptions', references to some element of the external world, not linked logically either to the narrated events or to the narrating voice. These inlays are either simply hard little lumps of the physical world, almost *chosiste* in their intensity, or similes, in both cases disturbing because they seem to be coming from an unidentified narrative position: 'A plume of steam released itself from the boiler-house, like a white hole in the flat vista. Outside in the corridor a girl was being pushed along in a wheel-chair while a nurse walked beside her reading a clip-board chart' (p. 127).

These inlays have the effect of stills from a film, instants that are already images in the sense of having been removed from (narrative, temporal) continuity and experienced as a pattern of figures rather than as an informative remark about the state of things in the world. These cuts and stills become dominant in the stunning middle section of the novel (especially Chapter 9), which 'recounts' the war experiences of Chapman and Irene, overlaying several scenes, switching time and perspective in a thoroughly dislocating way and destabilizing narrative point of view in the sequence of unrelated, disjuncted stills. This section, besides embodying and conveying the traumatized experience of temporality that is also the 'object' of the narrative, links this experience to other persistent concerns of Swift's fiction: the nature of (visual) experience, the boundary between event/thing and image and, given that the 'root' sequence of this disjuncted section is a family event, the taking of photographs in the Harrisons' garden during the war, to another major concern in Swift's work, the essentially wounded, dislocated nature of the time of the family. The disjointed bits of the text are like brittle, hard, skewed shards insisting on their discreteness. The fractured text, organized by refrain-like sequences ('The figures grouped, composed', p. 70) enacts this temporality and, in another chiasmic phrase, connects it explicitly to the motif and temporality of the photograph: 'Can you capture the moment without it capturing you?' (p. 222).

Swift's later novels develop his continuing interest in the nature of vision, image and experience. If *The Sweet Shop Owner* explores the human condition in terms of our relationship with objects and our objectified relationships with each other, *Shuttlecock*, concerned with the spiritual plight and regeneration of a man damaged by the influence of his war hero father, torturing himself and his family by being a bully, investigates the essentials of our intersubjective relationships in terms of the metaphor of looking or gazing. The novel presents an extremely diverse typology of situations of gazing, from scientific scrutiny to spying (Prentis spied on by his son), voyeurism and surveillance (for me, the novel's most memorable image is that of the hamster's unseeing eyes which 'seemed, under certain circumstances, to be about to spill, like drops of ink, from its head', (p. 5)). The root scene of the novel, repeated in several situations and variations, is one in which a naked person is looked at by someone else (the old inmate of the mental home who slowly undresses in the garden, the humiliating experiences of Prentis's father at the hands of the Gestapo in France, Prentis's father running away naked and coming face to face with a German guard, Prentis standing over his wife who is having a bath, Prentis giving a bath to his young sons, Prentis's dark anthropological observations about our behaviour in the Tube). Conceived as the intersubjective situation *par excellence*, this image would seem to define human relationships in terms of power and submission; this suggestion is reinforced, among many other episodes, by the founding scene of the novel, Prentis's boyhood memories of torturing his pet hamster, as well as by the claustrophobic, panopticon-like structure of his office (the boss, Quinn, is looking down on his clerks through a glass panel 'with the air of a scientist surveying some delicate experiment' p. 21).

The thematic and symbolic structure of the novel is probably best seen in terms of the layering of situations of power and situations of looking, a layering that promises interpretative coherence and stability but does not result in a perfect fit. On the one hand, every intersubjective situation (father and son, husband and wife, boss and subordinate) seems to be reducible to that of master and slave: even love and caring reveal their basic complicity with power, expressed in the desire to torture the creature we discover to be at our mercy ('It's a funny thing, isn't it, how you start off wanting to protect someone and then, for that very reason, you end up torturing them?', p. 180). This essential set-up seems to find its most expressive image in the act of gazing that necessarily acquires a colouring of sadism and object-ification. This strand of the novel is effectively reinforced by the text's links with the self-detesting narrator of Dostoevsky's *Notes from the Underground* and the existential parable of Kafka's story 'The Burrow', whose unidentified narrator defines ideal existence as that where one is unseen; existence, reduced to its essentials, reveals man as 'some burrowing animal' (pp. 108, 170). This extremely depressing but interpretatively neat conclusion, however, is challenged precisely by the deeper implications of some obvious power struggles that involve sadistic gazing. Quinn's experiment with power is one case in point: although his access to secret files provides him with explo-sive knowledge about others, the kind of knowledge the revelation of which could unleash a lot of pain and confer on him a great deal of power, he chooses to incinerate the incriminating files; his blatant manipulation (torturing) of Prentis is like the strategies of John Fow-les's magus figures: using and abusing power, ultimately in order to disabuse their victims, by educating them towards an acceptance of uncertainty. The other case indicates that the novel's strategy of ostensibly identifying a sadistic power relationship with gazing is questioned by the text itself, and this has to do with what was said earlier about the general implications of the rupture between abstrac-tion and lived experience. The act of looking (even if we consider only the root scene of looking at a naked person) always contains a contextual excess that escapes theoretical formulations, as is indi-cated by the scene in which Prentis is looking down at the naked body of his wife in the bath. 'She peers up at me with the frozen look of someone anticipating some attack and scared to provoke that attack by making a move of defence [...] here she is cornered and has no choice but to plead innocence' (p. 148). Even though the episode is explicitly linked to other instances of the root scene (it follows the father's prison memories of humiliating nakedness and is followed by reminiscences of Marian's work as a physiotherapist, having enormous power over her patients, see p. 149), this scene is different, simply by virtue of happening at this particular moment and in this particular context. Instead of generating sadistic or voyeuristic emotions, Marian's naked body evokes in Prentis memories of

bathing his sons when they were very young, of their 'tender...
pitiful... pink flesh' (p. 149), and Prentis finds himself overcome
by 'a sudden urge to wash my wife. To kneel down at the edge of the
bath and – with the utmost tenderness – to run the soap and the bath-
sponge over her body' (p. 149). At the end of the novel we are left
with a sense of the potential unpredictability of any intersubjective
situation rather than with the anthropologically or psychologically
defined necessity of sadism in human relationships, reducible to variations of the master/slave relationship.

Swift returned later to his exploration of image, vision, photography, and their relationship with a traumatized experience of temporality, most explicitly in *Out of This World*, where the explosive,
traumatic moment of the narrative (the violent death of Robert Beech)
is also the moment of photography: Sophie, Robert Beech's granddaughter, seems to have been as much traumatized by her father's
taking photos of the aftermath of the explosion as by the event itself.
The novel, using the motif of photography to explore the phenomenological nature of the boundary between thing and image ('An
image, my dear Sophie, is something without knowledge or memory.
Do we see the truth or tell it?', p. 76), connects this problem with the
essentially traumatic nature of all experience, of all events – in a
paradoxical way. On the one hand, Harry Beech, the legendary frontline news photographer, defines photography as a defence, as an
extinction of the self ('All you are is your eyes, all there is is in your
eyes', p. 121), and also in psychoanalytic terms as a means of detrau-
matizing a traumatic experience: 'A photo is a reprieve, an act of
suspension, a charm. If you see something terrible or wonderful, that
you can't take in or focus your feelings for, [...] take a picture of it,
hold the camera to it. Look again when it's safe' (p. 122). In this way
the photograph defuses a traumatic experience by accumulating into
itself the psychic energy that is generated by the experience but
for some reason cannot be released (abreacted): the photo is something like an externalized, harmless symptom. On the other hand,
the photograph is also a replica of the trauma itself, fixing 'an
instant which occurs once and once only, [yet] remains permanently
visible' (p. 205).

The photograph, then, besides being an instrument of detraumati-
zation, condenses into itself the paradoxical temporality of the
trauma as it is defined in *Waterland*: 'But then we've already stepped
into a different world. The one where things come to a stop; the one
where the past will go on happening' (p. 263, see also 284). The
traumatic event is irretrievably past, it is 'a unique, a momentous
event. [...]. It only happens once' (p. 237); on the other hand, it is like

the photograph in the sense of having been etched in the mind, of not being over because the psyche is unable to work through it: 'And, though, indeed, it only happened once, it's gone on happening, the way unique and momentous things do, for ever and ever, as long as there's a memory for them to happen in' (pp. 237–8; the temporality of the trauma is described in similar terms by Sophie in *Out of This World*, p. 109).

Several of Swift's novels (*Out of This World*, *Waterland*, *Ever After*) present the narratives of characters (in *Out of This World* some of the 'world's walking wounded', p. 174), represent attempts to tell, process and overcome a traumatic experience. The narratives, therefore, are outside the trauma but also marked by it, becoming symptomatic texts (this is indicated by the fact that Sophie Beech's monologues in *Out of This World* are addressed to her analyst, and also by the very successfully and evocatively presented transferential narrative situation in *Waterland*). Swift's interest in the act of story-telling began with *Shuttlecock* (p. 67), where Prentis's obsessive reading of his father's war memoirs offers a possible manual for the reading of the other texts: even though the book, or parts of it, may be a pack of lies, the way it is told remains perhaps even more interesting, and suggestive of what the father was 'like' than a purely factual account.

Waterland, Swift's most complex novel, and perhaps still his best, alongside *Last Orders*, practically identifies 'event' with trauma (as does Derrida in *Sauf le nom*) and presents the highly pathological, wounded (the Greek for 'wound' is '*trauma*') narrative of the history teacher Thomas Crick, who at one point abandons the teaching of history to his pupils and switches to the teaching of metahistory, recounting the story of his native Fenland, his paternal and maternal ancestors, as well as the story of his teenage years that involves abortion, murder and all manner of other kinds of death, that is, a massive dose of loss. *Waterland*, among other things, is a suggestive exploration of narrative not only as a way of working through traumatic experience but also as a culturally, psychologically and ethically defined human act. The novel's opening scene is, significantly, an episode that recounts an act of storytelling. Thomas Crick recalls a night when his father, the lock-keeper Henry Crick, told him and his half-witted brother, Dick, a story about the stars: 'Do you know what the stars are? They are the silver dust of God's blessing. They are little broken-off bits of heaven. God cast them down to fall on us. But when he saw how wicked we were, he changed his mind and ordered the stars to stop. Which is why they hang up in the sky but seem as though at any time they might drop . . .' (p. 1).

This scene accomplishes several things. It founds the narrative situation as a paternal act of bequeathing knowledge about the world; the opening chapter is the evocation of the Fens by means of the conferred authority of the father, through the father's naming and narrating acts. The fictional world is founded by a mistaken, catachretic act of naming (stars are God's blessing), just as in García Márquez's *One Hundred Years of Solitude*, where the patriarch José Arcadio Buendía's act of naming the ice (calling it 'the biggest diamond in the world') has a similar function. Wendy Wheeler, Adrian Poole in 'Graham Swift and the Morning After', 1991, (p. 153) and Fred Botting all associated Crick's (and Swift's) melancholic mode with the 'crisis of paternity' (Botting, 'History, holes and things', pp. 125–6), which, as Wheeler claims, indicates a more general 'failure of cultural and historical continuity, the failure, in psychoanalytical terms, of the "paternal" function of bearing and transmitting the cultural "law," but also [...] a divine father who no longer works' ('Melancholic modernity...', 1999, p. 66). This opening scene, introducing a father who is endowed with the knack of storytelling, seems to be a successful act of transmission, but only a limitedly successful one. It works only if complemented by the maternally inherited act and rationale of storytelling (Adrian Poole claims that Swift mourns also 'the voice of the mother' ['Graham Swift...', 1991, p. 163]). Storytelling 'was a knack which my mother had too – and perhaps he really acquired it from her. Because when I was very small it was my mother who first told me stories, which, unlike my father, she got from books as well as out of her head, to make me sleep at night' (p. 2). This sentence complicates the process of cultural transmission in several ways; leaving aside the class and gender implications of the passage (the mother, an Atkinson girl, would be familiar with books, that is, the written documents of the culture, whereas the father, one of the phlegmatic Cricks, represents oral narration), there is an essential difference in the function of storytelling implied in the two acts: for the father, stories are a means of transmitting knowledge about the world, whereas the mother's storytelling is essentially a performative act, the sense (point) of stories residing in their effect rather than their contents (it is not by chance that what Crick remembers here is the father's *story* and the mother's *storytelling*). The opening chapter thus establishes two kinds (and theories) of narrative situation, founding the essential ambiguity of Crick's narrative: in his text, the paternal narrative situation (a schoolmaster educating pupils) is subverted and transformed by the insistence of the maternal model.

Yet another important aspect of the father's story has to be mentioned, since the temporality of the entire novel is also established

here. The father tells a cosmological story of origins and of a suspended ending, of the suspended stars arrested in their fall. The world
of the suspended blessing is an essentially eschatological one, a world
that is waiting for the end, measuring itself and its time against its
imminent end. Crick's narrative is an eschatological story of a waste-
land that has lost its original fertility. The entire world and time of the
novel are overshadowed by the (biological and spiritual) infertility of
his marriage, the infertility of the present. The storytelling, besides
being a richly ambiguous act of teaching, confession, healing, remembering and forgetting, ought to be working primarily as a 'magic tale'
(p. 297), miraculously taking Crick and Mary back to before the
moment of loss.

The opening chapter thus establishes the ambiguous mode of
Crick's narrative (story *and* act) as well as its eschatological temporality. The story is about the impossibility of salvation, narrating the
death of Dick, 'That baby who, as everyone knows, was sent by God.
Who will save us all' (p. 284), and the death of Tom and Mary's baby
before he was even born. Crick constructs a gigantic narrative mechanism, including a complete mythology, metaphysics and metahistory,
as well as a magical narrative of inherited curse, writing himself into
all these (meta)narratives in order to be able to absolve himself, to
write himself out of his own story; the extremely powerful rhetorical
nature of the story, that is, Crick's pervasive presence in his narrative,
conceals a desire to write himself out of his own story, to be absent
from it. Instead of a confrontation with history, which is what he
would seem to be undertaking in true hermeneutic spirit, hoping to
learn who he is from history, he projects upon it the shape of his own
life, thus he is able to discover in history only what he has put into it
in the first place: the emptiness of his life, enclosed between the two
moments of the abortion and the returning of the baby his wife has
snatched from the supermarket. The chapter recounting the returning
of the stolen baby is inserted between the two chapters recounting the
abortion. In the book, there is nothing between the two moments,
repetition abolishes the time between, that is, the entire adult life of
Thomas Crick: this is the emptiness he discovers and recognizes as his
own wherever he looks: in his mythology, metaphysics, historiography and eschatology.

Crick's ambitious narrative project is made possible by his discovery that traumatic temporality is structurally identical with the temporality of eschatology. In a strictly formal sense, Crick's conception
of time is like that of the believing Christian who is already above
history, because the eschatological event (the embodiment of the word
in flesh in the figure of Christ) is potentially happening in every

moment. As Walter Benjamin put it, 'every second of time ... [is] the straight gate through which the Messiah might enter'.[6] Graham Swift's ongoing exploration of the time of trauma reaches its culmination here. Traumatic time is like the negative of eschatological time, every moment invaded by the same event that goes on happening in every moment, with the huge difference that the repetition of the traumatic anti-event hollows out every moment of time instead of making it, as eschatological temporality does, a moment of potential plenitude.

Waterland is perhaps the most negative in tone among Swift's novels, at least as far as the possibility of overcoming trauma, of spiritual reconciliation and regeneration is concerned. Precisely because it conflates the time of the trauma with eschatological time, the narrative offers no hope, no point of exit out of its multilayered circularity. This is why *Last Orders*, in many ways a neat rounding-off of many of Swift's major concerns, makes such a difference – and brings relief after the less successful *Out of This World* and especially *Ever After*. In terms of narrative organization, *Last Orders* is structured, like *Out of This World*, out of the alternating monologues of a couple of characters, thus posing in its structure the question, so prevalent in novels from *The Sweet Shop Owner* on, of narrative continuity versus disjointedness. Although the four pilgrims of the novel, taking the jar containing the ashes of their dead friend to Margate Pier in observance of his last wish, do not tell their respective stories in one instalment but in chronologically disrupted fragments, the effect is not that of disjointedness or discontinuity. The structural question, instead, seems to be that of figure and ground and, indeed, the individual narratives are as good as dissolved in the conglomerate of interrelated and intermingled tales. This is so partly because the text, wisely I think, abandons the exploration of trauma and traumatic time, and is therefore exempt from the almost gratuitous proliferation of traumas, which threatened to suffocate the two previous novels. Thus, although this is not a happy book at all, the multiple narrators and the disrupted chronology do not create a sense of a traumatized temporality of discrete moments that refuse to be synthesized into a continuity, simply because the novel, in the final analysis, recounts the story of a successful ritual of mourning, a ritual that is spiritually uplifting for all the participants or communicants.

Swift's changed strategy is also reflected in the perfectly calculated language of the novel, positioning itself somewhere between the two extremes of language use, the two possible responses to trauma, that characterize Swift's fiction. On the one hand, every novel contains an allegorical figure of silence, a catatonic character (in *Shuttlecock*

Prentis's father is suffering from 'language-coma', p. 40), living in a home and embodying some mystifying secret that another character is obsessively trying to excavate (Irene Harrison in *The Sweet Shop Owner*, Prentis's father in *Shuttlecock*, Sarah Atkinson and Mary Crick in *Waterland*, Joe's father in *Out of This World*, June in *Last Orders*). These figures are stuck inside this temporality (Bernard, 'Dismembering/Remembering Mimesis...' 1993, p. 129), also embodying the element beyond language that all the novels contain within themselves like a secret centre; in *Shuttlecock* 'it is not madness which is locked up and concealed like a crime', suggests Prentis, 'but something concealed behind madness' (p. 127). At the other extreme, as another strategy of responding to trauma, we have the loquacious, meandering, self-conscious, highly rhetorical and profoundly symptomatic filibustering of some earlier narrators, very effective in the case of Crick but much less so in that of Bob Unwin, the narrator of *Ever After*. The muted language of *Last Orders* avoids the sense of creating an ineffable secret centre around which the verbal world of the novel is orbiting. Returning to the world of the first novel, *The Sweet Shop Owner, Last Orders* chooses, again like the first novel, a very simple, partly very physical, partly metaphorical terrain for exploring the human condition: that of jobs, occupations, as they define identity within the community (one of the novel's refrains is 'What do you want to be'? [see pp. 96, 155, 159]). None of these characters, apart from Vic the undertaker, have become what they wanted to be, yet these failed lives and figures succeed in undertaking one successful act of mourning.

This leads us to another, perhaps the greatest, success of the novel. The text recounts and enacts a ritual of death, including a visit to the hallowed ground of Canterbury Cathedral, managing to avoid any earnestness or undue solemnity. It maintains a very skilfully calculated oscillation between the sacred and the profane, letting itself be gently tugged by an upward and a downward pull. The narrative and figurative universe of *Last Orders* is vertically organized by these two forces, and achieves, through the omnipresent sense of being a ritual, a tone that manages to suggest elevation without ever becoming sententious or sentimental. The novel pulls this off by means of a very gentle but clearly recognizable tendency to profanation, returning in this way to the world of objects so powerfully present in *The Sweet Shop Owner*. The central object of the pilgrimage is the very profane plastic jar containing Jack Dodds's ashes, and it is the – partly verbal – vicissitudes of this object, likened even at the very end to a box of cornflakes (p. 294), that dispel any ponderousness. It is Swift's triumph that the text is able to accommodate the grotesque tussle between Vince and Lenny for the jar (pp. 146–7) as well as the genuinely chastening experience of the ritual of mourning that tentatively raises, without being assertive, various possibilities of spiritual regeneration and reconciliation.

Notes

1   The finest of these include John Schad, 'The End of the End of History: Graham Swift's *Waterland*', *Modern Fiction Studies* 38.4 (Winter 1992), 911–25; Pamela Cooper, 'Imperial Topographies: The Spaces of History in *Waterland*', *Modern Fiction Studies* 42.2 (Summer 1996), 371–96; Fred Botting, 'History, holes and things', *Sex, machines and navels: Fiction, fantasy and history in the future present* (Manchester: Manchester University Press, 1999); George P. Landow, 'History, His Story, and Stories in Graham Swift's *Waterland*', *Studies in the Literary Imagination* 23.2 (1990), 197–211; Catherine Bernard, 'Dismembering/Remembering Mimesis: Martin Amis, Graham Swift', *British Postmodern Fiction*, eds. Theo D'Haen and Hans Bertens (Amsterdam: Rodopi, 1993), pp. 121–144.
2   Wendy Wheeler, 'Melancholic modernity and contemporary grief: the novels of Graham Swift', *Literature and the Contemporary: Fictions and Theories of the Present*, ed. Roger Luckhurst and Peter Marks (Harlow: Longman, 1999), pp. 63–79. The other important relevant article is Adrian Poole's 'Graham Swift and the Morning After', *An Introduction to Contemporary Fiction*, ed. Rod Mengham (Cambridge: Polity Press, 1999) pp. 150–67.
3   For Wendy Wheeler, for instance, Swift's work is representative of a postmodern attempt to address and overcome modernism's pathological temporality of melancholia.
4   Comprising a particular instance of what Husserl called the *Lebenswelt*.
5   These refrains constitute one of the trademarks of Swift; they are present in all the novels, the same sequence sometimes appearing in several texts (e.g. 'What you don't know can't hurt you').
6   Walter Benjamin, 'Theses on the Philosophy of History', *Illuminations*, ed. Hannah Arendt (London: New Left Books, 1973), p. 266.

Primary texts

The Sweet Shop Owner (London: Heinemann, 1980)
Shuttlecock (London: Allen Lane, 1981)
Waterland (London: Heinemann, 1983)
Out of This World (London: Penguin, 1988)
Ever After (London: Macmillan, 1992)
Last Orders (London: Macmillan, 1996)

Selected critical texts

Catherine Bernard, 'Dismembering/Remembering Mimesis: Martin Amis, Graham Swift' in *British Postmodern Fiction*, eds Theo D'Haen and Hans Bertens (Amsterdam: Rodopi, 1993)

Fred Botting, 'History, holes and things', *Sex, machines and navels: Fiction, fantasy and history in the future present* (Manchester: Manchester University Press, 1999)

Pamela Cooper, 'Imperial Topographies: The Spaces of History in *Waterland*', *Modern Fiction Studies* 42.2 (Summer 1996), 371–96

George P. Landow, 'History, His Story, and Stories in Graham Swift's *Waterland*', *Studies in the Literary Imagination* 23.2 (1990), 197–211.

Adrian Poole, 'Graham Swift and the Morning After', *An Introduction to Contemporary Fiction*, ed., Rod Mengham (Cambridge: Polity Press, 1991), pp. 150–67.

John Schad, 'The End of the End of History: Graham Swift's *Waterland*', *Modern Fiction Studies* 38.4 (Winter 1992), 911–25.

Wendy Wheeler, 'Melancholic modernity and contemporary grief: the novels of Graham Swift', *Literature and the Contemporary: Fictions and Theories of the Present*, ed. Roger Luckhurst and Peter Marks, (Harlow: Longman, 1999), pp. 63–79.

4 The Writing of Iain Sinclair: 'Our Narrative Starts Everywhere'

Rod Mengham

The work of Iain Sinclair – poetry, fiction, non-fiction – is unified by an obsessive focus on the repressed history of the contemporary landscape. It is a coherent project that is both gripping in and gripped by its fascination with particular territories, driven by its concern with the rival claims staked by those who would both make and tell the history of those territories. Particularly in its meditations on the condition of London, Sinclair's is an intense and impassioned writing that has always resisted 'official' versions, that has been haunted, almost literally, by ideas of, dreams of, and plans for, another London that has either been swept away or which perhaps has never come into being. In making the links between those who have contributed to the life of this other, fictional place, Sinclair's texts have established a sense of community across time-zones that must be weighed in the balance against the demands made on the metropolis by those who merely inhabit or manage its present organization of space. Since the publication of the first three novels, *White Chappell, Scarlet Tracings* (1987), *Downriver* (1991) and *Radon Daughters* (1994), there have been several quasi-documentary books, *Lights Out for the Territory* (1997), *Liquid City* (1999) and *Rodinsky's Room* (1999), collaborations (the first two with Marc Atkins, the third with Rachel Lichtenstein) which have wondered about what happens to a city when it becomes amnesiac, and which have taken seriously the responsibility of counting the cost of that amnesia and of holding it off.

Long before the publication of his first novel, Sinclair was already working out in his poetry the agenda that has sustained his writing in fiction and essay form ever since. One particularly crucial text in the development of his concerns was *The Horse. The Man. The Talking*

Head, originally published as a prose section in the long poem *Suicide Bridge* (1979). This represents the most sustained and systematic account of twentieth-century myth-formation in Sinclair's early work. It takes as its subject the figure of Howard Hughes, that industrial and media giant, who was one of the most dynamic presences behind the inception of modern consumer society, but who also attempted to reverse the direction that history was taking him in, in the most astonishingly dramatic of ways. Hughes's activities seemed to be universal: he had controlling interests in the aircraft industry, in the manufacture of poisons and weapons, he owned newspapers, printing-works, forests, radio stations, cinemas, film companies and teams of writers. He had at his disposal all the means of producing the simulacra of postmodernity. Sinclair considers him the key figure in the absolute confusion of the movies and the world: 'Realities oscillate: so that Shirley Temple can be leased from her studio to the Republican Party, or Ronald Reagan can graduate from playing epileptic juveniles for Don Siegel to the heavy in *The Killers* to chewing the rug in the Governor's Palace.'[1] Sinclair's text is itself, of course, produced in the post-Hughes era of media simulations and its own language is ambivalently tuned in to the airwaves; it simultaneously attaches itself to and resists the language of mass media transmissions: 'So the action cranes through horse skull into McCarthy land...with Presidential candidates mouthing, just-out-of-synch' (p. 100); 'opening shot silhouette figure, with credit titles over, entering from the left, death' (p. 102) and so on.

Hughes is made the paradigmatic figure of American culture, dubbed 'the intelligence of America', whose bizarre appearance at time of death (he was emaciated and had allowed his hair and nails to grow unchecked for about a decade) gives him the 'face of a man kept alive by time-surgery', a sort of cryogenic survivor of the civil war, who had lived through the industrial war boom of the forties into the postmodern era of 'image factories'. His personal history seemed to lay bare the fatal logic of a society dedicated to the inflation of celebrity status to a degree that the individual actually inhabiting that condition would implode. Stardom becomes the paradoxical guarantee of anonymity: to manufacture a star means to 'spray anonymity in gold light' (p. 100); to produce a subject through the glamorous extinction of individuality. Hughes is credited with having had the acuity to realize this and to have sought evasion from its controlling power over his own life by taking the initiative, by willing it to happen, by anticipating the process in his own actions. Thus he became a total recluse, refusing the invasions of the outside world to the extent of refusing food, attempting to 'reverse into the invisible', in Sinclair's phrase, to 'obscure the face, the source' (p. 100), and surrounding himself with Mormons, whose own self-suppression was in the service of a church that was a simulacrum of Christianity, locked into material interests that would instrumentalize religion as a form of social control. Hughes, therefore, transforms himself into a kind of trace element, as nothing more than a response to cues from the social environment, a mark 'on the transparent medium through which his heat had passed' (p. 103). His annihilation of self allows what Sinclair calls the 'energy' to 'step free', allows the cultural dominant to emerge in the place previously occupied by a myth of self-determination.

This is a thoroughly postmodern scenario in which the motivations for political action are irrelevant – their effect is the same as events on a screen, whether they have this motivation or that. In this context, Sinclair's deliberately perverse analysis is as viable as any other. The Kennedys' extravagant bids for media attention are seen as manic responses to the planned socialization of a code of signals that will reduce the value of a political commitment by its rate of exchange into that which will replace it as a spectacular version. Hughes proves the rule by his exceptional attempt to withdraw from the code, to withdraw himself from circulation in this economy of signs which produces a culture of inanition. Sinclair's text uncovers the socio-cultural mechanisms of the simulacrum. It offers itself as a critique of the American, and therefore global, hyper-reality. And yet the tailpiece to its theorization of Howard Hughes seems to reveal that Sinclair's own writing is unexpectedly beyond his control. Determinants crowd in of which he had previously been unaware, making it seem as if they had used him merely to produce what they had wanted. Suddenly, the author feels like one of Hughes's hacks being directed by remote control and asks himself, 'Who are you working for?' (p. 108). The writing is subject to an extraordinary, unstable tension between the maintenance of critical distance and the relinquishing of that distance.

Perhaps Sinclair's version of the life of Hughes is no more privileged than any of the others: 'one of many projections floating about just ahead of, or just behind, the event screen' (p. 107). It may be that his ability to tap into the lines of stress and surges of power he detects in contemporary history is a form of complicity with oppression rather than the disengagement of positive energy. Either his writing has a merely negative value, moving 'just ahead of the causal tide, but attached to it', or else it has a more positive role to play, actively facilitating the production of new social relations by getting ahead of events 'by one beat, [causing] the events to follow' (p. 108). Whether or not, is undecidable: the writer is within a charmed circle impossible to break out of, mesmerized by the charm of his own designs. To disclose the existence of certain patterns and connections may lead to their abolition, or it may, on the other hand, actually invite them to close in.

This early text provides a template for the preoccupations that Sinclair has explored relentlessly in his subsequent books. It expresses the nature of the relationship between the subject and history in terms of flows of energy which form recurrent patterns; art provides a means of access to these patterns, or it imagines them, but with a power that is difficult to control, with a difficulty expressive of the limitations on individual agency, hinting at the possibility that participation in history is a process of being taken possession of. History is also interfused with art, especially fiction, in the sense that fiction not only reflects the patterns of history, it also sometimes anticipates them, and may even trigger them. Sinclair's fiction includes propositions about historical reality, while his non-fiction views history as fictive. Genres overlap constantly in his writings, but so do individual texts, whether written by Sinclair himself, or by others. His compositions are full of allusions to texts whose rhetorical structures are echoed in his own work: the Sherlock Holmes stories, Conrad, Stevenson, T. S. Eliot ('The Waste Land'), Dickens (especially *Our Mutual Friend*); the centre of gravity for this allusive tendency is the history of writing about London. London was not the exclusive, but it was the major, focus of Sinclair's writings in the 1990s. *Radon Daughters* (1994) includes extensive scenes set in Oxford, Cambridge and the west coast of Ireland, while *Landor's Tower* (2001) concentrates on the border country between England and Wales, but the remaining books published during the last decade have returned again and again to the East End, to the City, to the Thames, to the estuarine marshes.

In Chapter 11 of Dickens's *Our Mutual Friend*, a bewildered Frenchman is challenged to make some sort of connection between the idea of Britishness as expressed in its institutions – what Mr Podsnap refers to as the 'British Constitution' – and the 'evidence' to be found actually in the streets of London. The Frenchman does not make any headway in his attempt to connect the idea to the reality. Neither does he get any help in trying to do so from the odious Mr Podsnap. In Atkins's and Sinclair's *Liquid City* (1999), another Frenchman, 'deranged' rather than just bewildered, is faced with a very similar dilemma; although he is physically in the streets, and surrounded by their 'evidence', he is unable to relate what he is seeing to what he thinks he should be seeing: '*Is* this London?' he queries, uncertain of how to connect the reality to the idea. On this occasion, however, the interlocutors are Marc Atkins and Iain Sinclair, who seem to have spent much of their lives and most of their shoe-leather in investigating the scale and nature of the question of where London begins and ends. London turns out to be a state of mind, a stratum of feelings, a set of memories, and the evidence for it is to be found quite precisely in the streets.

The two books *Lights Out for the Territory* (1997) and *Liquid City* (1999) are companion pieces; the first contains more text than photographs, the second more photographs than text, but both cover the same terrain and even many of the same events. They are also generic transformations of much of the same subject matter exposed initially in another pair of texts, *White Chappell, Scarlet Tracings* (1987) and *Downriver* (1991), where the point of view is a mobile one, but associated most frequently with the shared inquisitiveness of the narrator and the character Joblard, who resemble closely Sinclair himself and the writer and artist, Brian Catling. In all four books, the protagonists are constructed as fictional characters who inhabit a vividly realized social reality. In the fiction, Joblard and the narrator – in the 'non-fiction', Atkins and Sinclair – patrol the boundaries of the City of London and traverse its interior, dowsing for the lost routes of the historic city and the vanished contours of its original landscape. The books are effectively organized around a series of walks that avoid the circuitry of modern transport systems and the pace of contemporary city life: 'time on these excursions should be allowed to unravel at its own speed, that's the whole point of the exercise. To shift away from the culture of consumption into a meandering stream.'[2] These wanderings are not like the solitary adventures of the nineteenth-century *flaneur*, nor are their reveries highly subjective but collaborative, symbiotic attempts to discover and tap into the collective memories and shared experiences that energize particular buildings and patches of ground. 'Energy' and 'heat' are important words in the vocabulary used by Sinclair to describe the vitality now hidden or displaced that once animated a particular set of coordinates. Misalignment, creating disruptions in the field, is what particularly galvanizes the attention; the focal characters are fascinated by the removal of monuments from one place to another: by the excavation and repositioning of the Temple of Mithras, by the peregrinations of London Stone, by the deracinating of sculptures from the original Ludgate, which stood on the western flank of the old City wall. These markers, and others like them, are correlated, mutually defining and chthonic, in ways that a modern map of the same area will not register.

But if there is a 'sacred geometry' of London to be discovered, its precise extent and intricacy are impossible to determine. The focal characters clearly place themselves under obligations, to be ready, alert, responsive to patterns wherever these manifest themselves, but they are equally prone to anticipate, encourage and fictionalize the process. The words 'fiction' and 'documentation' enter into an increasingly close relationship, become intertwined, inextricable. A highly developed capacity to create patterns where none exist becomes simultaneously a risk, a drawback and a stimulus. In *Lights Out for the Territory* and *Liquid City*, writer and photographer circle around each other, their prose and images recording different levels, or layers, of reality while they take it in turns to work the documentary and fictive strands; on some occasions, Sinclair can be seen orchestrating the photographs that Atkins will take, while at other times, it is only an image captured by Atkins that provides the necessary cue for one of Sinclair's narratives. The constant mutual adjustments of the two media, the double-act refined by the footsore duo, with matching inbuilt resistivity meters but contrasting diets, desires and phobias, create a focus for the books' conceptual organization, and for the Sinclair *oeuvre* as a whole, which is fascinated by, and which returns again and again to, the contemplation of doubles, doppelgängers, contraries and amalgams: pairs of writers (Catling and Sinclair, Rimbaud and Verlaine), of bookdealers (Dryfeld and Nicholas Lane), of investigators (Holmes and Moriarty), murderers (Gull and Hinton), doctors and patients (Treves and Merrick) gangster twins (the Krays). Joblard and the narrator and Atkins and Sinclair are the Bouvards and Pecuchets of the urban desert, the Weggs and Venuses of the dust mounds, their artistic interdependence so complete in these books it becomes impossible to decide at any given moment which is the disarticulator, which the re-articulator, of the secret knowledge they struggle to unearth.

For Wegg and Venus (*Our Mutual Friend*), the buried secret in the mounds of filth had an alchemical sheen – once discovered, it would turn all the crap into gold. For Sinclair's symbiotic characters, the value of hidden things inheres in the degree of secrecy attached to them: 'Access should never be easy. If a story is worth excavating, it's quite right that the latter-day guardians should sod you about.'[3] Resistance and obstruction attract further and deeper investigation. Certain territories remain obstinately off-limits: the banking zones of the City, hemmed in by surveillance cameras, and the inner recesses of Lord Archer's apartment, even though Atkins and Sinclair wangle permission to inspect his art collection. This failure to penetrate the barriers set up by contemporary forms of power sharpens the instinct to decipher other, more occulted, versions: cabbalistic graffiti, coded statuary, defaced maps, abandoned objects are all collated and cross-referenced as evidence of an underlying system of meaning. It is in the end an aesthetic judgement which determines how far the quest will be taken; when Sinclair's investigating duos fail to gain physical access to the premises, they will gain access by other, textual, means. In many respects, refusal of access is a great liberator, as Sinclair recognizes in respect of the burning of Old St Paul's library during the Great Fire of London: 'they sealed away all the knowledge that was worth preserving ... Hot air reached the bundles of paper and parchment and they gleefully ignited. "They burned for a week until they were no more than a great mound of ash." And the amnesiac church was left to invent any past that took its fancy.' (*Lights Out*, p. 131). That last sentence indicates the scope for inventiveness that is seized on eagerly in the Sinclair projects, but it also suggests a nonchalance that he does not avail himself of. In fact, there is something unremittingly moral in Sinclair's obsession with the dynamic relationship between memory and forgetting.

The books have a double focus: on the ghosts of old buildings, lost imprints in the landscape, vanished rivers, missing earthworks; and on the record of what is disappearing every day, anticipating what will be remembered after its extinction, and what will be irremediably forgotten. Sinclair notes of Atkins that he is 'quick to notice vulnerable structures. He doesn't want to photograph anything that will still be there tomorrow.' (*Liquid City*, p. 66) This suggests the vocation of archivist, the primacy of conservation; but from another perspective, it is as if the real meaning of these buildings is only arrived at in Atkins's dark room: 'The care that Atkins lavished on his inanimate subjects (however swiftly he operated) ensured that every image was an elegy. There was no point in hanging on any longer, better to collapse in a rubble heap, exist in memory' (*Lights Out*, p. 277); (everything in life existing to end up in a book). This elegiac imperative informs the interest Sinclair shows in Rachel Whiteread's sculpture *House*, a life-sized cast of an end-of-terrace house in Wennington Green. *House* was exhibited for a few months and then demolished. For Sinclair, the demolition was both the guarantee, and the inauguration, of meaning: 'The sooner it was disposed of the better: only then could it work on memory, displace its own volume' (*Lights Out*, p. 239). But this form of remembering is validated only if it is unofficial, antinomian, iconoclastic. Civic memory is derided, official memorials regarded as symptoms of a collective amnesia: 'Memorials are a way of forgetting, reducing generational guilt to a grid of albino chess pieces, bloodless stalagmites. Shapes that are easy to ignore stand in for the trauma of remembrance' (*Lights Out*, p. 9). Despite their different purpose and function, public sculptures like Henry Moore's bronzes are assumed to produce similar effects of memory loss, insofar as they benefit from government or commercial sponsorship: 'These grave forms do not so much affect memory as displace it, decant their own weight, position themselves in our mappings of the city like railway termini.' (*Lights Out*, p. 265) By contrast, it is only abandoned, disused, semi-derelict structures that can be trusted to absorb the relevant experience and become repositories, like the 'monster doss house' in Durward Street, 'of memory, of pain. A reserve collection of urban nightmares' (*Liquid City*, p. 82).

It is canonicity that disqualifies buildings, works of art and texts from serious consideration by Sinclair; if they acquire any kind of official status, the energy does not pass through them. The paradox here, of course, is that his relentless mythologizing of forgotten and re-forgotten writers is nothing if not the setting-up of an alternative canon. But despite the authoritativeness of his prose, Sinclair disowns the authority his work gives him, not least in the subordinating of his own version of the world to that of various collaborators, and vice versa. What their making of connections reveals is the extent to which London is a text that is endlessly recomposed, and over which the individual artist or architect has no control. The most the individual interpreter can hope for is to construct perhaps a single sentence or a single image that will capture the process of recomposition in a 'credible form': momentarily, precariously, provisionally – too fleetingly to exert power over the process and authorize it. Sinclair wants to devise 'a single sentence to contain everything I knew', dreams of arriving 'at that nanosecond when the pattern was revealed, before it vanished forever' (*Liquid City*, p. 8). But any such encapsulation is merely a trigger for the next stage of the process; keeping the writer/investigator on the move in a city forever recomposing the boundaries of what London is, and what it isn't.

The methods of literary composition play a crucial role in testing the boundaries of authority and the criteria of authenticity. Despite his enthusiasm for collaborative work, Sinclair's own literary style is vividly idiosyncratic, its pressurized, ricocheting energies highly reminiscent of the volatility and percussiveness that characterize the Vorticist prose of Wyndham Lewis. Lewis is a writer Sinclair has shown a great deal of interest in, but the earlier writer's emphasis on the values of egoism and on the expression of the individual will is not obviously suited to exploring the implications of the question constantly asked by Sinclair's work: 'Do we slowly begin to understand only because we are about to become performers in the same

blind ritual?'[4] The paradox inherent in this tension between individual assertiveness and automatism is captured effectively in the
following passage from *Downriver* which introduces the figure of
David Rodinsky, later to be the subject of an entire book, written in
collaboration by Sinclair and Rachel Lichtenstein:

> The turn into Princelet Street, from Brick Lane's fetishist gulch of com-
> peting credit-card caves, is stunning. One of those welcome moments of
> cardiac arrest, when you know that you have been absorbed into the
> scene you are looking at: for a single heartbeat, time freezes.
>
> We are sucked, by a vortex of expectation, into the synagogue, and up
> the unlit stairs: we are returning, approaching something that has always
> been there. The movement is inevitable. But we also sensed immediately
> that we were trespassing on a space that could soon be neutralized as a
> 'Museum of Immigration': as if immigration could be anything other
> than an active response to untenable circumstances – a brave, mad,
> greedy charge at some vision of the future; a thrusting forward of the
> unborn into a region they could neither claim nor desire. Immigration is
> a blowtorch held against an anthill. It can always be sentimentalized, but
> never re-created. It is as persistent and irreversible as the passage of
> glaciers and cannot – without diminishing its courage – be codified,
> and trapped in cases of nostalgia. But we ourselves were ethical Luddites,
> forcibly entering the reality of David Rodinsky's territorial self: the
> apparent squalor and the imposed mystery.
>
> There *was* no mystery, except the one we manufactured in our
> quest for the unknowable: shocking ourselves into a sense of our own
> human vulnerability. We were a future race of barbarians, too tall for the
> room in which we were standing. We fell gratefully upon the accumula-
> tion of detail: debased agents, resurrectionists with cheap Japanese
> cameras.[5]

The enigma of Rodinsky is conveyed by the title of the later book:
Rodinsky's Room (1999). He was a Polish Jew, employed as caretaker
of the Princelet Street synagogue, who walked out of his lodgings, at
some point in the early 1960s, never to return. His room was locked,
and apparently left untouched for over thirty years. The prosaic
explanation for his absence, that he died of a stroke, was effaced by
the elaboration of a myth that romanticized his disappearance; the
myth seemed more adequate to the fascination exerted by the room
and its contents, which offered a time-capsule not only of post-war
Britain, but also of mid-century European Jewry.

Sinclair's treatment of the scenario is revealingly ambivalent. His
evocation of Brick Lane is a one-sentence exposé, a miniature denun-
ciation, whose chief purpose is to convey authorial disapproval by

means of jagged alliteration and punched-out assonance. Realism is suspended in the second sentence, with its anaesthetized reference to physical trauma, an unperturbed sensationalism which again draws attention to authorial expressiveness. However, the second paragraph identifies the point of view as shared not exclusive; the narrator is accompanied by yet another sidekick, this time the writer Fredrik Hanbury (a thinly disguised Patrick Wright). The symbiotic pair is acted upon, rather than taking the initiative, despite the allusion to Vorticism in the second clause. The mysterious force which appears to be controlling their movements is characterized as irresistible, and yet the chief agent of inevitability in this paragraph is the logic of style: it is a virtuosic command of phrasing, punctuation and rhythm which propels the act of reading rather than any supernatural design which propels the characters into action. The narrator and Hanbury appear at first to have been caught up in a process that corresponds to the involuntary convulsions defining the history of migration, but at this point Sinclair draws a line.

There is a self-consciousness about the way in which rhetoric is used to exert pressure on subject matter; a chronic inclination towards predicates of vigorous exertion (such as charging and thrusting) appears to direct the course of thought. The narrator handles style like a blowtorch held against an anthill, the release of energy and heat guaranteeing a certain level of conceptual activity. But Sinclair also makes clear the risks incurred by these methods of composition, the high-handedness with which other peoples' lives are appropriated as material and forced to conform to authorial expectation. The flamboyant casualness with which texts are organized around a lexicon of aggression involves a degree of 'trespassing': Sinclair's experimentalism concentrates on the agitating of language, the distressing of form, to a degree that will provoke the engagement of the reader, but that engagement can easily metamorphose into infringement, the act of reading become an experience of conscription. The value of Sinclair's writing derives partly from the seriousness with which it treats this problem, recognizing the scope of moral debasement in contemporary society, and turning the act of reading itself, the experience of literary language, into an ethical dilemma.

Notes

1   Iain Sinclair, 'The Horse. The Man. The Talking Head' in *Flesh Eggs & Scalp Metal: Selected Poems 1970–1987* (London: Paladin, 1989), p. 101. All subsequent page references are to this edition.

2   Iain Sinclair, *Lights Out for the Territory* (London: Granta Books, 1997), p. 7. All subsequent page references are to this edition.
3   Marc Atkins and Iain Sinclair, *Liquid City* (London: Reaktion Books, 1999) p. 63. All subsequent page references are to this edition.
4   Iain Sinclair, *White Chappell, Scarlet Tracings* (Uppingham: Goldmark, 1987), p. 58.
5   Iain Sinclair, *Downriver* (London: Paladin, 1991).

Primary texts

Back Garden Poems (London: Albion Village Press, 1970)

The Kodak Mantra Diaries, October 1966 to June 1971 (London: Albion Village Press, 1971)

Muscat's Würm (London: Albion Village Press, 1972)

The Birth Rug (London: Albion Village Press, 1973)

Lud Heat: A Book of the Dead Hamlets (London: Albion Village Press, 1975)

Brown Clouds (Newcastle: Pig Press, 1977)

Suicide Bridge: A Book of the Furies, a Mythology of the South & East (London: Albion Village Press, 1979)

White Chappell, Scarlet Tracings (Uppingham: Goldmark, 1987)

Flesh Eggs & Scalp Metal: Selected Poems, 1970–1987 (London: Paladin, 1989)

Downriver (Or, the Vessels of Wrath) a Narrative in Twelve Tales (London: Paladin, 1991)

Radon Daughters: A Voyage, between Art and Terror, from the Mound of Whitechapel to the Limestone Pavements of the Burren (London: Jonathan Cape, 1994)

Lights Out for the Territory: Nine Excursions in the Secret History of London (London: Granta Books, 1997)

Slow Chocolate Autopsy: Incidents from the Notorious Career of Norton, Prisoner of London (London: Phoenix House, 1997)

The Ebbing of the Kraft (Cambridge: Equipage, 1997)

Crash: David Cronenberg's Post-Mortem on J. G. Ballard's 'Trajectory of Fate' (London: British Film Institute, 1999)

Iain Sinclair with Marc Atkins, *Liquid City* (London: Reaktion Books, 1999)

Iain Sinclair with Rachel Lichtenstein, *Rodinsky's Room* (London: Granta Books, 1999)

Dark Lanthorns: David Rodinsky as Psychogeographer (Uppingham: Goldmark, 1999)

Sorry Meniscus: Excursions to the Millennium Dome (London: Profile Books, 1999)

Landor's Tower: or, The Imaginary Conversations (London: Granta Books, 2001)

Selected critical texts

Simon Perril, 'A Cartography of Absence: the Work of Iain Sinclair', *Comparative Criticism* 19 (1997), 309–39
Rachel Potter, 'Culture Vulture: the Testimony of Iain Sinclair's *Downriver*', *Parataxis: Modernism and Modern Writing* 5 (Winter 1993–4), 40–8

Part II

Urban Thematics

Part II
Introduction

After the Thatcherite experience of the 1980s, the British urban environment was transformed and polarized: an oasis of middle-class excess and greed was cultivated at the expense of those who remained outside it, while a growing awareness of the degree of urban deprivation involved put difficulties in the way of any self-assured class hegemony. Contemporary fiction achieved some measure of 'ironic distance' from a culture of greed and acquisition explored in a variety of ways. Will Self would reserve his greatest scepticism for a culture of inanition running counter to the inner and paradoxical drives of his characters, while Hanif Kureshi and Zadie Smith mapped the other identities effaced by Thatcherite ideology on the one hand, and by intellectual liberalism on the other. The ethnic plurality of London, and society's changing constructions of gender, are central concerns of this new generation of writers.

Self, meanwhile, parodies the aspirations of the professional classes by placing them cheek by jowl with an underworld of the dead, who are engaged in commercial activities, emotional enthralments, and social relationships, but all in a vacuum of non-life, of a parallel and empty existence. The text becomes a powerful indictment of the vacuousness of contemporary paradigms of living together. There is a larger dimension to this critical and narrative strategy, which goes beyond the development of a satirical method in pursuit of a meta-physical enquiry in Merleau-Ponty's sense.[1] The disturbing quality of a mythic framing of existence creeps into the most routinized and over-written of environments – inner London. Self's book *How the Dead Live* uses a map that superimposes an otherworldly exist-ence over that of the cartography of the city with which one is familiar. This creates a perceptual flux and oscillation, an experience of transformation whose conditions are highly specific. As Cassirer says:

> Life is not divided into classes and subclasses. It is felt as an unbroken continuous whole which does not admit of any clean-cut and trenchant distinctions. The limits between the different spheres are not insurmountable barriers; they are fluent and fluctuating. There is no specific difference between the various realms of life. Nothing has a definite, invariable, static shape. By a sudden metamorphosis everything may be turned into everything. If there is any characteristic and outstanding feature of the mythical world, any law by which it is governed – it is this law of metamorphosis.[2]

Modern urban fiction generates its own form of myth, a changeability often labelled as 'post-modern'. This term serves almost as a shorthand label for a whole new phase of writings concerned with the tensions of the city, which can no longer be seen as the domain of middle-class professionals alone, the territory of so much previous post-war urban fiction. The concept of new or forgotten identities came to the fore during the end of the twentieth century, emerging from the underclasses and the margins.

Conventional lives are transformed through a quite different context in the work of A. L. Kennedy. In her view, the condition of emptiness extends to the world beyond London, seeping into the urban and suburban spaces of provincial life. Her characters are engulfed by the world; they are individuals unable to direct much of their lives, their sense of self diminishing in direct proportion to the pressure of other narratives and to the density of events they are caught up in, in situations similar to those found also in Pat Barker's trilogy. Many of Kennedy's characters become like ghosts or marginal figures. Such residual and depleted responses to the city are recurrent in many of the new recognitions of urban identity found in contemporary British fiction. In all of the writing featured in this section, the allure of urban chic and of urban youth culture alike prove elusive. There are various frustrated attempts to provide ethical value systems for this new context, but new forms of suffering and identity crisis underlie the texts. The characters pattern their lives on rituals in the effort to resist the amorphous anonymity imposed by urban density, by the weight of numbers, and by the indifference of contemporary city-dwellers towards those around them.

Notes

1 Maurice Merleau-Ponty, *Sense and Non-Sense*, trans. Hubert L. Dreyfus and Patricia Allen Dreyfus (Evanston, Illinois: Northwestern University Press, 1964), pp. 26–40.
2 Ernst Cassirer, *An Essay on Man: An Introduction to a Philosophy of Human Culture*, (New Haven: Yale University Press, 1944), p. 81.

5 The Fiction of Will Self: Motif, Method and Madness

Liorah Anne Golomb

Some writers create a world, some a universe. Will Self creates a community. The community is defined by Self's peculiar themes and concerns, and populated with radical psychotherapists, archaeologists and artists; dead people residing in the suburbs; people who wake to find that chimpanzees have replaced humans; people who develop the sex organs of the opposite sex. Some characters wander into each other's stories like neighbours borrowing cups of sugar. Not only characters but places, clubs, titles, even fictional academic journals and granting foundations from one story turn up in another, sometimes off-handedly, sometimes providing another piece of the puzzle of a character's narrative, sometimes as an exact scene viewed from two perspectives. Think of this chapter, then, as a brief tour of Will Self's community, an orientation. I will introduce some of its prominent residents, call attention to the landscape of its themes and the architecture of its methods, and point out some of its blue plaques.

Will Self is, first and foremost, a master teller of tall tales. He has proven this with impressive consistency in his three novels, *My Idea of Fun*, *Great Apes*, and *How the Dead Live*; two novellas, *Cock and Bull*; three collections of short stories, *The Quantity Theory of Insanity*, *Grey Area* and *Tough, Tough Toys for Tough, Tough Boys*; and, with Martin Rowson, *The Sweet Smell of Psychosis*, an illustrated 'fable', as one blurb calls it. And all were written in the 1990s, along with various other short stories, articles, weekly columns, interviews and reviews.

The key to a good story is that it be presented as true, no matter how absurd it is, and for this to happen, a contract must be formed between the teller and the told. There is no story without a complicit set of ears. Self knows this; he is aware of his readers, anxious to draw them in, to have them experience the story along with him. Self can turn a reader from an anonymous voyeur to a guest within a couple of sentences. For example, consider the opening of the story 'Inclusion®' from *Grey Area*: 'You are holding in your hands a folder. The hands cannot be described by me, because they are yours, but the folder can' (p. 201). The statement, 'You are holding in your hands a folder,' is playful yet coercive; it brooks no dissent, whereas if Self had written, 'Imagine you are holding in your hands a folder', you could agree to imagine, or not.

'Inclusion®' is the name of a new psychopharmaceutical meant for the treatment of depression. It works by making the user intensely interested in any object, sound, conversation or scent within the range of vision, hearing, or smell of the user – but all without distinction or a sense of proportion, so that looking at a sports trophy is equally as interesting as watching one's children develop. 'Inclusion' also describes what is happening to the reader: we are being taken into the story. Not as a character; more like a privileged spectator who has been invited to watch from the wings. And the devout Selfist knows the players: Zack Busner, the radical psychotherapist who developed the drug; Anthony Bohm, the psychiatrist-turned-GP who illegally tests Inclusion® on Simon Dykes, a well-known artist; the Dykes family. They have appeared in earlier stories and will appear in later ones.

Self has said that 'There are two ways of getting someone to suspend disbelief. One is just to present a fantastic conceit – like Kafka – and the other is to very gradually try and convince somebody of something utterly preposterous'.[1] He uses the gradual method in the novelette *Cock*, the story of Carol and Dan, a dull young couple who occasionally engage in exceedingly dull love-making. *Cock* (designated a novelette – note the feminization – by Self) begins in the third person but somewhere into the second chapter the typeface switches to italic and the subject to the first person. The story is not coming directly from the author Will Self but is in fact being told by an odd little man on a train, and relayed to us, in turn, by the man stuck in the compartment with him. This narrative maze renders the ultimate narrator, Self, nearly invisible which, paradoxically, facilitates the fulfilment of the contract between reader and storyteller. We are now also stuck in that compartment, and the author, who could free us, is nowhere to be found.

The 'don', as our narrator refers to *his* narrator, pulls his listener into his story by setting up, in great detail, the history of Dan and Carol's relationship, Carol's discovery of autoeroticism, her subsequent discovery of a small lump below her clitoris, and the various stages of the lump's development into what it will become – a fully-functional penis. 'To be a woman with a penis in our society – it isn't an overwhelming distinction, is it? Well is it?' the don demands to know (p. 78). He is changing his role from narrator to malevolent Socratic inquisitor, and our narrator thinks he has found an opportunity to break the teller-told contract he has been forced into. He takes up his new role as pupil and answers the don, suggesting that Carol's penis is a metaphor for women's liberation, but the don will not release him: 'I'm talking about a fucking literal penis, shit-for-brains . . . ' (p. 79). This is but the first of the insults and innuendos to which our narrator will be subjected as the fusty, feeble old don gradually morphs into a terrifying and powerful threat.

Having been courteous to a fellow passenger, our narrator leaves himself open to this aural abuse and later, to oral, and anal, rape. The narrator is feminized, debased and raped, and when it is over, he is left powerless. He cannot even report the rape – he knows he would be held accountable for the indignity he suffered. As he cleans himself up in a pay toilet he imagines the constable's response if he reports having been violated:

> 'Now quite honestly, sonny, dressed in this get-up. I mean to say what do you expect if you venture out into the fictional night alone, looking like you do, acting like you did? . . . I think you should be prepared for what people are going to say. Because I reckon that they will be forced to conclude that you were asking for it. You actually wanted someone to perform to you. In fact, I'll go further. I think you wanted to be an audience. Oh, I don't doubt that you feel bad about it now, you feel used. But really, luvvie – come on. This is what you get if you sit there like a prat, listening to a load of cock . . . and bull' (pp. 144–5).

Were we, by extension, also 'asking for it'? The conflation of storytelling and rape will strike some as offensive and insensitive, but it might also be said that Self isn't minimizing the horror of rape – he is maximizing the danger of fiction. Self's fiction lurks in some dark corner of its author's mind; it surprises its victims, assaults them, penetrates them, and then goes on its merry way, leaving the victims to deal with the consequences.

Bull, the fable (again, Self's designation) accompanying *Cock*, takes the Kafkaesque road to suspension of disbelief. It begins: 'Bull, a large and heavyset man, awoke one morning to find that while he had slept he had acquired another primary sexual characteristic: to wit, a vagina' (p. 49). The sentence is, of course, reminiscent of Kafka's *Metamorphosis*, and in fact that is the name of the chapter. In this metamorphosis, though, a bull turns into a cow. John Bull, whose very name pegs him as an English Everyman, is a decent man, an amateur rugby player, not the brightest bulb in the marquee but a good sort. As in *Cock*, the development of a new sex organ is accompanied, apparently, by the appropriate hormones: Bull undergoes a cartoon feminization during which, in quick succession, he is seduced by his doctor, mistakes orgasm for love ('Will I see you again?' he asks the doctor, p. 235), feels betrayed, and gives birth to his 'love child' in (where else?) San Francisco.

Woody Allen has quipped that being bisexual doubles one's chances of getting a date. Being bisexed, however, has prevented Bull and Carol from having either healthy sex lives or any sort of social life. Bull is used and discarded by his doctor; a transsexual who befriends him is horrified at the sight of the vagina; in the end he winds up living a quiet life in Wales with his son. Carol's sex acts are acts of violence. Very few of the residents of Self's community get to experience sexual intimacy within the context of a loving relationship. Those who do, do not do so for long. *Bull* is a counterpoint to *Cock* in style as well as theme. It is a straightforward third-person narrative with a happy, or at least contented, ending. There is no menacing figure pulling us into a dark trap. But the creepy manipulator returns in Self's next work, *My Idea of Fun*.

My Idea of Fun is a novel about coming of age in the 1980s, featuring that oldest of themes, the son supplanting the father. The father-figure whom Ian Wharton must learn from, rebel against, and eventually become, is quite literally the embodiment of conspicuous consumption; his copious fat seems to have been carved from the bodies of powerless and exploited labourers. He is so thoroughly a consumer that, from time to time, he even consumes himself: 'I have eaten myself up and through some unprecedented act of gastromancy farted out my new incarnation,' he tells Ian (p. 73). With his girth, penchant for cigars, and odd manner of speaking, Mr Broadhurst, or 'The Fat Controller' as he prefers to be called, is reminiscent of a sinister W. C. Fields: 'You're wondering something, boy, cough it up, spit it out, expel it, vomit it forth. In short, tell me.' (p. 73) This odd creature becomes Ian's mentor and *de facto* guardian.

An appropriate reading of Self's text perhaps ought to emphasize the 'guard' in 'guardian'. Mr Broadhurst and Ian are both 'eidetic': they recall things in such vivid detail that they are able to recreate anything they have seen as though it were occurring at that moment. One practical application of eidesis is 'retroscendence'. As Mr Broadhurst explains, 'retroscendence enables us to take any element in our visual field and, as it were, unpack its history' (p. 110). To demonstrate, he guides Ian through the history of his underpants, beginning with the cotton plant. It is a remarkable scene, painted in words so vivid that the reader can envision each moment with almost as much visual clarity as Ian's eidesis gives him. We see the cotton pickers and their hard, hopeless lives; the raw material being sold to the only buyer, who pays next to nothing for it; its carding and spinning; the weaving into cloth by small children with cut and mutilated hands; the sweatshop workers cutting the cloth and sewing it up as underpants that the upmarket menswear store buys for a mere 50 pence apiece. Capitalist economics is clearly inhumane and inequitable, but 'The Fat Controller' is completely disinterested in its ethical repercussions. In fact he is, at best, contemptuous of humanity, and at worst, cruel to it.

Ian must pay for 'The Fat Controller's' tutelage by putting himself in his hands unconditionally. The extent of this commitment is made quite clear when Ian, now at university, is literally on the verge of having his first sexual experience: 'The Fat Controller' appears, freezes the girl with the pointing of his finger, and tells Ian that if he had penetrated her, his penis would have 'quite literally' broken off right inside the girl (p. 103). As in *Cock* and *Bull*, sexual intimacy is not possible.

Eventually Ian seems to be free of 'The Fat Controller'. He even wonders whether it has all been an extended eidetic fantasy built around some ordinary off-season tenant at his mother's seaside resort. At the urging of one of his professors Ian goes into therapy with a doctor whose unconventional treatment methods include putting Ian into a deep coma for a couple of days. At this point, what had been Ian's first-person narrative switches to the third person; he becomes, as the new narrator informs us, the object, not the subject.

Ian at last gives into his nature and performs increasingly repulsive acts of violence: his idea of fun. He regains narrative control, and tells us that he has married the woman The Fat Controller chose for him; they are expecting a child; and Ian is planning the cruellest act of all: telling his wife who and what he really is. And although he loves her, he can't help looking forward to the fun that destroying her will provide.

These 'nasty' books, as Self has called them,[2] represent only one small corner of Self's community. More frequently, Self's characters are not evil, only eccentric, delusional, or psychotic. And some of them are also academics.

In 'Understanding the Ur-Bororo', Self parodies the English, academe, and anthropology. As in *Cock*, the narrator of 'Understanding the Ur-Bororo' in *The Quantity Theory of Insanity* is not the story's subject, only a vehicle for the hearing of it – our surrogate. The actual protagonist is Janner, the narrator's friend from Reigate, a university 'moderately well known for its tradition of doing work on stagnating subsocietal groups' (p. 73). They meet again after several years' separation, and Janner recounts his fieldwork on an Amazonian tribe, the Ur-Bororo. Janner begins with a few introductory statements about the diet, language and belief system of the tribe before casting his line: 'Lurie penetrated to the reality of the Ur-Bororo and was horrified by what he found. He locked his secret away. Marston lived among the Ur-Bororo for only a few months and ended up suspicious but still deceived by them. It was left for me to uncover the secret springs and cogs that drive the Ur-Bororo's world view; it was left for me to reveal them' (p. 81). Who could resist such bait? By the time we learn that the Ur-Bororo refer to themselves as 'The People Who You Wouldn't Like to be Cornered by at a Party' (p. 82), or hear Janner quote the shaman saying, 'Quite right, jolly good, jolly good. That's the ticket' (p. 89), or meet Jane, Janner's utterly unremarkable Ur-Bororo wife and her trivia-spouting brother David – by this time we are quite ready to accept the inner reality of the story, even while knowing it to be a fiction; even knowing it to be a joke.

Self is a pointillist. His fiction is intricate, rich, dense with detail and very true, even when his story is about a man who has a mutually beneficial relationship with common household insects, or an afterlife that differs from life only in that it takes place in a different part of London, or the discovery of a motherlode of crack cocaine in a Harlesden house. That is the premise of 'The Rock of Crack as Big as the Ritz' and the plot impetus of its companion story, 'The Nonce Prize', which together bookend the collection *Tough, Tough Toys for Tough, Tough Boys*. The main characters are brothers Danny and Tembe, young black men who live in the slums and make a fine living dealing crack. Their situation could hardly be further removed from their creator's. Self's father was a professor, his mother worked in publishing; he was raised in a middle-class London suburb, earned his MA at Oxford, and is one of the fortunate few who earn good money doing good writing. Self's use of street drugs got him in trouble (most notably, he was fired from his job with the *Observer* when it was learned that he snorted heroin on John Major's election plane). But he never landed in jail, much less in the paedophiles' ward, as Danny does. So it seems audacious of Self to author these stories and yet have Danny's prison-writing instructor advise his student – to good effect – to write what he knows. Audacious, because unlike *Cock* or *Bull*, for example, these stories are not sheer fantasy, even if crack cocaine isn't really mined as though it were coal. In a fantasy, Danny's talent might have helped him. It is much more credible that a black prisoner in a predominately white society is not likely to catch a break. Somehow, in writing seriously about that which he cannot know first-hand, Self has managed to draw perhaps his most sincerely tragic character.

Along with academics, the other well-represented group in Self's community are psychotherapists. 'Design Faults in the Volvo 760 Turbo: A Manual' from *Tough, Tough Toys for Tough, Tough Boys* is the story of the adulterous affair between Dr Bill Bywater, a psychiatrist, and Serena, an upper-crust sexpot, as it progresses from the early snogging-in-the-car stage, through the copulating-in-grassy-areas-along-the-roadside stage, and finally, to Bywater's overwhelming sense of guilt. In Bywater's state of mind, the Volvo's manual reads like the *Kama Sutra*. Headings from the manual become quite suggestive: 'Instruments and Controls', 'Body and Interior', 'Starting and Driving', and finally, 'Wheel and Tyres'. That last may seem innocent enough until we notice, along with Bywater, the subheading, 'Special Rims', or the caption of the photo of a sexy woman changing a tyre: 'Stand Next to Body', or worst of all, in boldface, the caution, '**Make sure that the arm is lodged well in the attachment**' (p. 170).

Upon reading those words, Bywater realizes the futility of his therapy. He has been eradicating every instance of the word 'Volvo' with white correction fluid, hoping to exorcize his obsession with Serena's vulva. He turns instead to the car itself and paints over every instance of its name. When that fails he seeks out his friend Dave Adler, a car mechanic and former Freudian psychiatrist. But Dave is out; in fact he is 'lower[ing] himself carefully into the inspection pit of the Bywaters' marital bed. He has the necessary equipment and he's intent on giving Vanessa Bywater's chassis a really thorough servicing. As far as Dave Adler is concerned a car is a means of transport, nothing more and nothing less' (p. 174).

The name Dave, incidentally, has a particular significance in Self's fiction. 'Dave' indicates the unspectacular, the undistinguished; conformity, niceness, perhaps; in a word, stereotyped middle-class Englishness. Dave-Dave Hutchinson is the kindly pharmacist in 'Chest', reasonably content, comfortably merchant class, deferential to the wealthy and snobbish Dykeses. In *Cock*, there is mention of Dan's drinking buddy Dave; his main function in the story is to allow Self to name Dan's AA sponsor 'Dave Two'. *Tough, Tough Toys* contains the story 'Dave Too', in which the world becomes increasingly populated with Daves: Old Dave, Fat Dave, the Ur-Dave. The narrator, whose name we never learn, has a girlfriend who changes her name to Davina and wants to be called Dave; his psychiatrist changes his name from Colin to Dave. Self never reveals the cause of this Davism, so the reader is free to invent one; the image that sprang to my mind was a sort of 'Invasion of the Body Snatchers': individuals being systematically replaced by Regular Joes, or in this case, Daves. When the narrator complains to his psychiatrist about this profusion of Daves, the doctor uses King David to form a theory of 'secular ultramontanism'. 'But it is Daves, not David,' says the narrator, to which the doctor replies, 'Oh come on, what's in an id' (p. 81). One wonders if Self didn't build the entire story, if not his entire Dave trope, on this pun.

Bill Bywater and Dave Adler are only two of the therapists in Self's repertoire. He has, in fact, an entire mental health community, and at its centre is Dr Zack Busner. His narrative is told over the course of several stories and a novel: Dr Busner as a somewhat pretentious graduate student, then as a pop psychologist who has made a fortune on a Rubik's cube-type object called 'The Riddle' (intended to help people see inside themselves); we know that he has had a lucrative but unrespected career as a television personality; we see him running 'Concept House', a highly unconventional institution, and later, in charge of a ward where both the patients and the doctors are mad. And at last sighting, Zack Busner is the ageing alpha male in his group of chimpanzees in *Great Apes*. All the while he has maintained a habit of rolling up his brown knitted tie.

Zack Busner and many of Self's recurring characters, predominant themes, and favoured motifs have their genesis in Self's first book, the short-story collection, *The Quantity Theory of Insanity*. The epigram preceding the collection's first story, 'The North London Book of the Dead', hints at one such motif: 'However far you may travel in this world, you will still occupy the same volume of space.' The attribution reads, 'Traditional Ur-Bororo saying' – the Ur-Bororo being, as we know, a tribe of Self's invention. As trivial and self-evident as the saying is, it is well-chosen. Self's work is filled with an awareness of proportion, volume, mass, distance, space, time.

In 'The North London Book of the Dead' and again in *How the Dead Live*, Self expands upon the Ur-Bororo's philosophy, taking the notion of occupation of space beyond this world and into the next. In the short story, the narrator sees his recently deceased mother on the street, speaks to her, and learns that the dead go neither to Heaven nor Hell, nor do they simply cease to exist. The dead move to another part of London, there to continue in much the same way they did in life. The son reasons that the dead keep dying, and there is only so much space in North London: 'How come people don't notice all the dead people clogging up the transport system?' (p. 11). These and other sensible questions go unanswered in 'The North London Book of the Dead'. Such particulars are more thoroughly addressed in *How the Dead Live*, but the explanations do not really add anything. As with everything Self writes, the hows and whys that set the story in motion are not only unimportant, they are virtually beside the point. Even if the mother in 'North London' is not clear on how it all works, there it is: the dead live, work, and attend support meetings alongside the living.

Stories such as 'Scale', 'Between the Conceits', and 'The Quantity Theory of Insanity' exemplify Self's apparent fascination with measurement. The Quantity Theory of Insanity, the concept providing the collection's title, is based on the premise that there is a quantifiable proportion of sanity in any given community or social group. A sample hypothesis: 'If you decrease the number of social class 2 anorexics you necessarily increase the numbers of valium abusers in social class 4' (p. 127). In the story of the same name, we learn the theory's origins, comprehensive history, and how it has been applied and misapplied via a journal entry written by Harold Ford, the man who developed it. He is attending an interdisciplinary conference centred around his theory. His keynote address is an attempt to demystify Quantity Theory, which has been altered beyond recognition and put to unintended and often unethical uses (not unlike the currently chic and virtually ubiquitous Quantum Theory). Once again, Self removes himself from the narrative and brings the reader into the privileged position of being able to read the journal. It is written in total sincerity and in perfect imitation of the language of psychology and the social sciences, complete with references to articles in *Practical Mental Health*, the *Journal of Psychology*, and a favourite on the shelves of Self's fictional reference room, *The British Journal of Ephemera*. Self parodies academe so smoothly that it almost passes you by. Would it be entirely unthinkable to run across an article entitled 'Some Aspects of Sanity Quotient Mechanisms in a Witless Shetland Community' (p. 149)? Or that in the 1970s (certainly not now), a researcher could gain a grant to 'do some research towards a book on aspects of grant application' (p. 116)?

In *Grey Area*, 'Between the Conceits' is a first-person ramble in which the narrator believes himself to be one of eight Londoners who control all the others. Each of the eight, who range from an incontinent slob to a titled woman, has a particular number of Londoners in his or her camp. By gesture, thought, strategy, even bodily function, the Eight Who Count control their people. The narrator (who ranks himself third from the top in the class system) tells us:

'I stretch, then relax – and 35,665 white-collar workers leave their houses a teensy bit early for work. This means that 6,014 of them will feel dyspeptic during the journey because they've missed their second piece of toast, or bowl of Fruit 'n' Fibre. From which it follows that 2,982 of them will be testy throughout the morning; and therefore, 312 of them will say the wrong thing, leading to dismissal; hence one of these 312 people will lose the balance of his reason and commit an apparently random and motiveless murder on the way home.' (pp. 9–10)

The narrator of 'Scale' is a morphine-addicted divorced father who feels he has lost his sense of scale, even while being surrounded by it. He lives next to a model village built to scale; he attempts to remove the scale in his kettle; his track marks form a road map, to scale, of England; it was the bathroom scales that revealed his infidelity and led to his divorce; he keeps a scaly lizard as a pet. All that's missing are musical scales. In one of his other lives, as a columnist for *Building Design*, Self writes in *Sore Sites*, 'One of my main preoccupations as a writer of Surrealist fiction is the conundrum that the very notion of scale presents us with – time and time again...There seem to be several different complexes or gestalts bound up in the notion of scale' (p. 57).

In both of these stories from *Grey Area* – 'Between the Conceits' and 'Scale' – the narrators' preoccupations are manifestations of their mental states. Narcotics addicts and schizophrenics often try to maintain a sense of control by keeping records, creating rituals and categorizing. In 'Between the Conceits', the narrator is in reality a lonely bachelor living with his infirm old mother and suffering from an obsession with the class system. Addiction to narcotics has robbed the narrator of 'Scale' of his wife, his children and his home, in addition to his sense of scale. It is no secret that Self, himself a father and husband, was addicted to heroin, an experience that no doubt accounts for his skill at infusing 'Scale' with a sense of painful truth, even while having its narrator author a thesis ludicrously entitled, 'No Services: Reflex Ritualism and Modern Motorway Signs (with special reference to the M40)' (p. 94).

Bringing everything full circle is Self's latest novel, *How the Dead Live*. Its most obvious antecedent is the early story 'The North London Book of the Dead': both feature the parallel world of the dead as experienced by an old, cynical, ex-pat American mother. But whereas 'The North London Book of the Dead' is essentially an extended joke, *How the Dead Live* is an earnest, complex and ultimately poignant first-person narrative.

As she lies in hospital dying of breast cancer, Lily Bloom (whose name at once recalls the flower symbolic of death, vernal rebirth, and the hero of Joyce's *Ulysses*,) recounts her life and its several disappointments, not least of which are her daughters, one a cold, calculating capitalist, the other, a wasted junkie. Lily takes the reader through dying, death, and finally, through her tragic rebirth.

In afterlife Lily is tormented not by her sins or regrets for things left undone, but by bits, quite literally, of herself. She is at all times accompanied by a pop-song-loving calcification of a foetus that died in, but was never discharged from, her womb, and by her son, who as a child was struck by a car and killed. Waiting for her at home are the Fats, the hideous globular embodiments of the weight Lily has gained and lost in her lifetime. She has a guide, Phar Lap Jones, her own Virgil, to show her the ropes of death, and he makes certain that his charge gets out of the house: Lily works in an office alongside the living and keeps appointments with the bureaucrats of death. She attends informational meetings for the Newly Dead. They don't realize it but she even visits her children, seeing at least as much of them as she did when she was alive. Death, as envisioned by Self, is no place to rest in peace.

Every story, novella and novel of Self's stands on its own solid footing. But the more of them you read, the more you will be 'included' into the community. Turning up the Easter eggs Self has scattered throughout his work is like a game where the prize is a wink from the author and a feeling of being in the know. Not every piece of the puzzle fits; while Busner's narrative is consistent and can be plotted along a line, Simon Dykes's is not. Dykes meets his end in the story 'Chest' by breathing the carcinogenic, post-apocalyptic air he notes near the end of 'Inclusion®'. He then pops up quite alive in *Great Apes*, although he is older, divorced from Jean (his wife at the time of his death in 'Chest'), and peripherally involved in the London club scene. On top of everything, he has become a chimp who believes himself to be a man. He winds up under the care of Dr Busner, who is much the same as always, but hairier. Bill Bywater's narrative seems consistent enough, but if you read his two stories in the order in which they appear in *Tough, Tough Toys*, he presumably drives off the road to his death in the title story only to turn up in the very next story betraying his wife with Serena.

Self's writing is at once personal and impersonal, often springing from his own experiences but not confined by them. To give but one example, Self has, in common with Bill Bywater, removed the insignias from his own Volvo, but not because the word resembles 'vulva': Self was attempting 'to be left with the Platonic ideal of a car'.[3] He has transcended trite labels of being 'dangerous', a 'bad boy' or a drug-culture writer. And perhaps the most remarkable thing about him – more remarkable than his brilliant imagination, voluminous vocabulary, or extensive knowledge of diverse subjects – is his stamina. Having hit the scene in 1991 with *The Quantity Theory of Insanity*, Self has been firing off powerful works of fiction and non-fiction like a machine-gun ever since, and he shows no signs of letting up. No doubt Will Self still has decades' worth of writing in him and we will still be reading his work in decades to come.

Notes

1   Anna Henchman, 'Will Self: An Enfant Terrible Comes of Age', *Publishers Weekly*, 8 September 1997, 52–3.
2   Henchman, 'Will Self', 52.
3   Chris Hall, 'Dead Man Talking', *Spike Magazine*, 2000, http://www. willself.org.uk, unpag.

Primary texts

The Quantity Theory of Insanity (London: Bloomsbury, 1991)
Cock & Bull (London: Bloomsbury, 1992)
My Idea of Fun: A Cautionary Tale (London: Bloomsbury, 1993)
Grey Area and other Stories (London: Bloomsbury, 1994)
Junk Mail (London: Bloomsbury, 1995)
The Sweet Smell of Psychosis, illus. Martin Rowson (London: Bloomsbury, 1996)
Great Apes (London: Bloomsbury, 1997)
Tough Tough Toys for Tough Tough Boys (London: Bloomsbury, 1998)
How the Dead Live (London: Bloomsbury, 2000)
with David Gamble, photographer, *Perfidious Man* (London: Viking, 2000)
Sore Sites (London: Ellipsis, 2000)

Selected critical texts

Chris Hall, 'Dead Man Talking', *Spike Magazine* (http://www.willself. org.uk) 2000.
Anna Henchman, 'Will Self: An Enfant Terrible Comes of Age', *Publishers Weekly*, 8 September 1997, 52–3.
http://www.willself.org.uk. An extensive collection of links to all things Self available on the Internet, including interviews, literary criticism, book

reviews, audio and video files, and first chapters of some of Self's novels. Produced by spikemagazine.com.

A. O. Scott, 'Trans-Atlantic Flights', *The New York Times Book Review*, 31 January 1999, 5, 7.

Katherine Sender, 'To Have and To Be: Sex, Gender, and the Paradox of Change', *Women and Language*, 20.1 (1997), 18–24.

Tom Shone, 'The Complete, Unexpurgated Self', *Sunday Times Magazine*, 5 September 1993, 38–42.

6 Hanif Kureishi's *The Buddha of Suburbia*: 'A New Way of Being British'

Anthony Ilona

One cannot see the modern world as it is unless one recognizes the overwhelming strength of patriotism, [of] national loyalty. [...A]s a *positive* force there is nothing to set beside it [...]. It is *your* civilization. It is *you*. However much you hate it or laugh at it, you will never be happy away from it for any length of time. The suet-puddings and the red pillar boxes have entered into your soul.

George Orwell, 'The Lion and the Unicorn: Socialism and the English Genius'

The vastness of England swallows you up, and you lose for a while your feeling that the whole nation has a single identifiable character. Are there really such things as nations? Are we not forty-six million individuals, all different? And the diversity of it, the chaos! [...W]e call our islands by no less than six different names, England, Britain, Great Britain, the British Isles, the United Kingdom and, in very exalted moments, Albion. Even the differences between north and south loom large in our own eyes. But somehow these differences fade away the moment that any two Britons are confronted by a European.

George Orwell, 'The Lion and the Unicorn: Socialism and the English Genius'

Writing in 1941, amid the crisis of a protracted world war, Orwell saw an urgent need to understand the limits of nationhood. His observations above illustrate a common problem in the general conception of national identity; whether national identity is determined by some *intrinsic* quality or whether it is determined in relation to something *extrinsic*.

In Orwell's first observation above, the identity of the nation is deemed to have an intrinsic or *essential* quality, for which the perennial cultural signposts of 'suet-puddings' and 'red pillar boxes' are a 'positive force' that permeate the 'soul' of the nation's inhabitants. In the second, national identity is figured as a more dynamic *relational* concept for its definition through contact with a specified and demarcated outsider (the 'European'). Yet both observations are burdened with fallacious notions of interaction and diversity.

As an essentially determined phenomenon, national identity, in Orwell's view, relies on a mass conception of unilateral sameness within a group or community of individuals. Here identity is formed and nurtured by a sense of timeless cultural tradition (the consumption of suet-puddings, the ubiquity of red pillar boxes), rigid principles of social classification ('North' vs. 'South'; 'Albion' vs. Europe) and, of course, arcane notions of ethnic origin ('it is *you*'). These are conditions that can provide a perceived community with a sense of certainty and purpose in circumstances where, as is the case during world wars, 'self-doubt and anxiety [...] become routine'.[1]

As a relational phenomenon, the identity of a community is perceived as whole only through interaction with another perceived community or group. Though Britain's national identity is, as Orwell sees it, a mutable construct ('we call our islands by no less than six different names'), it is only so in a negatively reinforced way. That is, Britain's national wholeness appears to be at its most cohesive when positioned in relation to some externalized and excluded Other. The condition of being an individual (or group) distinct from the surrounding environment can only be understood through an appreciation of the complementary network of 'interaction[s]' which that individual (or group) has with their surrounding environment.[2] This tethered idea of individual and environment defines the *relational* quality of identity formation. This conception of identity as relational is seen as useful to times of increasing proximity between peoples from different regions and cultures.[3] Yet, in the second of the Orwell citations above, there is a limited relationality; one that refers to a perceived external social organism (the 'European') only for the sake of self-determination. That is, internal cohesion is legitimated by reference to alterity.

Thus, the development of a genuinely interactive vision of British national identity – one that might, in Orwell's opinion, admit a sense of its constitutive 'diversity', even 'chaos' – is here retarded by a fixation with the need to legitimate an internal oneness in the mass-conception of 'Britishness'. Here, the rhetoric of the relational in the second Orwell epigraph above overlaps with the rhetoric of essential-ism in the first. Though differences among 'us' ('North' and 'South') may well match and be contiguous with differences between 'us' and 'them' (Britons and Europeans, say), the common impulse, according to Orwell, is to deny both internal diversity and its potential for overlap with the extrinsic world. This concerns boundaries of exclu-sion that might better hold in place an imagined sameness within the geographical borders of 'Albion'.[4] Any link with Europe invoked in terms of identity formation is curtailed by the extrinsic quality of their difference from 'us'. In his examination of the socio-political dis-course of British nationalism entitled *The Break-Up of Britain: Crisis and Neo-Nationalism* (1977), Tom Nairn calls attention to this dupli-city:

> There is no coherent, sufficiently democratic myth of Englishness – no sufficiently accessible and popular myth-identity where mass discon-tents can find a vehicle. This is the source of the disconcerting lurch from a semi-divine Constitution and the Mother of Parliaments to the crudest racialism.[5]

More disconcerting than the 'lurch' between ethical extremes, per-haps, is the fact that such uncomplicated idealism as possessing a sublimely 'divine' Constitution and a prototypically supreme Parlia-ment should be allowed to circulate unchecked in nationalist dis-course. Such self-glorification at the core of national identity remains the divisive factor for its persuasive subsumption of internal human diversity beneath the 'myth' of an overarching schema, destiny or purpose. Such myth defines the totalizing delusion that the nation is a necessary or essentially homologous entity.

Set against such recurrent essentialism in conceptions of nationhood is the problem of stipulating a non-exclusive notion of national iden-tity, one that acknowledges what Joseph Nuttin calls the 'actual and potential interactions between individual and environment'.[6] Such identity formation would recognize internal diversity and its specific relation (and potential for relation) to the extrinsic world.

This mutable concept of nationalism is a consistent feature of the work of the British-born writer, Hanif Kureishi. The representation of nationhood in his work is in direct contrast to essentialist notions of British national identity. Kureishi's call for a 're-vitalized and broader self-definition'[7] in the evaluation of the concept of Britishness runs like a mantra throughout his fictional and non-fictional writing. The aim of this chapter is to show how Kureishi uses his prose as a mechanism for establishing terms for 'a new way of being British'[8]; a less insular and more flexible approach towards notions of diversity, interaction and change. To this end, specific attention will be given here to Kureishi's acclaimed novel, *The Buddha of Suburbia* (1990),[9] a text where the issue of an openly interactive and mutable concept of national identity is critical. Arguably this allows Kureishi to explore qualities of identity formation through dramatizing the specular limitations in mass conceptions of nationhood, exposed in the quotations from Orwell's essay above.

I

There is the general belief that British national identity has 'changed and become more forward looking and gently inclusive over the last fifty years'[10] or so. It is claimed that this is attributable to the presence of migrant workers and refugees arriving from the outreaches of its former empire just after the Second World War and to the 'discourse of freedom and equality they brought with them'.[11] If such a degree of progressive social change in the conception of British identity is to be conceded, one must also accommodate disjuncture and suspension in this process due to relational anxieties about the instability and indeterminacy of British identity precipitated by such change. In the decade following the inaugural arrival of the first post-war migrant workers from the colony of Jamaica in June 1948, such anxieties began to surface in the central institutions of Britain. I shall discuss this period of post-war social *relations* in Britain and evidence of an authorized capitulation to the *essential* in British national discourse as a means of better understanding the strategies used in Kureishi's work to critique the discourse of national identity.

The advent of migrant workers and refugees from the British Caribbean, Eastern Europe, Ireland, South Asia and West Africa was not necessarily received with the 'forward-looking' mentality that is claimed for the nation's perspective on social tolerance nowadays. Set beside the well-documented experiences of social exclusion, ideological conflict and economic disadvantage of the time is a set of discursive manoeuvres through which the state actively sought to cling to the image of cultural and racial singularity, motivated by fear of being 'swamped' by 'aliens'.[12] One key discursive event in this early post-war period signals a self-conscious effort to demarcate the concept of an integral national unity against the unmanageable alterity that had washed up on British shores. This event is notable for the way in which it renders an ambivalent self-legitimating relationality in the process of safe-guarding British nationhood. This event demonstrates how the process of identity formation is sublimated into the institutional mechanisms of the nation-state. A brief look at this discursive event is necessary here for the way in which it reveals a certain duplicitous anxiety in the ongoing effort to sustain a cohesive and well-bounded notion of Britishness.

The event in question is the prodigious work done in 1953 by a number of governmental and voluntary organizations in the production of social statistics about the black segment of the new migrant communities in Britain. This was in compliance with the diktat of a covert ministerial committee. Sociologists Clive Harris, Bob Carter and Shirley Joshi offer an account of the event.

> Early in 1953 a confidential meeting of ministers took place at the Colonial Office. The case for legislative control, it was stressed, needed empirical demonstration. This meant gathering information about unemployment and National Assistance, 'numbers', housing, health, criminality and miscegenation, which it was hoped would confirm that black immigrants posed insoluble problems of social, economic and political assimilation. The already widespread surveillance of black communities by the police was supplemented by surveys undertaken by the Ministry of Labour, the National Assistance Board, the Welfare Department of the Colonial Office, the Home Office, the Commonwealth Relations Office, the Departments of Health, Housing and Transport as well as voluntary organizations. A working party on 'The Employment of Coloured People in the UK', set up by the cabinet in 1953, used the findings to produce a report which assessed the strengths and weaknesses of the 'strong case'. This report formed a central part of cabinet discussion in 1954–5 concerning the need to control black immigration and was to be regularly updated throughout the 1950s.[13]

Remarkable in this account is both the partial nature of the research ('criminality', 'miscegenation') and the numerous institutional sites (Departments and Offices) required to produce compliant evidence of the incompatibility of the black migrant community. Contrary to Michael Eldridge's assertion in his essay entitled, 'The Rise and Fall of Black Britain' that, 'no one in Britain *consciously* set out to delineate a black public sphere until 1966',[14] there is more than just the aim of a cultural getting-to-know-you session being undertaken here; more than ten years prior to the inauguration of the Caribbean Artists' Movement of which Eldridge speaks. The almost militaristic commitment given over to the agenda of the 1953 report exemplifies the breadth and depth of the work needed to establish what Michel Foucault has termed a 'field of frequencies'[15] – a complex network of signs and practices – in which state institutions and legislative bodies make official a policy of social demarcation. 'Step by step', as Peter Fryer notes of the same post-war period in his book, *Staying Power: The History of Black People in Britain* (1984), 'racism was institutionalized, legitimized, and nationalized'.[16]

It is from this discursive platform of the 1953 report on the social condition of black migrants that a representative economy could be deployed in the articulation of the non-white migrant constituencies in Britain as an homogeneous and qualitatively different – if not altogether inferior – social entity. The heterogeneous African, South Asian and African Caribbean groups in Britain now became a single, empirical Other; enunciated in a single discursive sign, 'black'.[17] In her introduction to the critical anthology entitled *The Rhetorics of Self-Making*, the social anthropologist Debbora Battaglia acknowledges the self-legitimating power of discursive interaction with others:

> The 'Self' is [. . .] a reification continually defeated by mutable entanglements with other subject[s] [. . .]. [It is] a chronically unstable productivity brought *situationally* – not invariably – to some form of *imaginary* order, to some purpose, as realized in the course of culturally patterned interactions.[18] (*my italics*)

In their commissioning and mediation of the 1953 report on the case for legislative control of black immigration, the 'confidential' ministerial committee created a field of discursive frequencies that could be actively retuned, depending on what Battaglia terms the 'situatio[n]', to augment a vision of the threat posed by black immigration to national unity. Hence, as Bob Carter et al. note above, the 1953 report's successive annual revisions as policies for reducing the numbers of black migrants were prepared for parliamentary debate.

Foucault has said that a discursive formation has no one consequence but rather a 'field of relations' in which its effects are 'far-reaching' and various.[19] As such, the discourse of surveillance and demarcation generated by the 1953 report might find a genealogical line extending forward to the tensions and crises that led up to the north Kensington riots of 1958, in which racial conflict played the greater part. It might also be traced as far forward as 1971 and the vocabulary of the Conservative MP, J. Enoch Powell, who called for a 'Ministry of Repatriation' for non-white residents in Britain on the passing of the Immigration Act of that year. This was an Act of Parliament which ended all primary immigration for black and Asians from the former colonies to Britain. Tom Nairn captures the discursive anxiety of the Powell era when he says that, 'In the obscene form of racism, English nationalism had been reborn'.[20]

I stress these issues here to highlight the belated quality of identity formation in its relational, interactive mode. The *desideratum* of a homogeneous cultural identity in Britain is rehearsed not through direct reference to internal qualities (suet-pudding, red pillar boxes etc.) but through the process of negative reinforcement, through the compulsive demarcation and exclusion of a perceived internal stranger/invader. Thus, Britain's internal entanglement with its ex-colonial subjects (Africans, South Asians, West Indians) in the post-war period becomes an unyielding preoccupation of the nation's custodians – its politicians, parliament, police etc. This involves a compensatory anxiety since the process of identity assertion, on a national scale, is here characterized by an oscillation towards establishing a discourse of Otherness before any shift towards the discourse of sameness can take place; then back and forth again as that primary Other loses its valency as a principle of exclusion (i.e. becomes assimilated or expunged). The critic Homi K. Bhabha understands this compulsive vacillation between discursive extremes as a 'doubling of the national address'.[21] He describes its ramifications in psychoanalytic terms:

> The problem is, of course, that the ambivalent identifications of love and hate occupy the same psychic space; and the paranoid projections 'outwards' return to haunt and split the place from which they are made.[22]

Following this logic of psychic recapitulation, I want to make the case for a restaging of this discursive 'doubling' in the work of Hanif Kureishi. Kureishi, as a British-born descendant of those earlier migrant groups, purposefully restages and circumscribes the contradictory motion in nationalist discourse between positivist assertion (essentialism) and negative reinforcement (relationalism) in his work.

II

Many of the themes of Hanif Kureishi's work mediate his own experience of interaction between people of different backgrounds and cultures in Britain. Born in 1954, to a Pakistani father and an English mother, Kureishi was raised in Bromley, Kent. Growing up in the suburbs, there were few points of identification outside the family circle for a young Briton of mixed heritage. 'When I was at school,' he says in an interview with Colin MacCabe:

> You were a hippie, or you were a rocker, or you were a skinhead. And a lot of the boys that I'd actually grown up with, since I was four or five, became skinheads. And I remember the shock of that. I remember one guy who was a very good friend of mine, coming to my house, and he had cropped hair and he had braces. [...]he was completely different and it was shocking[...]. And then being thought of as 'Pakis'[...] being chased down the streets by boys I'd been to school with.[23]

This formative experience registers a kind of trauma ('shock') in the young Kureishi because he is instantaneously made aware of just how much his Pakistani heritage compromises the bond between himself and his schoolmates. That acquaintances of his should seek identification with the anti-Asian dogma of the skinhead cult infuses a sense of estrangement in the young Kureishi's self-perception, which Frantz Fanon in 1952 described in terms of a premature internalization and objectification of one's bodily self-image as the repository of negativity.[24] Such self-objectification reverberates throughout Kureishi's *oeuvre* and is evident even in such later works as the novel *Intimacy* (1998) and the short-story collection, *Midnight All Day* (1999) where more reflexive motifs of lovelessness, self-denial, social anonymity and displacement preside over themes of race and ethnicity.

Early experiences of alienation and exclusion informed Kureishi's decision to validate himself through the process of writing:

> When I was fourteen, I made up my mind to be a writer [...] little of life need be lost or wasted if words could secure it, control it, reconstitute it. [...T]o write is to claim primacy for one's version of experience, and even a form of revenge.[25]

Thus on leaving King's College, London, where he studied philosophy, Kureishi began the process of filtering his experience through a range of literary genres and artistic media. Early employment as script-typist at the newly established Riverside Theatre and as factotum at the Royal Court Theatre in the late 1970s eventually led to the staging of his first full-length play, *'The King and Me'* in January 1980. Between 1980 and 1983, Kureishi wrote a series of plays which, in form, were influenced by dramatists as various as Anton Chekhov, Oscar Wilde, Samuel Beckett and Joe Orton[26] but whose titles alone – *The Mother Country* (1980), *Outskirts* (1981), *Border-line* (1981), *Birds of Passage* (1983) – reflect themes consistent with his earlier experience of social marginalization and conflict.

By the mid-1980s, Kureishi had gained widespread critical acclaim for his filmed screenplays, *My Beautiful Laundrette* (1984, nominated for an Oscar), *Sammy and Rosie Get Laid* (1988) and *London Kills Me* (1991). *My Beautiful Laundrette* is the most organic of Kureishi's dramaturgical works, given the closeness of its setting and character-ization to the details of his own upbringing.[27] This play depicts with unmediated realism the crude and passionate forces of interaction between different cultures residing in 1980s' Britain. The play centres on the relationship between two Londoners, Omar and Johnny. Omar, a Briton of Pakistani heritage, exploits the enterprise culture of the Thatcher era by establishing himself in the Laundromat busi-ness. Johnny is an ex-school colleague, whose transgressions in the world of petty crime are stifled by Omar's offer of employment. As their relationship develops into an homosexual affair, tensions arise due to their uncommon hierarchical roles – Johnny, the native Brit, is Omar's 'man Friday' in the workplace – and to Johnny's misguided allegiance to the racist dogma and violence of the National Front's political campaign.

Responding in part to provocation by Salman Rushdie, Kureishi shifted his focus in the 1990s from dramaturgy to prose.[28] He has published three novels to date, *The Buddha of Suburbia*, *The Black Album* (1995) and *Intimacy*, and the short-story collections, *Love in a Blue Time* (1997) and *Midnight All Day* (1999). Only one play, *Sleep With Me* (1999), has been premiered in this latter period. On the whole, these more recent works reveal a broadening of thematic concerns to encompass religion – as with the short story 'My Son the Fanatic' in *Love in a Blue Time* – and the psycho-sexual deca-dence of the metropolitan middle classes (*Intimacy*, *Midnight All Day*). Kureishi justifies this general shift towards prose by saying that, 'what you write goes to the reader unmediated: there are no directors, or anybody else involved'.[29] Hence, also, a marked gravita-tion towards a more reflexive, 'intimate' voice in which to communi-cate the internal consequences of social alienation and displacement in these latter works. To this effect, one of the most powerful prose works produced by Kureishi is an earlier non-fictional essay entitled, 'The Rainbow Sign'. As an appendix to the playscript of *My Beautiful Laundrette* first published in 1986, this essay is meant to elucidate themes of the screenplay through autobiographical reference. Yet, in giving primacy to Kureishi's experiences of social and cultural mar-ginalization and exclusion in his homeland, England, it also provides trenchant insight into the failure of national discourse to adequately enunciate its relation to internal diversity and, in consequence, external difference. A brief look at this essay should lend additional insight into the representational devices utilized in Kureishi's fictional prose.

In 'The Rainbow Sign', Kureishi gives an account of his early life growing up in Britain and of his first visit to Pakistan as a young adult where he has many relatives. The essay is divided into three sections – 'England, 'Pakistan', 'England' – with the final section offering an homecoming perspective which has benefited from an understanding of a discursive overlap in the alternative concept of national identity provided by the sojourn abroad.

In this essay, Kureishi offers a personal perspective on the various contradictory manoeuvres that underscore nationalist discourse. In Britain, the perpetuation of essentialist Orwellian notions of the 'soundness and homogeneity of Britain' and the timelessness of its 'gentle manners' and 'tolerance'[30] are, in Kureishi's view, blind to the exclusionary signs and practices that infect the nation's political, social and cultural life. From the politics of J. Enoch Powell and Duncan Sandys, to the televisual and print media, the classroom and the playground, Kureishi demonstrates how the principle of Othering and exclusion is woven into the fabric of the nation with dehumanizing psychological effect:

> From the start I tried to deny my Pakistani self. I was ashamed. It was a curse and I wanted to be rid of it. I wanted to be like everyone else [...].
> I reckoned that at least once every day since I was five years old I had been racially abused. I became incapable of distinguishing between remarks that were genuinely intended to hurt and those intended as 'humour'.
> I became cold and distant [...].[31]

Here, survival in Britain requires a denial of self and a total assimilation to the cultural and sub-cultural characteristics associated with 'white' British identity. Everywhere in Kureishi's novel *The Buddha of Suburbia* this process of self-negation is evident in the young protagonist Karim:

> We wasted days and days dancing in the Pink Pussy Club, yawning at Fat Mattress at the Croydon Greyhound, ogling strippers on Sunday mornings in a pub, sleeping through Godard and Antonioni films, and enjoying the fighting at Millwall Football Ground, where I forced Changez to wear a bobble-hat over his face in case the lads saw he was a Paki and imagined I was one too. (p. 98)

Karim's efforts to enjoy the heterogeneous lifestyle that remains available to him in a culturally diverse Britain demands vigilance against those custodians of national homogeneity (the Millwall-supporting 'lads') via self-erasure. In forcing Changez to wear a bobble-hat over his face, Karim tries to erase the sign of a subcontinental heritage that, alongside his Britishness, also constitutes his identity. This exemplifies what Paul Gilroy describes as the powerful semiotics of the body as 'arbitrat[or] in the assignment of cultures and nationalities to peoples'.[32] It also demonstrates just how deeply the signs and practices of social exclusion can be internalized by those excluded.

Similarly, in Pakistan, Kureishi describes the contradictory impact of the 'new Islamization'. The revival and reinforcement of Islamic law as governmental policy that occurred in Pakistan in the late 1970s had, according to Kureishi, imbued the nation with a moral mission that stifled democracy, artistic cultural life, progressive civil rights for women and neglected a large underclass of economically deprived citizens. Admittedly, Kureishi's own ethical stance is obscured by his secular, Western system of values. Yet, slogans like 'there need only be one party – the party of the righteous'[33] betray a 'return to ignorance' and essentialism, in Kureishi's view, for its instituted reliance on 'revelation' and 'scripture'[34] rather than reason. Kureishi notes that not even the strain of metaphysical piety in the discourse of a nation under rule of military dictatorship (Pakistan was then under the rule of the Bhutto regime) is free from what Joseph Nuttin terms its 'complementary motivation'.[35] As Kureishi sees it, a prominent feature in the reinforcement of national identity in Pakistan is anxious comparison to what is deemed the 'moral vertigo' of the 'godless societies' of the West. England, in particular, is a popular point of reference:

[T]he old men in their clubs and the young eating their hamburgers took great pleasure in England's decline and decay. The great master was fallen. Now it was seen as strikebound, drug-ridden, riot-torn, inefficient, disunited, a society which had moved too suddenly from puritanism to hedonism and now loathed itself.[36]

A similar view is taken by Rafi, the doomed protagonist of Kureishi's screenplay, *Sammy and Rosie Get Laid*. Rafi's belief that he can escape crimes committed in his homeland via exile in London is undermined by the city's cosmopolitanism. Its secular and decadent heterogeneity he describes pejoratively as 'world war', 'out of control' and comparable with 'Beirut'.[37]

Set against this comparative motivation in the discourses of nation-hood, found both in England and in Pakistan, is Kureishi's realization that neither Britain nor Pakistan is a satisfactory locus of identifica-tion, 'I couldn't rightfully lay claim to either place'.[38] What seems intrinsic to both nations is not communal wholeness, stability, direc-tion, certainty or sanctity, but rather an irrational principle of intoler-ance towards human diversity and mixture. Indeed, for Kureishi – born in England, with both Pakistani and English relatives – the process of identity formation must now reside in its negative capabil-ity. That is, it must reside in a distancing and circumscription of the self-serving causes of identity with its ambivalent 'lurch', as Tom Nairn put it, between the essential and the relational, between same-ness and difference in the discourse of nationhood. As Kureishi says in 'The Rainbow Sign': 'I wasn't a misfit; I could join the elements of myself together. It was the others, they wanted misfits; they wanted you to embody within yourself their ambivalence.'[39]

In this light, Kureishi's first novel, *The Buddha of Suburbia*, can be read as a rendition of the act of self-determination through the exter-nalization of the ambivalent discourse of national identity. The tech-nique used for this process of externalization in Kureishi's text is, I claim, the concept of performance; of 'playing not-me'.

III

It is the existential condition of migrancy that proves a significant trope in the reconfiguration of identity as an wholly interactive and mutable rather than fixed and timeless idea in *The Buddha of Suburbia*. Here, it is the concept of continual relocation, the ongoing encounter and interaction with the extrinsic world, the transformative negotiation between the idea of home and changing locations abroad, that be-comes a constant over and above the oscillatory return to a reified vision of Self. Salman Rushdie has considered this uncircumscribed conception of identity in his famous essay, 'Imaginary Homelands':

> We [...] have been forced by cultural displacement to accept the provisional nature of all truths, all certainties. We cannot lay claim to Olympus, and are thus released to describe our worlds in the way in which all of us, whether writers or not, perceive it from day to day.[40]

This includes the provisional veracity given to notions of national identity as a pre-given concept of geo-cultural or ethnic similitude. Caught between two or more worlds, with fragmented memories of home and incomplete assimilation abroad, the migrant subject develops a diminished sense of national belonging. In his call for the flexible use of the 'imagination' over the half-truths of past or present, there or here, Rushdie appeals to the authority of liminal and changing interaction that defines the migrant experience over and above the discursive shackles of nationalism with its contradictory doctrine of *e pluribus unum*.

In *Buddha*, Kureishi occupies a similar stance. The propulsive condition of migrancy is a transformative force in this text that undermines bounded notions of identity and nation. He uses the condition of migrancy in two subtle ways; first to highlight the compulsive and contradictory referral to the alterity of the extrinsic world as a means of maintaining the idea of inward homogeneity, stability and timelessness; and secondly to displace such outward projectionism by referring the trope of migrancy to the instability and diversity of the intrinsic life of the nation.

The first and second conditions are demonstrated in *Buddha* through corresponding transformations undergone by Karim's father Haroon, the eponymous Buddha of suburban Bromley. In the first instance, Haroon, working as a clerk in the Civil Service during his early years of migration from India to England, is given to lamenting the continual sense of estrangement he feels in the new environment: 'His life, once a cool river of balmy distraction, of beaches and cricket, of mocking the British, and dentists' chairs, was now a cage of umbrellas and steely regularity.' (p. 26) Here, the uniformity of British life with its added dysfunction of inclement weather provides the motivation for Haroon's comparative reflections on the more fulfilling life enjoyed in his homeland, India. Yet, a major contradiction is evident here in just how much an antipathetic reference to Britain ('mocking the British') defines Haroon's sense of belonging to India. Haroon's identification with India is doubly tethered to the sign of India's perceived Other, the 'British'. His migration to Britain somehow cannot deny the interactive influence of Britain in the constitution of Indian national identity.

In the second instance, Kureishi places the terms of this contradiction inside Britain's national borders. In an essay entitled 'The Semi-Detached Metropolis: Hanif Kureishi's London'(1996), the critic John Clement Ball offers a perceptive analysis of how larger relations between 'home' and 'abroad' are transposed onto the intrinsic landscape of suburbs and city. This is represented in the figure of a revitalized Haroon who, having left his job and split with his wife, undertakes a mock migration from Bromley to West Kensington with his lover Eva, Karim and Charlie (Eva's son). Ball says:

[The] move from the suburbs to 'London proper' becomes a local, miniaturized version of postcolonial migrancy and culture-shock – the move from ex-colony to metropolis. This London not only includes 'the world' in the sense of peoples, it also replicates within its borders the world's spatial patterning.[41]

Here, Ball refers to Kureishi's utilization of London as a positive sign of diverse social and cultural interaction. London, then, with its ever-changing cultural diversity and incompleteness, is revalued as a mecca for the migrant subject, whether from Bromley or Bombay. Such is the view of Karim:

There was a sound London had. It was [...] people in Hyde Park playing bongos with their hands; there was also the keyboard on the Doors's 'Light My Fire'. There were kids dressed in velvet cloaks who lived free lives; there were thousands of black people everywhere, so I wouldn't feel exposed; there were bookshops with racks of magazines printed without capital letters or the bourgeois disturbance of full stops; there were shops selling all the records you could desire; there were parties where girls and boys you didn't know took you upstairs and fucked you; there were all the drugs you could use. [...] I was twenty. I was ready for anything. (p. 121)

There is cultural diversity but without the threat of exclusion by violence, which Karim senses earlier with Changez at the Millwall football ground. In London there are enough migrants and 'black people' for Karim not to necessarily fit in or share an identity with, but enough for him not to feel exposed to those who do share an exclusive sense of belonging. In the tradition of the *bildungsroman*, the novel of development from innocence to maturity, the move from Bromley to West Kensington is also, for Karim, an escape from the inhibitions of adolescence to adult freedom. Likewise, Charlie's punk-rock band is named, more decadently, 'The Condemned' from its suburban incarnation as 'Musn't Grumble'; Eva indulges in hosting a string of parties and finds a new, glamorous career as an interior designer; and the new, revitalized Haroon establishes a profitable career as guru to the directionless metropolitan bour-geoisie. As Ball states: '[The small-scale migration] as performed by Karim, Charlie, Eva, and the "new" Haroon, result in sensual pleas-ures, cunning, and the exploitation of identity as a fabricated image.'[42]

In conclusion, I'd like to take up this last point – 'identity as a fabricated image' – with regard to Kureishi's depiction of London as the site in which identities shift and are performed.

IV

Everywhere in Part Two of *Buddha*, London is celebrated as a location of cultural diversity without the stifling tensions seen in the suburbs. London provides the space in which Kureishi can communicate a conceptually unbounded interactive notion of British identity; one that incorporates a variety of different ethnicities and cultures. Here, identity is projected as relational and changeable but never taken as seriously as, say, Anwar takes it with his customary arrangement of marriage and anachronistic response of fasting when his daughter, Jamilla, resists. Kureishi's London, with its 'thousands of blacks', is internally influenced by the culture of minorities as well as by emergent cultural groups like the punk movement. Different identities are not only celebrated here but performed on a huge scale. Like his father Haroon, the fake-Buddha, Karim also engages in performing his ethnic identity when he takes up the role of Mowgli in Jeremy Shadwell's theatre production of *The Jungle Book* (pp. 140–3), and again when Karim later enlists Changez as his muse – despite warnings to the contrary from the latter – in Matthew Pyke's more edgy dramaturgy. Pyke himself sums up the 'double-consciousness' required in the act of performing one's identity:

> What a strange business this acting is, Pyke said; you are trying to convince people that you're someone else, that this is not-me. The way to do it is this, he said: when in character playing not-me, you have to be yourself. To make your not-self real you have to steal from your authentic self. A false stroke, a wrong note, anything pretended, and to the audience you are as obvious as a Catholic naked in a mosque. The closer you play yourself the better. Paradox of paradoxes: to be someone else successfully you must be yourself! This I learned. (p. 219)

This statement, more about the craft of acting than anything else, encapsulates the flexible way in which Karim's generation see identity as a relational and mutable concept. Different identities are easily assimilable, easily performed. In his introduction to the reader *Black British Culture and Society*, Kwesi Owusu, revising but not contradicting Pyke's terms, describes the way in which the act of performance engages with the politics of representation: 'Performance forms act accordingly in the struggle for identity. [...] It is the assertion of an "I am" [...] precisely in the face of others who are saying that "you are not".'[43]

For the 'new' Haroon and his son Karim, identity in London becomes a dynamic, flexible and interactive concept. Playing 'not-me' is also playing another version of what I am, an easy shifting of

the boundaries of identity, playing with the vacillating signs of positive approval and negative stereotype as the route to an elevated sense
of self-knowledge and worth. Perhaps the more symbolic example of
this performance of identity is evident in the transformation undertaken by Charlie. Having acquired success and fame with his band
The Condemned, the restless Charlie has undergone another migration across the Atlantic, to New York. Karim observes the hitherto
stoical Charlie thus:

> I walked down the street, laughing, amused that here in America
> Charlie had acquired this cockney accent when my first memory of
> him at school was that he'd cried after being mocked by the stinking
> gypsy kids for talking so posh. Certainly, I'd never heard anyone talk
> like that before. Now he was going in for cockney rhyming slang, too.
> 'I'm just off for a pony,' he'd say. Pony and trap – crap. Or he was going
> to wear his winter whistle. Whistle and flute – suit. He was selling
> Englishness, and getting a lot of money for it. (p. 247)

As writer, director and producer of plays, films and novels centred
on British life, Kureishi is also engaged in the art of performance.
Through the representation of Charlie – a 'posh' indigenous Englishman mimicking a working-class accent for more credibility abroad –
Kureishi is in some sense selling his own version of an openly interactive, performative concept of British identity back to the British.
Simon Gikandi takes a comparable view of Kureishi's strategy in his
book, *Maps of Englishness: Writing Identity in the Culture of Colonialism* (1996):

> Kureishi's reticent identification with Englishness is based on the belief
> that, in England, he can valorize the logic of a secular and enlightened
> culture and use it against the unreason of the racists. This way he will
> posit himself as the true Englishman and cast the racists as aberrations
> from the national norm.[44]

Such intent is confirmed towards the end of Kureishi's essay, 'The
Rainbow Sign'. Here Kureishi, having given account of his sojourn in
Pakistan, comes to a radical understanding of this need to promote a
viable, more flexible alternative to existing notions of what it means
to be British. His comments provide an apt *dernier cri* to the Orwellian predicament that opened this discussion:

> It is the British [...] who have to learn that being British isn't what it
> was. Now it is a more complex thing, involving new elements. So there
> must be a fresh way of seeing Britain and the choices it faces. Much

thought, discussion and self-examination must go into what this 'new way of being British' involves and how difficult it might be to attain.

The failure to grasp this opportunity for a revitalized and broader self-definition in the face of a real failure to be human, will be more insularity, schism, bitterness and catastrophe.[45]

Notes

1   See Paul Gilroy's chapter, 'Identity, Belonging and the Critique of Pure Sameness' in his *Between Camps: Race, Identity and Nationalism at the End of the Colour Line* (London: Allen Lane/Penguin, 2000), p. 108.

2   See Joseph Nuttin, *Motivation, Planning, and Action: A Relational Theory of Behaviour Dynamics*, trans. Raymond P. Lorion and Jean E. Dumas (NJ:Leuven University Press/Lawrence Erlbaum Associates, 1984), p. 58–9.

3   Gilroy, 'Identity, Belonging . . .'.

4   Benedict Anderson, *Imagined Communities: Reflections on the Origin and Spread of Nationalism* (London: Verso, 1983), p. 36.

5   Tom Nairn, *The Break-Up of Britain: Crisis and Neo-Nationalism* (London: New Left Books, 1977), p. 294.

6   Nuttin, *Motivation, Planning and Action*, p. 58.

7   Hanif Kureishi, 'The Rainbow Sign' in *My Beautiful Laundrette and the Rainbow Sign* (London: Faber and Faber, 1986), p. 102.

8   Ibid.

9   Hanif Kureishi, *The Buddha of Suburbia* (London: Faber and Faber, 1990)

10   See Onyekachi Wambu's (ed.) introduction to the celebratory anthology, *Empire Windrush: Fifty-Years of Writing about Black Britain* (London: Victor Gollancz/Cassell, 1998), p. 22.

11   Ibid.

12   Words used in J. Enoch Powell's anti-immigration speech titled 'Still to Decide', delivered in 1972. Cited in Wambu, *Empire Windrush*, p. 139–40.

13   See Bob Carter, Clive Harris and Shirley Joshi's chapter, 'The 1951–55 Conservative Government and the Racialization of Black Immigration' in *Inside Babylon: The Caribbean Diaspora in Britain*, eds. Winston James and Clive Harris (London: Verso, 1993), pp. 58–9.

14   Michael Eldridge, 'The Rise and Fall of Black Britain,' *Transition*, issue 74, vol.7, no.2, 35.

15   Michel Foucault, *The Archaeology of Knowledge* (London: Tavistock Publications, 1972), p. 51.

16   Peter Fryer, *Staying Power: The History of Black People in Britain* (London: Pluto Press, 1984), p. 381.

17   Stuart Hall argues that such a discursive enunciation defines the moment when racism finds structured and 'legitimate form [...] at the heart of British political culture'. See his essay, 'Racism and Reaction' in *Five Views of Multi-Racial Britain: Talks on Race Relations Broadcast by BBC TV* (London: Commission for Racial Equality/BBC Television Further Education, 1978), pp. 29–30.

18   Debbora Battaglia (ed.), *The Rhetorics of Self-Making* (Berkeley, CA: University of California Press, 1995), p. 2.

19   Foucault, *The Archaeology of Knowledge*, p. 51.

20   Nairn, *The Break-Up of Britain*, p. 51.

21   Homi K. Bhabha, 'DissemiNation: Time, Narrative, and the Margins of the Modern Nation' in *Nation and Narration* (London: Routledge, 1990), p. 300.

22   Ibid.

23   Colin MacCabe, 'Interview: Hanif Kureishi on London', *Critical Quarterly*, vol. 41, no. 3 (Autumn 1999), p. 39.

24   'What else could it be for me but an amputation, an excision, a haemorrhage that splattered my whole body with black blood? [...] All I wanted was to be a man among other men,' Frantz Fanon, *Black Skin, White Masks* (London: Pluto Press,1986), p. 112.

25   See Kureishi's introduction to *Outskirts and Other Plays* (London: Faber and Faber, 1992), p. x.

26   Kenneth C. Kaleta discusses Kureishi's intertextual influences in his critical biography, *Hanif Kureishi: Postcolonial Storyteller* (Austin, TX: University of Texas Press, 1998), pp. 26–7.

27   This is discussed in Kureishi's interview with MacCabe.

28   Ibid., pp. 42–3.

29   Ibid., p. 42.

30   Kureishi, 'The Rainbow Sign', p. 100–1.

31   Ibid., pp. 73 and 76.

32   Gilroy, 'Identity, Belonging...' p. 24.

33   Kureishi 'Rainbow Sign.', p. 90.

34   Ibid., p. 92.

35   Nuttin, *Motivation, Planning and Action*, p. 64.

36   Kureishi 'Rainbow Sign', p. 92.

37   Hanif Kureishi, *Sammy and Rosie Get Laid: The Script and the Diary* (London: Faber and Faber, 1988).

38   Kureishi 'Rainbow Sign', p. 81.

39   Ibid., p. 75.

40   Salman Rushdie, 'Imaginary Homelands' in *Imaginary Homelands: Essays and Criticism, 1981–1991* (London: Granta Books, 1991), pp. 12–13.

41   John Clement Ball, 'The Semi-Detached Metropolis: Hanif Kureishi's London', *Ariel*, vol. 27, no. 4 (October 1996), 21.

42   Ibid., p. 24.

43   Kwesi Owusu (ed.), 'The Question of Performance', *Black British Culture and Society: A Text Reader* (London: Routledge, 1999), p.x.
44   Simon Gikandi, *Maps of Englishness: Writing Identity in the Culture of Colonialism* (New York: Columbia University Press, 1996), p. 204.
45   Kureishi 'Rainbow Sign', pp. 101–2.

Primary texts

Fiction

The Buddha of Suburbia (London: Faber and Faber, 1990)
The Black Album (London: Faber and Faber, 1995)
Love in a Blue Time (London: Faber and Faber, 1997)
Intimacy (London: Faber and Faber, 1998)
Midnight All Day (London: Faber and Faber, 1999)
Gabriel's Gift (London: Faber and Faber, 2001)
Dreaming and Scheming (London: Faber and Faber, 2002)

Screenplays

My Beautiful Laundrette and the Rainbow Sign (London: Faber and Faber, 1986)
Sammy and Rosie Get Laid: The Script and the Diary (London: Faber and Faber, 1988)
London Kills Me: Three Screenplays and Four Essays (London: Faber and Faber, 1991)
Outskirts and Other Plays (London: Faber and Faber, 1992)
My Son, the Fanatic (London: Faber and Faber, 1997)

Selected critical texts

John Clement Ball, 'The Semi-Detached Metropolis: Hanif Kureishi's London', *Ariel*, 27:4 (October, 1996), 7–27
Simon Gikandi, *Maps of Englishness: Writing Identity in the Culture of Colonialism* (New York: Columbia University Press, 1996)
Kenneth C. Kaleta, *Hanif Kureishi: Postcolonial Storyteller*, (Austin, TX: University of Texas Press, 1998)
Colin MacCabe, 'Interview: Hanif Kureishi on London', *Critical Quarterly*, 41:3 (Autumn, 1999), 37–56
Ruvani Ranasinha, *Hanif Kureishi* (Tavistock: Northcote House, 2001)
Gayatri C. Spivak, 'In Praise of *Sammy and Rosie Get Laid*', *Critical Quarterly*, 31:2 (Summer, 1989), 80–8
Nahem Yousaf, 'Hanif Kureishi and "the Brown Man's Burden"', *Critical Survey*, 8:1 (1996), 15–22

7 Zadie Smith's *White Teeth*: Multiculturalism for the Millennium

Dominic Head

On the jacket of the first hardback edition of *White Teeth* (2000) the photograph of Zadie Smith is intended to give out several unmistakable signals. This bespectacled and studious writer, the publisher is telling us, has achieved a maturity of vision that is unusual for someone in her twenties. But we also note, if only subliminally, the Afro hairstyle, and the complexion which betokens a mixed-race identity.

These details become worth remarking upon with the publication of the paperback edition a year later. Now the author has lost her glasses, and sports long, straight dark hair – a makeover that evokes a stereotype of sultry seductiveness. With the seriousness of the author established, it seems that the publisher could attend to other areas of her marketability. But there is a more important aspect to the new image. Smith now has an Asian look, and this demonstrates an indeterminate ethnicity. For the author of a book that purports to speak authoritatively to a wide range of ethnic experience – including Caribbean British and Asian British experience – the ability to adopt different guises suggests a substantive hybridized identity that goes beyond the more cynical marketing objectives. And what this implies about the author is certainly true of her novel's scheme: *White Teeth*, through its complex plot, its diverse range of characters, its broad post-war historical sweep, and its insistent and summative portrayal of a *de facto* hybrid cultural life, is artfully constructed as the definitive representation of twentieth-century British multiculturalism.

The hype surrounding *White Teeth* began in 1997 when Zadie Smith, at the age of twenty-one and still a Cambridge undergraduate, signed a contract with Penguin for a six-figure sum, on the basis of eighty pages of her first novel. Smith, who hails from Willesden Green, born of a Jamaican mother and an English father, had been identified as the epitome of multicultural Britain – or certainly as someone who could be marketed as such and touted as 'the first publishing sensation of the millennium'.[1]

The really remarkable aspect of Zadie Smith's dramatic appearance on the British literary scene, however, is that *White Teeth* turned out to be just as significant as the hype had proclaimed; so good, in fact, that reviewers were unable to shoot it down. Successive reviews emphasized the book's rich and entertaining treatment of Black-British life. Among the high-profile reviewers, Caryl Phillips's commendation is especially noteworthy: in Phillips's view, Smith 'recognizes and celebrates' the 'helpless heterogeneity' of post-colonial Britain in a novel that is 'restless and wonderfully poised'. The 'helplessness' is that of a mongrel nation 'still struggling to find a way to stare into the mirror' and accept its complex history, with its concomitant pain. Smith's novel, concludes Phillips, is an 'audaciously assured contribution to this process of staring into the mirror'.[2]

The claim that has been made for *White Teeth*, then, is large indeed. The implication is that Smith has found a way of harnessing the novel's capacity to embrace heterogeneity, and has used it to give convincing shape to her presentation of an evolving, and genuinely multicultural Britain.[3] The complex problem of post-colonial identity and national affiliation, exacerbated in a post-war Britain facing the challenges of the end of Empire and the process of national redefinition that ensues, begins to find some kind of resolution in the intricate, but satisfying plot of *White Teeth*. In terms of literary history this seems especially significant since evocations of post-colonial migrant experience in post-war Britain have been haunted by a sense of social failure. The fictionalized migrant self, from Moses Aloetta in Sam Selvon's *The Lonely Londoners* through to V. S. Naipaul's self-portrait in *The Enigma of Arrival* and beyond, is always vulnerable and often embattled.

This is sometimes due to the transitional nature of twentieth-century post-colonial expression, where post-colonial identity is properly conceived as *process* rather than *arrival*;[4] but the presentation of vulnerability has just as frequently to do with the inhospitable nature of British, and especially English society, often portrayed as unsympathetic to the goals of a living, interactive multiculturalism. Zadie Smith seems to speak for a third generation of post-war Black British experience, a generation for which the concepts of 'migrancy' and 'exile' have become too distant to carry their former freight of disabling rootlessness. *White Teeth* does not avoid the fact of ethnic tension but, in its self-conscious mode of end-of-millennium *tour de force*, it presents the social problems of ethnicity as the shared problems of a diverse citizenship with a common 'home'.

In this view, some element of social integration is taken as given. The problem with 'integration' is that it often means 'assimilation' within a host culture that is insensitive to cultural diversity, and many novelists have been concerned by this new, internal form of cultural imperialism. Salman Rushdie, in an essay from 1982, alerts us to the difficulties of understanding race in Britain, where, following E. P. Thompson, he discovers 'the last colony of the British Empire'.[5] This new internal empire manifests the disastrous tendency to colonize or demonize aspects of racial difference, thus poisoning its own natural development. Indeed, Rushdie's essay exhibits deep concern about the failure of Britain to embrace its post-colonial future, and sees this as 'a crisis of the whole culture, of the society's entire sense of itself'. The misperception of racial and cultural difference extends to those apparently benign attempts at 'integration', which Rushdie sees as code for a nullifying assimilation. He is particularly dismissive of 'multiculturalism', a term, he feels, which too often conceals mere tokenism.[6]

Rushdie's essay locates the need for an alternative approach to ethnic diversity, an approach that will avoid glib multiculturalism on the one hand, and flat assimilation on the other. He is defining the cultural space of the post-colonial migrant, and is insisting that this space is of crucial significance to all inhabitants of the new emerging culture.

A question to ask is whether or not the term 'multicultural' is really as damaging as Rushdie suggests. If one speaks of 'Black-British' identity, does this already denote some kind of capitulation? To the contrary, A. Robert Lee indicates that 'hybridizations like "Asian-British", "Caribbean-British" or "African-British"', which can be further 'particularized into, say, Brixton-Jamaican, Cardiff-Bengali, Liverpool-Nigerian', contain also 'their own internal dynamics of heterogeneity and . . . tension'.[7] This cultural space of migrant and post-migrant identity is, necessarily, transitional, an interactive site in which multiculturalism must be redeemed as an active, conflictual process. In the post-war era we have witnessed an ongoing practice of redefining and rewriting the nation from within, and eventually, the emergence of what Bhabha terms 'a hybrid national narrative'.[8] If, for most of the post-war period, writers have had to confront the obstacles to this meaningful hybridity, perhaps we have begun to see the emergence of a literature in which it begins to be realized.

Before advancing in more detail the case for *White Teeth* as an exemplary instance of this new phase, it is worth bearing in mind the social and political obstacles that have presented themselves prior to this more propitious moment. If there has been a pervasive misperception about 'race' abroad in society, this has been compounded in the post-war era by the confused and contradictory immigration policies of successive governments. The British Nationality Act of 1948 confirmed the right of entry to Britain for the citizens of Empire, who were deemed British subjects; since then, however, there has been a steady attrition of these rights. The post-war 'open door' policy was ended by the 1962 Commonwealth Immigration Act, which introduced a system of employment vouchers, subject to quota, for Commonwealth immigrants. Further restrictions on East Indian Asians (1968) were followed by the Immigration Act (1971), which limited domicile to those born in Britain, or whose parents or grandparents were of British origin. Perhaps the most significant redefinition of nationality and citizenship was enshrined in the 1981 British Nationality Act, which abolished the automatic right to British citizenship for children born in Britain. This Act was designed to restrict the naturalization of immigrants' children, but in the process it removed from the statute book an ancient birthright.[9]

This brief sketch of some of the legislation demonstrates, first, that the acceptance of the subjects of the former Empire in the 1940s and 1950s – who were in some cases positively encouraged to migrate to the 'mother' nation – rapidly evaporated in the light of economic change and political expediency; and, second, the shifting policy shows that identity based on national affiliation is a political construction. The Janus-faced response to the citizens of Empire has helped to foster a denial of post-colonial obligations and a rejection of the post-colonial heritage.

There is now a strong tradition of Black-British writing which challenges this culture of denial, gradually expanding the ways in which fiction might treat of migrant experience and the tensions which attend it. For the post-war period, the issue becomes pressing with the arrival of the 'Windrush generation' of West Indian immigrants in the late 1940s and 1950s, named after the *Empire Windrush*, which docked at Tilbury in 1948. Immigrants from the West Indies viewed England not merely as a land of opportunity, but also as a kind of home, a mother country whose history, culture and literature were familiar to them from their school textbooks. In close-up, however, things looked very different.

The experience of disillusionment is artfully rendered in the technically exuberant fiction of Sam Selvon, who migrated to England in

1950. If the arrival in the inhospitable mother country was demoralizing, the literature that evolved out of this experience began to transform 'English literature' by appending to it a form of migrant post-colonial expression which rewrote the cultural centre. This is especially true of Selvon's London novels, with their formal project to 'creolize' the English novel.[10] But this is also a geo-political gesture, an attempt to stake a claim to the spaces of the city. The new colonization of London is epitomized in *The Lonely Londoners* when the character dubbed 'Sir Galahad' waits for his white date at Piccadilly Circus, and is overwhelmed by a sense of being at the centre of things.[11]

More usually, place, and the quest for settlement have been problematic for the migrant writer. If V. S. Naipaul's *The Enigma of Arrival* is an elaborate attempt to insert the migrant self into the English landscape (and Naipaul into the canon of English literature), the great effort involved, and the contradictions discovered in the process serve, paradoxically, to confirm the inhospitability of England to this project.

Salman Rushdie is interesting in this connection, since he does not participate in the attempt to reclaim a particular geographical place, whether urban or rural, or to rethink national identity in relation to it. Rather, Rushdie is the chronicler of the unfettered migrant sensibility, that version of post-colonialism which unhooks historical tradition from place, and which creates new, self-conscious kinds of identity from a fragmentary vision. History is vital to Rushdie's method, but his own brand of magic realism is defined by the imaginative transformation of 'fact', in the process of reimagining history. This is a claim that is often made on behalf of significant post-colonial fiction, the assertion that it creates the freedom to rewrite 'official' colonial history. Yet this is also a turning away from the particular difficulties inherent in the actual geographical experience of the migrant self in post-war Britain. The project taken up by Selvon and Naipaul in their different ways – of articulating the new colonization of England – is effectively ignored in Rushdie's technique.

Bhabha's work on the interrelationship between 'nation' and 'narration' suggests a way in which actual political identities might be located more precisely. Bhabha considers 'the cultural construction of nationness' to be 'a form of social and textual affiliation', and he describes a complex tension between two contradictory (but interacting) forces: the 'pedagogic' tendency to assert an authoritative national identity based on 'pre-given or constituted historical origin or event', and the 'performative' process of reconstruction, an on-going 'living principle' which 'must erase any prior or originary presence of the nation-people'. The two processes act on the people, ensuring that they are doubly inscribed 'as pedagogical objects and performative subjects'. What emerges from this double inscription is not oppositional or confrontational; indeed, it is cast as something which is at once more productive and inevitable:

> The minority does not simply confront the pedagogical, or powerful master-discourse with a contradictory or negating referent. . . . It interrogates its object by initially withholding its objective. Insinuating itself into the terms of reference of the dominant discourse, the supplementary [minority discourse] antagonizes the implicit power to generalize, to produce the sociological solidity.

The tendency of that which is supplementary to *question* is conceived as 'a meditation on the disposition of space and time from which the narrative of the nation must *begin*'. Consequently, the supplementary impulse is also that which has the power to effect a 'renegotiation of those times, terms, and traditions through which we turn our uncertain, passing contemporaneity into the signs of history'.[12]

This gives 'cultural difference' a very particular edge. In Bhabha's terms, 'cultural difference . . . addresses the jarring of meanings and values generated in-between the variety and diversity associated with cultural plenitude' – no bland multiculturalism, this – and so 'it represents the process of cultural interpretation formed . . . in the disjunctive, liminal space of national society'. (That term 'liminal', it is worth noting, is well suited to Bhabha's purpose, since its two meanings – 'inhabiting a borderland', as well as 'incipient' or 'just emerging' – are simultaneously implied.) Bhabha's process of 'dissemi-Nation' is one by which 'the radical alterity of the national culture will create new forms of living and writing', and will do so by rearticulating 'meaning, time, peoples, cultural boundaries and historical traditions'.[13] I take it that these metaphors of space begin to have meaning only when applied to a particular geographical place.

The issues I have been tracing are all given a satisfactory treatment in Zadie Smith's *White Teeth* (2000). This novel, part celebration, part cautionary tale, is an apt summation of the triumphs and the limits of British multiculturalism at the end of the century. But it also embodies a potential solution to several of the difficulties that have beset earlier migrant writers in the post-war years. Where Rushdie and others have worried about integration and assimilation, Smith presents integration as a productive, two-way street; where the magic realists have distanced themselves from a sustained engagement with place, Smith's novel is mostly located in London; and, conscious that misperceptions about race have often hampered the development of a multicultural society, Smith reserves her most scathing satirical commentary for a new kind of racial misperception, associated with the experiments of genetic engineering.

The book's anchor is the relationship between Samad Iqbal, a Bengali Muslim, and Archie Jones, whose lifelong bond stems from serving together in the Second World War. This pre-given, and resonant national history supplies the 'pedagogic' pole (in Bhabha's terms) against which the 'performative' reinscription of the national culture takes its meaning. There is a crucial moment in the war episode when Samad and Archie capture a French scientist, who is purported to have worked on the Nazi sterilization programme. Since they have not been involved in direct action, Samad feels they must seize this opportunity to play a part in the destruction of the 'great evil' that they have hitherto 'failed to fight'. At this 'moral crossroads', decides Samad, Archie must kill the scientist, to identify himself with England's future.[14] Archie takes the prisoner off, and returns, limping, after a shot is heard (p. 105). Samad assumes the deed has been done, but a mystery is installed which links the novel's principal themes: the complexity of national identity and ethnicity, and the moral problems which complicate the active assertion – or, worse still, the attempted control – of ethnicity.

Smith asks us to question the extent to which the attitudes of Samad and Archie amount to a reliable understanding of 'first generation' immigration and its reception. But the novel also embeds the representativeness of its characters more deeply, both historically and culturally. The identity of Samad is determined partly through his pride in his great-grandfather, Mangal Pande, whose actions are rumoured to have triggered the Indian Mutiny. Archie's sense of self, on the other hand, is rooted in the transformative experience of being saved from suicide (by a halal butcher): a revelation results, and within hours, in a new state of euphoria, he meets his future wife, Clara, whose Jamaican mother was sired by a colonial Englishman.

Magid and Millat, Samad's twin sons, are used to demonstrate the competing claims operating on the second-generation migrant. Horrified at Magid's willingness to absorb English culture, Samad has him sent 'home' to Bangladesh to be educated in 'the old ways' (p. 185). When he returns, however, he is the quintessential Anglo-Indian, having embraced the advice of an esteemed Indian writer that 'we must be more like the English' (p. 248). His willingness to defend genetic engineering – which Smith deploys somewhat archly as the millennial symbol of Western culture – locates him within a four-square secular Englishness. Millat, by contrast, joins a militant

Islamic group, with an 'acronym problem': Keepers of the Eternal and Victorious Islamic Nation (KEVIN) (p. 255). The need 'to purge oneself of the taint of the West' is one of the four guiding principles of KEVIN (p. 380); but since Millat's identity is fashioned by Hollywood, and specifically by the gangster movie, this affiliation is dubious. Here Smith identifies an important contradiction: in Britain, such militant religious youth groups thrive partly by virtue of the very cultural values they denounce.

Yet in the satirical portrayal of the Islamic militants, Smith presents the cultural clash in a balanced manner. When the Rushdie affair blows up, Millat's 'Crew' take a trip to Bradford to participate in the ritual book-burning. (Their cultivated lilting walk, a kind of 'funky limp' makes them appear to be 'slouching towards Bradford' in the manner of Yeats's 'rough millennial beast'.) They manufacture their outrage, untroubled by their ignorance of the book's contents: 'you don't have to read shit to know that it's blasphemous', insists Millat (p. 202). But Smith is also at pains to insist that 'fundamentalism' can be a by-product of prejudice and discrimination. If Millat is ignorant about Rushdie, he well understands his own disenfranchisement, and so 'recognized the anger' ostensibly directed at Rushdie, 'thought it recognized him, and grabbed it with both hands'. (p. 202) The internalized 'knowledge' of racist interpellation and ethnic suppression generates a groundswell of justified rebelliousness waiting to be unleashed.

Given Smith's understanding of cultural misrecognition it is remarkable that this does not generate a stark and unproductive opposition. The focus, instead, is the sense of cultural confusion. It is this aspect, which lends the book a serio-comic tone, that is particularly evident in the admirably orchestrated conclusion, where several important strands are interwoven. The final episode involves the launch of a high-profile genetic experiment, the 'FutureMouse©', a mouse engineered to live for exactly seven years, and to suffer predetermined genetic defects, including susceptibility to carcinomas, at set intervals (pp. 369–70). FutureMouse© is the work of Marcus Chalfen, and it is the Chalfens that bear the main brunt of Smith's social satire. This family of seemingly well-adjusted middle-class rationalists appears to embody a normative model of genetic health and stability; but the family is also a model of asocial exclusiveness: the Chalfens, having no friends, interact only with their extended family, 'the *good genes*'. The boredom that results from this enclosed perfection, with the family members seeming 'like clones of each other' leads the Chalfens to reach out, and to interfere in the lives of Magid and Millat, and in that of Irie, daughter of Archie and Clara (p. 271). Thus a mild but debilitating form of eugenics is halted by its interaction with diverse migrant bodies, though this necessary 'grafting on' is misperceived by the Chalfens as a channel for their own condescending patronage. Smith explodes the stereotypical middle-class Englishness of the Chalfens and demonstrates that the notion of biological 'purity' is destructive, not just as a biological falsehood, but also as a historical falsehood: the Chalfens are 'immigrants too (third generation, by way of Germany and Poland)' (p. 283).

In the concluding episode Smith links these concerns explicitly with the issue of genetic engineering. Here, various campaigning organizations converge on the launch of FutureMouse© with their separate plans of disruption. Millat and the Islamic militants, for whom genetic engineering is blasphemous interference in the work of Allah are there, for example; and when Millat pulls a gun with the intention of shooting at the scientists on the stage, Archie (for all the principal characters are here assembled) leaps to intercept the bullet heading for the ageing geneticist and mentor that Marcus Chalfen has been publically crediting with the groundwork for FutureMouse©. Of course, this is none other than the Nazi collaborator Perret that Archie – it is now revealed – had decided to free rather than execute, but who had shot him in the leg when the opportunity arose: Archie is shot in the leg once more, in the process of saving the man for a second time (p. 461).

In the novel's ending the genetic experimentation of Marcus Chalfen is linked overtly to Nazi eugenics. But this does not serve simply as a caution against the dangers of biological or racial control. In saving the dubious Perret once more, Archie demonstrates a tacit conviction in common humanity. From the point of view of ethnicity, this signals Smith's conviction: that we are all hybrid post-colonials, biologically as well as culturally, and the pursuit of pure ethnic origins is a pointless objective. And in celebrating this hybridity, Smith embraces its contradictory and haphazard nature. Smith, then, is dismissive of a 'Happy Multicultural Land' (p. 398) in the present, but she anticipates a time when integration will be so pervasive that 'roots won't matter any more because they can't because they mustn't because they're too long and they're too tortuous and they're just buried too damn deep' (p. 450).

After the attempted shooting, the twins Millat and Magid are totally confused in the testimony of eye-witnesses. So, as the true culprit cannot be identified, a reduced punishment for the attempted attack is shared by both of them. The two extreme responses of the migrant self – the willing integration of Magid and the repudiation of Millat – are thus both corrected and channelled into a symbolic communal project: they are both required to do community service working in a millennial garden.

In the crucial final scene, Samad initially feels betrayed by the lie – the pretence of killing Perret – that Archie has sustained for fifty years. Then he has a moment of revelation: '*This incident alone will keep us two old boys going for the next forty years. It is the story to end all stories. It is the gift that keeps on giving*' (p. 455). Samad realizes that he and Archie will continue to share in the retelling of the past in the joint construction of their history. And this participative generation of history is the narrative lifeblood of all post-colonial futures, ensuring the characters' double inscription as pedagogical objects and performative subjects.[15]

White Teeth is a celebration of the contingent and chaotic stuff of social life, an enactment of haphazard but vibrant multiculturalism. This is the book's central (and unavoidable) theme; and its directness is certainly a strength. But there is also a less clear-cut intellectual theme fairly close to the surface. As I have indicated, Smith's dismantling of the grounds for racism corresponds, interestingly, with certain implications of contemporary work in genetics. The genome project, for example, produces knowledge that tends to imply a kind of totality or 'species being'.

However, *White Teeth* is sharply critical of genetics in its contemporary guise: Smith is conscious that the attempt to manufacture genetic identity might lead to a new form of eugenics, and here there is an intriguing contrast between Smith's millennial world-view and the cultural perspective typified by the critic Donna Haraway. Smith's FutureMouse© is based on the actual OncoMouse[TM], an engineered 'brand' of laboratory mouse bred for cancer research, with a cancer-inducing bit of DNA.[16] Haraway, while alert to the moral and ethical difficulties which are concentrated on the 'first patented animal in the world', is nevertheless enthused by the transgressive implications of 'transgenic creatures' like OncoMouse[TM], creatures which dramatize the kind of 'border-crossing' that 'pollutes lineages'. In the case of a transgenic organism, as Haraway understands, it is 'the lineage of nature itself' which is crossed, so that nature is transformed 'into its binary opposite, culture'. 'Culture', here, is employed loosely to denote anything resulting from human activity; and it is made to carry a particularly heavy load of credulity in relation to a manufactured breed of mouse, available in several genetically defective varieties.

The curious dimension of Haraway's argument is her willingness to align the transgressive potential associated with a transgenic creature like OncoMouse[TM] with a challenge to racism. Her reasoning is this:

in the criticism of biotechnology, she feels, there is a mystification of natural purity which is 'akin to the doctrines of white racial hegemony' in the US. Thus Haraway hears 'the dangers of racism in the *opposition* to genetic engineering and especially transgenics', and so brands the enemy of technoscience by default also the opponent of the 'mess[y]', 'dangerous', 'thick' and 'satisfying' multiculturalism she wishes to promote.[17] This reasoning, however, is underpinned by a simple confusion: racism confines itself to a single species; transgenics is concerned with cross-species interference.

In contrast to the influential Haraway, Zadie Smith's novel stands as testimony that such a rich and heterogeneous multiculturalism can be realized textually by the writer positioned broadly in opposition to technoscience. Whether her acquaintance with Haraway is first- or second-hand, Smith's vision offers an alternative route to the dismantling of racial culture.[18]

There is a final point of comparison which is revealing of the respective visions of Smith and Haraway, and this concerns the frameworks in which their arguments are embedded. Haraway employs a semi-ironic pastiche of Christian imagery, ostensibly to make her readers address often concealed questions about 'the sacred-secular dramas of technoscientific salvation history'. To this end, she presents OncoMouse[TM] as 'a figure in the sense developed within Christian realism'. Thus even though the promise is secular (a cure for cancer), OncoMouse[TM] emerges as 'a Christ figure' whose 'story is that of the passion'. Her avowed intention is to offer an allegorical challenge to the globalizing impetus of the 'New World Order, Inc.'; but the implications of transgenic transgression (the production of species hybrids) make the anthropomorphism more than an allegorical device. Here Haraway tips over into an investment in the literal. If this transgression is intentional, it still serves to undermine the critical purchase that is claimed for the allegorizing impulse. The loss of critical distance, together with her portentous evocation of the 'timescapes of the end of the Second Christian Millennium', indicates a tacit approval of the new secular forces of salvation. Thus, despite her equivocations, Haraway's rhetorical framework reinforces the claims for OncoMouse[TM] and the global potential of technoscience for the third millennium.[19]

Smith's framework is quite different, in that the effects of colonial and twentieth-century history are consistently felt in the struggle for identity in a particular present. Thus, Smith's method serves to 'funnel' attention inwards towards a specific historical and geographical present, which is diverse and secular. Haraway's rhetorical structuring, by contrast, 'funnels' outwards to a global, post-Christian scientific utopia of the future. This kind of mysticism is explicitly rejected at the end of *White Teeth* when the wounded Archie Jones sees FutureMouse© scurrying off down an air vent: '*Go on my son!*', he thinks, on Zadie Smith's behalf (p. 462). Smith puts her faith in 'the liminality of the people' (in Bhabha's phrase) and the ways in which identity is *culturally* engineered.[20]

Smith's vision has the coherence and solidity afforded by one specific context: in this case the post-colonial history of Britain. She resists the kind of futuristic global trend which Haraway finds a way of endorsing, and rejects that transnational alliance of scientific and economic enterprise which postmodernity entails. There is a different kind of general implication in Smith's novel, however, a utopian projection which emerges from the particular instance. *This* utopian impulse chimes with the aspiration of sociologist Paul Gilroy as laid out in *Between Camps* (also 2000). Gilroy's 'transitional yearning' for a new kind of shared future is partly urged by the memory of the war against Nazism. His desire to 'liberate humankind from race-thinking' is intended also as a liberation from '"encamped" national cultures'. Gilroy projects a world which has progressed beyond nationalism, and which is united in the common recognition of a single human race. This is not intended as a simplification of existing distinctions, but rather an extension of them, a development of the logic of hybridity which is very much in the spirit of Zadie Smith. In Gilroy's vision, humanity might come to recognize that given principles of differentiation have become outmoded, and a kind of 'planetary humanism' might emerge instead.

The key recognition, however, is that a planetary humanism is only imaginable as a consequence of the post-colonial migrant experience, and the complex stages of renegotiating identities and national boundaries which are yet to be undertaken. As Zadie Smith well understands, the stage of interregnum in the quest for multicultural utopia is the one that still applies to the British context.[21]

Notes

1   See Christina Patterson, 'A Willesden Ring of Confidence', interview with Zadie Smith, *Independent*, Weekend Review, 22 January 2000, 9; Christian House, 'J. Alfred Prufrock meets Homer Simpson', review of *White Teeth*, *Independent on Sunday*, Culture Section, 23 January 2000, 10; Stephanie Merritt, 'The Books Interview', interview with Zadie Smith, *Observer* Review, 16 January 2000, 12. (The quote is taken from this source.)

2 Caryl Phillips, 'Mixed and Matched', review of *White Teeth*, *Observer Review*, 9 January 2000, 11.

3 In a sober review, Daniel Soar remarks upon Smith's descriptive infelicities, and some of her more obvious observations, indicating that such occasional weaknesses are probably inevitable in a young writer. See 'Willesden Fast-Forward', *London Review of Books*, 22: 18, 21 September 2000, 30–1.

4 I am drawing on Helen Tiffin's formulation in 'Post-Colonial Literatures and Counter-Discourse', *Kunapipi*, 9 (1987), 3, 17–34.

5 Salman Rushdie, 'The New Empire Within Britain', in *Imaginary Homelands: Essays and Criticism 1981–91* (1991; London: Granta Books, 1992), pp. 129–38 (130).

6 Ibid., pp. 129, 137.

7 A. Robert Lee, 'Introduction', *Other Britain, Other British: Contemporary Multicultural Fiction*, ed. Lee (London: Pluto Press, 1995), pp. 1–3 (2).

8 Homi Bhabha, 'DissemiNation: Time, Narrative, and the Margins of the Modern Nation', in *Nation and Narration*, ed. Bhabha (London: Routledge, 1990), pp. 291–322 (318).

9 For a useful summary of the legislation, see Dennis Kavanagh, *British Politics: Continuities and Change*, third edition (Oxford University Press, 1996), pp. 32–4.

10 On the question of Selvon's style, see Mark Looker, *Atlantic Passages: History, Community, and Language in the Fiction of Sam Selvon* (New York: Peter Lang, 1996).

11 Sam Selvon, *The Lonely Londoners* (1956; Harlow: Longman, 1998), p. 90.

12 Bhabha, 'DissemiNation', pp. 292, 297, 302, 306.

13 Ibid., pp. 312, 317.

14 Zadie Smith, *White Teeth* (London: Hamish Hamilton, 2000), pp. 102–3. Subsequent page references to this edition are given in the body of the essay.

15 There is not space here to consider the recurring motif of teeth in the novel. But it is worth noting that this motif is used in such a way to suggest important links between colonial and post-colonial history, through a device which reminds us, inevitably, of the theme of common humanity.

16 OncoMouse™ was patented in 1988, and licensed to Du Pont.

17 See Donna J. Haraway, *Modest _ Witness@Second _ Millennium.FemaleMan© _ Meets _ OncoMouse*™ (London: Routledge, 1997). Specific reference is made to pp. 253, 80, 58, 56, 60, 80, 61, 62, 264.

18 In her research, Smith admits to having 'read one "incredibly boring" book about onco-mice and cancer genes in mice', and to consulting with informed friends. See Patterson, 'A Willesden Ring of Confidence', 9.

19 Haraway, *Modest _ Witness*, pp. 47, 79.

20 Bhabha, 'DissemiNation', p. 302.

21   Paul Gilroy, *Between Camps: Race, Identity and Nationalism at the End of the Colour Line* (London: Allen Lane / Penguin, 2000), pp. 2, 12, 18, 328.

Primary texts

Zadie, Smith *White Teeth* (London: Hamish Hamilton, 2000)

Selected critical texts

Homi Bhabha, (ed.), *Nation and Narration* (London: Routledge, 1990)

Donna J. Haraway, *Modest _ Witness@Second _ Millennium.FemaleMan©_ Meets _ OncoMouse*™ (London: Routledge, 1997)

Christian House, 'J. Alfred Prufrock meets Homer Simpson', review of *White Teeth*, *Independent on Sunday*, 23 January 2000, 10 (Culture section)

Dennis Kavanagh, *British Politics: Continuities and Change*, third edition (Oxford University Press, 1996)

A. Robert Lee, (ed.), *Other Britain, Other British: Contemporary Multicultural Fiction* (London: Pluto Press, 1995)

Mark Looker, *Atlantic Passages: History, Community, and Language in the Fiction of Sam Selvon* (New York: Peter Lang, 1996)

Stephanie Merritt, 'The Books Interview', interview with Zadie Smith, *Observer* Review, 16 January 2000, 12

Christina Patterson, 'A Willesden Ring of Confidence', interview with Zadie Smith, *Independent*, Weekend Review, 22 January 2000, 9

Caryl Phillips, 'Mixed and Matched', review of *White Teeth*, *Observer* Review, 9 January 2000, 11

Salman Rushdie, 'The New Empire Within Britain', in *Imaginary Homelands: Essays and Criticism 1981–91* (1991; London: Granta Books, 1992), pp. 129–38

Sam Selvon, *The Lonely Londoners* (1956; Harlow: Longman, 1998)

Daniel Soar, 'Willesden Fast-Forward', *London Review of Books*, 22: 18, 21 September 2000, 30–1

Helen Tiffin, 'Post-Colonial Literatures and Counter-Discourse', *Kunapipi*, 9 (1987), 3, 17–34

The Fiction of A. L. Kennedy: the
Baffled, the Void and the (In)visible

Philip Tew

Appearing among the 'new wave' of 1990s Scottish writers, A. L.
Kennedy published three collections of short stories, *Night Geometry
and the Garscadden Trains* (1990), *Now That You're Back* (1994),
Original Bliss (1997); and three novels, *Looking for the Possible
Dance* (1993); *So I am Glad* (1995); and, *Everything You Need*
(1999).[1] This chapter focuses primarily on the first collection and
key themes from her first two novels. What marks out her most
effective prose is not simply its regionalism, but its tentative rendering
of the objective and emotional territory of the quotidian, an urban
understatement. Characteristically Kennedy sketches the simultan-
eous banality and profundity of life's minutiae. The narrator of the
title story, 'Night Geometry and the Garscadden Trains', is bewildered at the termination of the number of empty trains at Garscadden
station. She appears to lack a centre to her life, without a stable
conception of her own identity, negated by personal crises. Typically,
Kennedy centres on defeated individuals, each self undermined both
by life's topographical qualities and more profound, underlying fear-
tures. The woman's apparently mundane reflection broadens thematically, assimilating what appears an associative jumble of ideas:

> So many things are stupid, though. Like the fact that the death of my
> mother's dog seemed to upset me more than the death of my mother.
> And I loved my mother more than I loved the dog. The stupidity of
> someone being killed by the train that might normally take them home,
> things like that. There seems to be so much lack of foresight, so much
> carelessness in the world. And people can die of carelessness. They lack
> perspective.

I do, too. I know it. I am the most important thing in my life. I am central to whatever I do and those whom I love and care for are more vital to my existence than statesmen, or snooker players, or Oscar nominees, but the television news and the headlines were the same as they always are when my mother died and theirs were the names and faces that I saw.[2]

The narrator seems threatened and excluded by the overly rational. For her, this public world of news and events is existentially oppressive, dwarfing the individual, where the logic of the rational is perceptually problematic, since in effect it creates the conditions for an ultimately incomprehensible and thoroughly hostile environment. 'To return to the Garscadden trains, they are not important in themselves; they are only important in the ways they have affected me. Lack of perspective again, you see?'[3] This counter-rationality centralizes Kennedy's urban vision, her bemused individuals existing within a void, defined by social invisibility. Kennedy's writing confirms this vision through its curt style, the evocations of cruelty, and its elusive quests for female identity. Kennedy's world-view resonates with a critical awareness of life's paradoxes, a view that is best exemplified through comparison with theoretical or critical ideas offering a similar perspective, such as those of Maurice Merleau-Ponty. Kennedy's observations echo his central concepts of a perceptual flux and his notion of conceptual paradoxes in the most mundane of elements of life. Such perspectives allow Kennedy's litany of cultural referents to seem both almost gratuitously superfluous and irrelevant, and yet simultaneously very revealing in terms of her narrators' ongoing practical *and* ontological anguish. Each is concerned with a partial revelation of 'The revolt of life's immediacy against reason'.[4]

In a recent interview Kennedy insisted on her work's simplicity. 'It's always the same aim. I keep things very, very simple. Having got a cast together, I'm trying to find out more and more about what they want, what they want to do, and how do I make them real?'[5] Similarly, her characters quiz themselves, undertaking repeatedly an ersatz metaphysical questioning, seeking reality in lives that resist such immediacy. Kennedy evokes both life's incomprehensibility and the implacable indifference within social structures, mirroring key concepts from Merleau-Ponty, most particularly the sense that: 'Perception does not give me truths like geometry but presences.'[6] Hence, the apparent geometry – or more accurately the unfathomable movement – of the Garscadden trains and that of the couple's shifting sexual relationships ('night geometry') are interconnected. Both remain vague and potentially unreadable for the woman. Both refuse the ultimate logic of rationalization and yet each constitutes for this troubled woman some significance. She intuits an overarching, yet ill-defined meaning, not fully comprehending either patterns or their boundaries. Reading life is imprecise. For Kennedy, mirroring Merleau-Ponty, 'Communication in literature [...] arouses [...] meanings in the mind through enticement and a kind of oblique action.'[7] Furthermore, why should death associatively underscore this commuter's feelings of sexual frustration? Kennedy's notion of finitude echoes Georges Bataille's proposition that: 'the luxury of death is regarded by us in the same way as that of sexuality, first as a negation of ourselves, then – in a sudden reversal – as the profound truth of that movement of which life is the manifestation'.[8] Death and betrayal blur for this woman, yet tellingly both are overwhelmed by the facts of a repetitive urbanicity, the externality of life failing to satisfy her inner need for a profound emotional vocabulary or register. Immersed in a quotidian landscape, all that remains is to seek some elusive definition in the minutiae of its concrete facts.

Kennedy's narrator puzzles over issues peripheral to the central, yet initially unexpressed, fact of her husband's infidelity. 'I have never understood this. In the years I have waited on the westbound side of my station, the number of trains to Garscadden has gradually increased; this increase being commensurate with my lack of understanding.'[9] Her heightened anguish seems obliterated by such irrelevant public facts and the spaces with which they are associated. This objective, definable series of events seems to demand greater attention and relevance than her inner feelings; the effect of her representation of them is to mediate and almost displace her own concept of her life and its bemusing qualities, as if they were secondary to the external things of her existence. Almost mute, lacking full comprehension, what the narrator attempts to actualize and concretize is complex time, a pattern of being and social engagement hidden within the unpromising material of urban repetition. Life is an accelerating series of journeys and crises, the lost individual becoming an alienated observer conditioned by the interplay of larger forces. The trains seem neither for her benefit, negating their apparent purpose of transportation, nor can she fathom any underlying system. In Kennedy's fiction, such forces of convention and social behaviour fragment constantly, the world of apparent factuality remaining tantalizingly insubstantial, with a kind of virtual reality in the Bergsonian sense.

> Representation is there, but always virtual – being neutralized, at the very moment when it might become actual, by the obligation to continue itself and to lose itself in something else. To obtain this conversion

from the virtual to the actual, it would be necessary, not to throw more light on the object, but, on the contrary, to obscure some part of its aspects, to diminish it by the greater part of itself, so that the remainder, instead of being encased in its surroundings as a *thing*, should detach itself from them as a *picture*.[10]

In response to her metaphysical doubts, Kennedy's protagonist perverts the logic and certainty of the public, physical trauma of a real disaster. For her the emotional possesses greater immediacy. After interrogating her past experiences and her ontological disorientation, she ascribes her feelings at the discovery of her husband in bed with another woman not to her emotional disruption but to that of her journey, conflating the ideas, drawing upon another vocabulary by referring symbolically to the event as a train disaster within her life. This betrayal is numbing, but so too are years of repetitive commuting that she associates with the marriage. Removing her experience from its context, she transforms her unconscious everyday fears and her daily travel frustrations, and projects these into her current emotional condition. She cannot access her inner reality directly, but her chosen phrase has a distorted logic, since her return home from an abandoned wait for a train precipitates her discovery. Hence, an unconscious *train* of minor public frustrations initiates her most private *disaster*. The implicit pun is painful and evocative, comically rendering her potential collapse of identity. There is something both bathetic and poignant in the conditions of this revelation.

Kennedy's style mirrors a sense of such perverse interrelationships perceived in events; her references, interconnections and causality are chiefly tangential. According to this betrayed wife's account:

> Contrary to popular belief, people, many people, almost all the people, live their lives in the best way they can with generally good intentions and still leave absolutely nothing behind.
>
> There is only one thing I want more than proof that I existed and that's some proof, while I'm here, that I exist.[11]

Kennedy uses a colloquial vocabulary, conveying the familiarity of the apparently commonplace, but below the surface of the narrative and descriptive events exists an ontological sense that is more radical. Such sub-textual elements articulate the Bergsonian notion that an implicit reality underlies all existence, where '*There is a reality that is external and yet given immediately to the mind.* [...] Not *things* made, but things in the making, not self-maintaining *states*, but only changing states, exist. Rest is never more than apparent, or, rather, relative.'[12] For the despairing woman, change is read as if it constituted another bereavement, its disruptive effect revealing the depths of her unconscious pain at her sexual betrayal. Yet despite the range of potential emotional responses even these traumas cannot overwhelm the monotonous urban flux, as if such lives are denied a density or profundity outside of the habitual.

The female perspective is dominant in Kennedy's work, with recurrent notions of gender and difference. Elsewhere in *Night Geometry*, in 'Tea and biscuits', another narrator ruminates:

> I was wearing stockings. I like them because they feel good, but I thought that he would like them, too. I didn't imagine he would see them, or that he would know I had them on, but I thought that he would like them if I did.
>   Nothing in his kitchen had names on, not even the coffee and tea. Some of it was in jars that you could see through, but for the rest, you would have to remember where everything was.[13]

Repeatedly Kennedy insists on the unreadable and unfathomable. In this fragment of inconsequential description neither a common-sense transparency nor any apparently normal epistemological certainty can frame coherently even the domestic. Any understanding of events, objects and behaviour is agreed upon provisionally in such mundane environments. In this unfamiliar kitchen everything appears elusive; the jars persist objectively, but their relevance is only guessed. In their randomness objects defy ascription or penetration, and more broadly all relationships remain impenetrable. People create barriers, so only a reading of outer meanings is possible. Note that the feminine is encased, literally stockinged, its definition symbolized and marked by containment, commodification, an implied fetishism and outer limitation. This extends to all forms of expressibility. Paradoxically, only through such symbolically charged objects can Kennedy's women seek any viable communicative significance and presence. Symbolically the jars seem impenetrable and yet are literally transparent, signifying a paradoxical duality central to Kennedy's writing. Each of her social and emotive settings, like these containers, is both revealing and curiously inscrutable, mirroring Merleau-Ponty's concept that: 'each one knows that he himself and the others are *inscribed* in the world; what he feels, what he lives, what the others feel and live, even his dreams or their dreams, his illusions and theirs, are not islets, isolated fragments of being: all this, by reason of the fundamental exigency of our constitutive nothingness, is of *being*, has consistence, order, meaning, and there is a way to comprehend it'.[14]

Significantly, despite the stocking-wearing preparation, any sexual urge is easily displaced by other domestic concerns. For Kennedy's characters erotic exploration or obsession is undercut by uncertainties and by recurrent contractions of their emotional range. The female narrators find themselves physically at odds with the social world's ill-defined libidinal expectations, uncertain as to the trajectories or meanings of desire. M. [for Mercy] Jennifer Wilson declares bluntly in *So I am Glad*: 'Sex. I don't know what it means... [...] I can only remain bemused when I consider that on a depressingly regular basis I would render myself, and perhaps my companion, insensible with fatigue for no reason I could ever ascertain.'[15] Here lies a paradoxical clarity, for as Merleau-Ponty says: 'Everything is obscure when one has not thought out the negative; everything is clear when one has thought it as negative.'[16]

The betrayed wife of 'Night Geometry' concludes: 'We have small lives, easily lost in foreign droughts, or famines; the occasional incendiary incident, or a wall of pale faces, crushed against grillwork, one Saturday afternoon in Spring. This is not enough.'[17] Kennedy offers such people little more. *Night Geometry* maps a landscape full of public dualities and minor cruelties, representing a multiplicity of inner contradictions. The children in 'Translations' alternately try to feed and stone a stray dog with a broken paw. Imperfection, injury and indecision characterize the urban existence. In 'Didacus', one of Kennedy's literally small women, Jean, has been unfaithful, copulating with her manager in his car at night in a graveyard; she returns home by bus to the inadequate flat that she shares with her partner, Brian. In the tiny room they avoid the central issues of this crisis, but she complains finally, '"There's no room in here with the bed down. It's like a padded cell."'[18] This is ironic given that her infidelity was enclosed within the even smaller space of the car adjacent to the implied narrow containment of the coffin. Psychically relationships and sex are associated with deathliness. Jean begins her inner reconciliation to the facts of their life by tendering to Brian's hand injured by metal from the swarf at work. Their injuries and their containment are doubled, represented both symbolically and literally. The opening of 'The seaside photographer' combines puzzlement and a baldness of statement, suggesting it seems too exhausting to articulate everyday despairs with any rhetorical and discursive flourish: 'I came to the library and I don't know why.'[19] Agonizing over failing to communicate with her maternal grandfather, the protagonist memorializes her loss and the uselessness of narrative:

> I have no magic for you and there is nothing I have learned to make. If, in the world, I could, I would write you whole and well. I would write

you smiling through windy sunshine and strolling with your wife, the thin boards of the promenade beneath you, reaching up to a seaside photographer. I would wish myself unborn and you as you were in a holiday picture. A picture I have lost.[20]

Their separation is something against which it appears the writer has no power, the protagonist representing Kennedy's inability to offer her own characters any transformative possibilities. 'All I can do is write you words you cannot read and feel them between us.'[21]

The interplay of elements in the first novel, *Looking for the Possible Dance* (1993), typify Kennedy's fictional mood and method. Margaret Hamilton, *in media res* recollects herself as a child standing outside the adult world of the local dance hall alongside her father. The flashback possesses significant qualities. Briefly, Margaret appears emotionally at one with her father (and the universe itself) as he indicates the contrast between his own life and that of the celestial void, echoing somewhat whimsically what he imagines is an unspoken and unheard message from the moon, creating a memorable moment. Curiously even in retrospect his motives and fantasies baffle his daughter:

> 'Everything else is a waste of time. Do you hear me? Everything else is a waste of time. You hear me, Margaret? You understand?'
> Margaret was outside in the night, standing behind the Methodist Church Hall. Her ears, numbed after hours of music, were rushing with the sudden quiet, as if she had dipped her head inside a sea-shell, or a big tin box. Margaret's father was sitting on two empty beer crates, breathing in and out enormously, his legs extended flat ahead of him and both his hands folded, hotly, round one of her wrists.
> 'See there's the moon, Princess. Do you see?'
> 'Yes.'
> His swaying finger seemed to nudge at the fat, white circle; leave a little mark. [...]
> All of that, up there. Mi-rac-u-lous. And they see us and we look up at her and it's wonderful. She's telling us, 'Everything is a waste of time.' That's what she says. You hear her. That's what she says.[22]

The narrative acquires an almost banal simplicity symbolically and stylistically. The repetitiousness of his dialogue reinforces the sense that the idea of this appeal for something quite impossible appears to be part of the man's whimsical self-fashioning rather than a parental fantasy or narrative. As the text stresses, even when questioned, her father cannot account for his intentions or actions concerning the incident, remaining something he has forgotten entirely. The authorial failure to place the purpose of attending the *ceilidh*, rather than creating any sense of mystery or curiosity, seems fatalistic and reverberates with a tone of resignation at the loss generally of purposeful specificity. The prose style refuses any mythic or symbolic synthesis, rather creating a world of flatness, of immediacy, and curtailment, a lack of complex causality. Such feelings of bafflement and incomprehension are the major characteristics of the most successful of Kennedy's narratives. The father's underlying message reinforces the negativity of both his and his daughter's understanding of everyday life. The very visibility of her father's actions, his gesture of touching the celestial, is mediated by the child's vision of its literalness. The legacy of this memory remains impressionistic and certainly ambivalent. She can invoke her father at the sight of the moon and this reaffirms both her confusion and her sense of the logical impossibilities of life. Moreover, the memory is underpinned by remembering his subsequent feeling that her father had wasted his life and the narrative moves on suggestively to her own recent unemployment. Ultimately this is not a nostalgic text, but its themes define a lineage of loss and failure. Underlying the narrative is a sense of negation and paradox, themes concerned with the conditions of loss. Any sentimentality is further offset by Margaret's ongoing recollection of the stages of her father's physical decline.

Margaret fails to find in the past any territory on which she might establish any coherent sense of her origins, or any trajectory towards a unified understanding. There remains simply the fact of recording their love for each other in the lost immediacy of their shared existence. The facts of her life are sparse, the fragmentary past intermingled with Margaret's current life and journey to London for a job interview. The resurrection of her childlike consciousness haunts her, and both in the feelings of the recollections and in responding to them, her overwhelming sense is one of confusion. As the past recedes and as the journey accelerates, the former becomes the centre around which the wider narrative develops, with progressive episodes from the initial relationship with her father to sketches of her own confusions and frustrations, charting her tensions and a potential escape represented by London. Her overwhelming and ongoing sense of unhappiness undermines any lingering sense of the potentially prelapsarian quality of the initial image of her childhood instruction and parental intimacy.

Even this apparent scene of innocence is framed by a series of counter-intuitive contradictions implied by her present lack of understanding, which has more than unconscious implications of negativity for Margaret. She admits through her later recognition of a pattern of convincing lies purveyed by her father, that this fantasy has elements of self-deception. His initial comment may evoke a magical message from the moon itself but this is partly to negate human affairs making them irrelevant. The contrast of her small life to the succession of stars and its universal perspective is indicated graphically by her father, and for Margaret there remains in that memory an ongoing sense that her life continues to be dwarfed by greater forces. These magical elements of her father's fantasy although presented narratively, remain 'invisible' within the currency of everyday emotions available to her. Yet there is a sense of invisibility or the hidden void that frames the characters themselves, their obscurity being metonymically part of something ineffable.

For Margaret, the adult world seems both confusing and full of inconsequentialities. It edges toward confusion, a realm where 'Rationality is neither a total nor an immediate guarantee. It is somehow open, which is to say that it is menaced.'[23] This notion of menace summarizes the mood of Kennedy's writing, which purveys a simple and yet potentially profound sense of loss and anguish at the opening spaces between objects and events. Kennedy's is a world most readers are compelled to recognize as close to their own bleaker and inadequate experiences. For, as Kennedy insists, when questioned about human character and identity in terms of fiction, 'I try to think of my people as real. I am the first reader of my work – if I can't find my people real, no one else will.'[24] In her fiction rationality's usual mediatory and solicitous role in our lived experience is negated or reduced so that it appears far from efficacious, and survives at best in fragmentary form.

Significantly one important character in the first novel (a figure who serves as a correlative of the action and indicator of central themes) is a learning disabled boy, James. Margaret meets him as a fellow traveller on her London-bound journey. He is almost completely unable to speak and consequentially denied the possibility of an opinion or any sensibilities by those supposed to be his carers (in this sense an ironic term). James's condition is an extreme case of a 'void' of apparent inexpressiveness, a speechlessness to which other characters finds themselves emotionally and socially condemned, suffering a similar denial of agency and self-worth. Kennedy explains about the evolving structure of this first novel: 'The thing I did realize was that a journey threaded through a book without terribly much plot would provide it with a beginning, middle and end and make me feel safe. Until the last draft James Watt wasn't quite so prominent, but one of the three editorial suggestions I got was to increase his presence and do something with it. That seemed to make sense.'[25]

However serendipitous his expansion, what the presence of the boy does highlight is that for many human beings in practice logic and rationality can be denied, especially for the less fortunate or the marginal. This is part of the internal logic of a world where Margaret's education with its guilt and denial of local language may seem absurd in retrospect, but her 'education was in no way remarkable, it merely took the Scottish Method to its logical conclusion, secure in the knowledge that no one would ever complain because, after all, it only affected children'.[26]

The narrator of the novel codifies this scheme of influence for the reader, and we may note that the seventh of its ten commandments (for it surely parodies Scottish Calvinistic leanings) reads 'Joy is fleeting, sinful and the forerunner of despair.' This establishes the ethical and emotional structure and dynamic of Kennedy's work, with its movement towards a feeling of woefully partial epiphany that cannot remove personal confusion. Nevertheless, Kennedy herself responds to the suggested idea of a 'subtextual nastiness to life' that might underpin her work with 'I don't think life is especially unpleasant. I also don't think it's especially pleasant. I don't make qualitative judgements on the alternative reality, which the elements of any given fiction seem to suggest. I put a great deal of work into leaving my imagination undefended. [...]'[27] The inference is that the dynamics of the work follow an almost external, life-world logic or influence, but certainly not that of ratiocination. The first novel offers a structure typical of her writing, with its series of interlinked vignettes or episodes, loosely centred upon themes of questing (or 'looking') for an elusive meaning (to life and events) within often very inauspicious and trivial journeys in space and time (each of which memorializes various rites of bafflement).

For Kennedy, neither speech nor language renders the full extent of communicative possibility since 'Word-meaning [is] itself an enigma [...]. language is itself a world, itself a being – a world and a being to the second power, since it does not speak in a vacuum, since it speaks *of* being and *of* the world and therefore redoubles their enigma.'[28] Significantly, a moment of enduring epiphany in *Looking for the Possible Dance* is rendered when Margaret encounters a literally wordless event; she is taught in a workshop to breathe fire and it is in this unexpected manner of using her vocal equipment that she extends her range of expression towards a suggestion of transcendence beyond the verbal and beyond its emotional and rational restraint: 'At first she closed her eyes, but the fourth time, she just watched what her breath could produce. It was like her soul coming out. She'd always known her soul would be that colour.'[29] 'Production' here is taken beyond the thing and towards 'the desire that man always had to find himself, to regain an intimacy that was always strangely lost'.[30] In contrast to such a moment, Kennedy's dialogues are almost entirely guttural exchanges, a series of exhalations and limitations from which inferences can only be extruded against the silences of unspoken language and a contextuality of which the characters express little. This creates a muted space of potential reference, an associative range of likely possibilities. The shocking punishment of Colin, nailed by criminals to his floor, a crucifixion of sorts, remains a grotesque extension of Kennedy's general bafflement and hurt, a pathological rendition of the social forces evident in the marginalization and emptiness found in her landscapes.

The directness and simplicity of Kennedy's prose and the situations she creates can be disrupted by the unexpected and incongruous, as with the resurrection in *So I am Glad* of Cyrano de Bergerac, apparently as a vagrant lost in urban obscurity. By this undercutting of a grandiose cultural figure, Kennedy implies a sense of events possessing quite a different trajectory to the immediately perceived. Underlying truths may contradict the banalities of life's topography. Protagonist Jennifer ruminates: 'This is one thing I can say in my favour – if I have no idea of your mental state, I will ask you for more information. Many people base a lifetime's personal relations solely on guesswork.'[31] Kennedy evokes her life-world obliquely within anecdotal fragments suggesting incomprehension and chaos. In a story 'The poor souls' the narrator declares that: 'Once I met a woman on a train who was terrified of snow and now I can understand a little of why that was. But I can't be sure what other people think, or of what she thought. Perhaps she was only scared of freezing to death.'[32] In 'The last' Kath concludes: 'The century was ending, which meant nothing, but it felt significant. It worried her. It was another thing that worried her.'[33] Underlying negativities are crucial since 'The very movement by which a *this* is pronounced in my life, or this life in the world, is but the climax of negation, the negation that destroys itself'.[34] Kennedy comments of creativity 'It's about an absence of the self. [. . .] You go away from yourself – you're absent for an indeterminate period of time as far as you can remember. It's a meditative occupation.'[35] This negation is relevant to the world-view expressed, for the 'absence of the self' extends to the characterization. In Kennedy's prose, ascription is never definite or confident, it exists within a matrix of interrelated formulations and is therefore always partial and incomplete.

Kennedy's characters, although baffled, remain at least intuitively aware of an underlying series of meanings, possibilities and elusive readings. They appear frustrated by their frame of reference, half aware of their limited scope of expressiveness, for as Bourdieu says 'The interactions, which are accepted at their face value by people [...] conceal the structures that are realized in them. It's one of those cases in which the visible, that which is immediately given, conceals the invisible which determines it.'[36] Kennedy invokes the apparently invisible as a potential alternative to the visible. If the Garscadden trains themselves are definite, real objects cannot offer any sense or proportion, other realities are intuited. She attempts to refuse any total solipsistic despair by perceiving in people an innate social and communicative ability that remains a vital inner necessity, however equivocal its rational meaning or justification.

In *Looking for the Possible Dance*, the eighth commandment in what is in a sense both a macabre and mocking 'Scottish Method of Education' set of instructions reads 'Life is a series of interwoven ceremonies, etiquettes and forms which we will never understand. We may never trust ourselves to others.'[37] In response to this Calvinistic antagonism, which nevertheless retains its own contribution to some concept of truthful awareness, Kennedy's characters seem so bemused that they retreat within themselves in crisis, only capable of the most mundane ritual social behaviour even after great tribulations. 'Days ticked by, through and beyond Christmas. On Christmas Day there was no snow and no sign of snow. Margaret and Colin cooked part of a turkey, boiled a pudding, ate until they felt lightheaded and then lay on the sofa together feeling domestic. Margaret gave Colin a sweater.'[38] That they follow convention (which they mock) and express little about their feelings may convey something that can be noted beyond the simple fact of these characters' limitations.

Kennedy's interiority is not ultimately solipsistic, for in expressing the paucity of personalized space she offers an understanding of why people are drawn to inhabit external spaces. They indulge in a banalization on one level, but offer resistance on another, for as Guy Debord indicates, there is a significance to be found in the patterns of modern living and their ritualistic inanity. 'What spectacular antagonisms conceal is the *unity of poverty*. Differing forms of a single alienation contend in the masquerade of total freedom of choice by virtue of the fact that they are all founded on real repressed contradictions. Depending on the needs of the particular stage of poverty that is supposed at once to deny and sustain, the spectacle may be *concentrated* or *diffuse* in form. In either case, it is no more than an image of harmony set amidst desolation and dread, at the still centre of misfortune.'[39] For Kennedy's characters the mundane articulates some sense of a 'desolation and dread' for which they will never find the appropriate verbal or emotional language or register.

For Kennedy, the individual's relationship to the past is consistently problematized. For Margaret, a traumatic collective experience in her schooldays defies narrative possibility or understanding. It is not a question of accuracy, but as Kennedy suggests, a surplus of reality that forces a kind of diffusion of the factuality of this episode of her life. She struggles to understand the memory of her schooldays, uncertain of the truthfulness of her own recollection given its pathological and cruel aspects.

> Margaret can't quite describe her school; if she tries, things seem to get away from her. She can't be sure if what she remembers is totally true or not. [...] Over the years, she has invented sequences for effect, but only because the reality makes no sense.
>
> She can shut her eyes and watch a huge, square-headed man gradually take off his jacket to belt a boy. The boy has blond hair and is almost obscenely smaller than the man.
>
> 'Sometimes, when I belt a boy, I only take my arm back to here.
>
> 'Sometimes, when I belt a boy I lift my arm, right up, as far as it will go.
>
> 'Sometimes, when I belt a boy, I take my jacket off.
>
> 'For you boy, I'm going to take my jacket off, then I'm going to roll up my sleeve and then I'm going to make you very, very sorry.'
>
> The horror of it stayed with the class, all day. No one would go near the blond little boy, in case whatever badness he had around him would spread to them.[40]

Meaning is found in mundane events, in such understated and banal moments of excess. The performativity, the repetition and casual brutality are paradigms of a ritualistically oppressive world, offering key themes found throughout Kennedy's fiction. Subjection and brutality are marginalizing forces. Her characters are subjects constrained by the weight of the past rather than drawing upon it to transcend the conditions of the present. Her characters are troubled and uncertain, their interactions negating any potentially unifying aspirations. The only solace is a sense of invisibility that curiously offers more than simply feeling void. 'Each perception is mutable and only probable – it is, if one likes, only an *opinion*; but what is not opinion, what each perception, even if false, verifies, is the belongingness of each experience to the same world, their equal power to manifest it, as *possibilities of the same world*.'[41]

A further pattern negates Kennedy's moments of epiphany and potential transcendence. Repeatedly, her characters resubmit themselves to the logic of external reality (society's oppressive epistemological realm) even though they find themselves questioning its legitimacy. Typically, in *So I Am Glad*, Jennifer instinctively finds her life unsettling, verging on becoming an almost uninhabitable space. Yet she declares:

> A few things have happened to alter my condition, but it would still be broadly true to say that I am calm... [...]
>
> But I am quite happy to tell you that what appears to be peace and calmness is, in fact, empty space – or, to be more exact, a pause. I am not calm, I am unspontaneous. When something happens to me, I don't know how to feel.[42]

Yet Jennifer does react to a drifter, Savinen, who claims to be – and his claim increasingly becomes convincing to her – Cyrano de Bergerac. He feels that he has been reborn somehow, a subject initially he avoids.[43] In the excessive mundanity of their lives (which Jennifer catalogues successively as if perceptually she were numb) his miraculous rebirth pales into significance against the minutiae of their burgeoning relationship. In the fight against Savinen's drug addiction 'we began to be Savinen's jailers. It took a little time, but we learnt to pre-empt his thinking and police his actions.'[44] The mystery of the stranger's provenance is subsumed into the urban realities of the oddly constituted inhabitants of the house and their panoptic strategies.

Always liminal, Kennedy's small people are reduced by both their psychic and material conditions. Within everyday events they are subsumed in a kind of overwhelming anonymity set against an indifferent landscape. 'It is through openness that we will be able to understand being and nothingness, not through being and nothingness that we will be able to understand openness [...] this is because nothingness, the anonymous one in me that sees, pushes before itself a zone of void where being no longer only is, but *is seen*.'[45] From the vicissitudes of ordinariness, Kennedy reworks the contemporary experience of selfhood, with an admission of a void that emphasizes the contradictions of a modern world obsessed with selfhood and yet where lives seem increasingly decentred. In so doing Kennedy makes of anonymity a kind of negative transcendence, because by depicting everyday life in such a fashion as to convey a sense that these 'little' people are threatened by overwhelming forces she radicalizes their very anonymity:

> These are small people. On the whole, on the average, on the pavements, the people here are small.

Small in body.
And we are speaking of a time here when small things were thought
unimportant and the figures who now fill our bus stops were withered
by lack of belief. In the larger world they were steadily forgotten and
they woke up every morning, lost in their beds.[46]

As *So I Am Glad* opens, Jennifer records an intense lack of engagement and her level of unease about feeling inadequate. 'I don't understand things sometimes.'[47] Jennifer extends this sense both to objects
and people:

I hate secrets. No that's a lie, and here I was hoping to tell you the truth.
Start again.
    I hate to be on the blind side of a secret. That's more like it.
Sometimes I'll be shown, let in on, something that seems a real secret
to me, I'll be allowed to stand right up against it and look all I like, but
I still won't understand. I might as well be staring at a length of algebra,
an unknown language – it will have no meaning for me. Worse than
that, I will know that it must have a meaning for somebody else. So I'm
stupid. No one needs to hide this from me, it is, quite simply, beyond
me. I am on the blind side.[48]

From this 'blind side' and motivated by its paradoxical suggestion of a
knowingness, Kennedy infuses her narrative with Merleau-Ponty's
recognition: 'That if we are to be able to speak of falsity, we do
have to have experiences of truth.'[49] Jennifer's uncertainties are sup-
plemented by moments of a complete lack of control, such as the
curious epiphany when, in a sexual fantasy game, carried away with
sado-masochistic anger, she brutally beats her ex-boyfriend (an episode left undeveloped relative to her other concerns). Furthermore,
drawing on the scene, Kennedy, through her protagonist, refutes one
of the self-sustaining tropes of British bourgeois narrative by making
her protagonist both self-contradictory and downright nasty. 'Well, I
only told you I was calm. I never even suggested I was calm. I never
even suggested that I was nice. There would be no reason to believe
that, just because I'm writing this, I ought to be any worse or better
than anyone else. Than you.'[50] Kennedy challenges her reader,
rejecting their probable assumption that either characters or society
are pleasant. Hers is a world where the closed doors are opened, and
even pathological behaviour remains shabby and squalid. She over-
turns an inner sense of deep, structural moral virtue foundational for
British fiction, and reminds the reader that all worlds are shared and
contradictory, an admission that: '*What* I see is not mine in the sense
of being a private world.'[51]

Defining the quotidian as a void centred on bafflement is a risky venture, since with Kennedy's destabilizing of expectations, where a world-view of negative capabilities emerges within the interstices of art, this context depends upon an empathy with this world of 'nobodies', and some discovery of a critical truthfulness within the themes evoked by confronting such a 'void.' As Will Self notes, *Everything You Need* (1999) in this light appears wrongly focused. Set on an isolated island, inhabited by writers funded by a trust, novelist Nathan Staples has enticed there a putative young writer on a fellowship. She is in fact his daughter, Mary Lamb, who is unaware of her father's identity, thinking him dead. The complex plot dynamics fail to cohere in the manner of Kennedy's earlier work, partly because of the novel's extended nature and lack of apparent structure. As Self comments 'There was no real sense of the following in the book: who, what, where, when or why. [...] But as for that all important 'why' question, I'm afraid the only answer to her lack of one, is that she doesn't apply any intellectual rigour to the conception of her books whatsoever; and once more – she's proud of it.'[52]

Self's objection has a critical corollary. Kennedy's novel offers a vision of unfathomable desires and a critique of concepts of 'writerliness'; the only potential void can be our reading process and not that of an external world that alienates and baffles humanity. The writers' acts are too knowing and perhaps too precisely analytical of the writer's environment for any sense of any such overwhelming object relations to be sustained.

Kennedy replaces the ersatz, and yet threateningly familiar ordinariness of her previous fictions, with a reflexive, self-absorbed narrative primarily about narration itself. The ostensibly oddball dozen writers are improbably the island's only inhabitants, which removes them from the social order in a new way for Kennedy. Rather than metaphysical isolation in the midst of the urban indifference, that can offer an echoing and yet chaotic void full of invisible people, the separation in *Everything You Need* is now literal. All of the wonderfully dramatic understatement found in the frustrated, bullying and virtually anonymous schoolteacher so despised by Jennifer, is transfigured into the protagonist Nathan's suicide attempt in the opening scene and the imaginatively crazed tall tales of Joe about Mount Sinai and his notions of revelation. Unlike Colin's physical suffering, inflicted by a pathological culture, there is no marginality and pathos in the plight of Lynda who exposes her pierced and consequently infected labia to Mary for sympathy. The water phobia of Nathan's faithful dog, Eckless, has a vaudevillian touch without comedy. The attempts at pathos and mundanity no longer synthesize. Kennedy has lost her way, abandoning her landscape of the truly void and the invisible, one that constituted the parameters of the recognizably quotidian.

Previously she had charted so effectively a conception of life much like Merleau-Ponty's in *Sense and Non-Sense*, where he says 'We are in the world, mingled with it, compromised with it.'[53] Kennedy needs the truly unexceptional to achieve her dynamics of narrative understatement, where intuitive plotting, symbolism and a density of pathos all combine with urban blight and exploitation. Incidents like Nathan's prediction for the future in a sealed jar in *Everything You Need*, with yet another of the novel's peculiarly gratuitous and unrevealing moments, add little to her range or sustain her aesthetic effect. 'He punched one fist tenderly into its opposite palm. "Oh, good. Just to confide for a moment. I generally predict our education system will have declined to new levels of disrespect and disarray. I would like just once, to be proved wrong."'[54] In *So I Am Glad*, Jennifer's first-hand summary of her bemusement after one of her bouts of masochism towards boyfriend, Steven, has a cumulative *naiveté*. Her confession encapsulates many of the narrative's positive engagements with unknowingness with its ironic understatement, in a manner that appears to offer an almost accidental poignancy.

> I'm trying to say that I don't understand what happened next. But then, why should I? My life had always been fairly incomprehensible, why should it change for the better that morning, why not for the worse? I didn't understand my mother or my father. I didn't understand my country, its past, its present, its future, its means of government or the sense of its national anthem and flag. When I was young I didn't understand the other children and the adults were just as bad. Then I became an adult and nothing had changed. I didn't understand Steven, or anyone else of my intimate acquaintance, up to and of course including me. I never did really understand me.'[55]

In her most recent novel, *Everything You Need*, one suspects that Kennedy has failed to understand her own literary strengths and capacities in terms of their iterative qualities of that very unknowingness and the vulnerability of the most ordinary of characters trapped in their occluded visions of urban pathos. Kennedy has lost her *naiveté*.

Notes

1   A. L. Kennedy has achieved considerable critical attention, winning the following awards: *Mail on Sunday*/John Llewelyn Rhys prize in 1990 for

Night Geometry and the Garscadden Trains; Scotsman Saltire award for the best first Scottish book for *Night Geometry and the Garscadden Trains* in 1991; Somerset Maughan award in 1993 for *Looking for the Possible Dance*; *Granta* selection of twenty Best of Young British novelists 1993; and Saltire Scottish Book of the Year award joint winner in 1995 for *So I am Glad*.

2   Alison Kennedy, *Night Geometry and the Garscadden Trains* (London: Phoenix, 1993) pp. 24–5.

3   Kennedy, *Night Geometry*, p. 25.

4   Maurice Merleau-Ponty, *Sense and Non-Sense*, trans. Hubert L. Dreyfus and Patricia Allen Dreyfus (Evanston, Illinois: Northwestern University Press, 1964), p. 3.

5   Cristie March, 'Interview with A. L. Kennedy, Glasgow, March 17, 1999,' *The Edinburgh Review*, 101 (1999), 99–119, 100.

6   Maurice Merleau-Ponty, *The Primacy of Perception and Other Essays on Phenomenological Psychology, the Philosophy of Art, History and Politics*, ed. James M. Edie (Evanston: Northwestern University Press, 1964), p. 14.

7   Ibid., p. 8.

8   Georges Bataille, *The Accursed Share: An Essay on General Economy, Consumption* vol. I., trans. Robert Hurley (New York: Zone Books, 1988), pp. 34–5.

9   Kennedy, *Night Geometry*, p. 24.

10 Henri Bergson, *Matter and Memory* (New York: Zone Books, 1988), p. 36.

11 Kennedy, *Night Geometry*, p. 34.

12 Henri Bergson, *An Introduction to Metaphysics*, trans. T. E. Hulme (London, Macmillan, 1913), p. 55.

13 Kennedy, *Night Geometry*, pp. 1–2.

14 Maurice Merleau-Ponty, *The Visible and the Invisible*, trans. Alphonso Lingis (Evanston, Illinois: Northwestern University Press, 1968), p. 63.

15 A. L. Kennedy, *So I Am Glad*, (London: Jonathan Cape, 1995), p. 2.

16 Merleau-Ponty, *Visible and the Invisible*, p. 64.

17 Kennedy, *Night Geometry*, p. 34.

18 Ibid., p. 50.

19 Ibid., p. 122.

20 Ibid., p. 126.

21 Ibid., p. 126.

22 A. L. Kennedy, *Looking for the Possible Dance* (London: Secker & Warburg, 1993), p. 1.

23 Merleau-Ponty, *Primacy of Perception*, p. 23.

24 A. L. Kennedy, 'Re: Interview', unpublished e-mail to Dr Philip Tew, 2 August (1998), p. 1–2, 2.

25 A. L. Kennedy, 'Re: contact, apologies, queries etc.', unpublished e-mail to Dr Philip Tew, 2 November (1998), pp. 1–4, 2.

26   Kennedy, *Possible Dance*, p. 15.
27   Kennedy, 'Re: Interview', p. 2.
28   Merleau-Ponty, *Visible and the Invisible*, p. 96.
29   Kennedy, *Possible Dance*, p. 95.
30   Bataille, *Accursed Share*, p. 129.
31   Kennedy, *So I Am Glad*, p. 31.
32   Kennedy, *Night Geometry*, p. 102.
33   Ibid., p. 138.
34   Merleau-Ponty, *Visible and the Invisible*, p. 64.
35   March, 'Interview', 107–8.
36   Pierre Bourdieu, *In Other Words: Essays Towards a Reflexive Sociology*, trans. Matthew Adamson (Cambridge: Polity, 1990), p. 127.
37   Kennedy, *Possible Dance*, p. 15.
38   Ibid., p. 203.
39   Guy Debord, *The Society of the Spectacle*, trans. Donald Nicholson-Smith (New York: Zone Books, 1994), p. 41.
40   Kennedy, *Possible Dance*, pp. 17–8.
41   Merleau-Ponty, *Visible and the Invisible*, p. 41.
42   Kennedy, *So I Am Glad*, p. 5.
43   Ibid., p. 173.
44   Ibid., p. 162.
45   Merleau-Ponty, *Visible and the Invisible*, p. 99.
46   Kennedy, *Night Geometry*, p. 47.
47   Kennedy, *So I Am Glad*, p. 1.
48   Ibid., p. 22.
49   Merleau-Ponty, *Visible and the Invisible*, p. 5.
50   Kennedy, *So I Am Glad*, p. 129.
51   Merleau-Ponty, *Visible and the Invisible*, p. 57.
52   Will Self 'address etc.' (unpublished e-mail message from Will Self to Dr Philip Tew with full original version of interview article on A. L. Kennedy later published in part in *Independent on Sunday* Review in 2000), 1 February (2001), unpaginated.
53   Merleau-Ponty, *Sense and Non-Sense*, p. 147.
54   A. L. Kennedy, *Everything You Need* (London: Jonathan Cape 1999), p. 90.
55   Kennedy, *So I Am Glad*, pp. 65–6.

Primary texts

Night Geometry and the Garscadden Trains (Edinburgh: Polygon, 1990; London: Phoenix, 1993)
Looking for the Possible Dance (London: Secker & Warburg, 1993)
Now That You're Back (London: Jonathan Cape, 1994)
So I am Glad (London: Jonathan Cape, 1995)
Original Bliss (London: Jonathan Cape, 1997)

Everything You Need (London: Jonathan Cape, 1999)
On Bullfighting (London: Yellow Jersey Press, 1999)

Selected critical texts

Cristie March, 'Interview with A. L. Kennedy, Glasgow, 17 March, 1999,'
   The Edinburgh Review, 101 (1999), 99–119

Part III

Cultural Hybridity

Part III
Introduction

The theme of cultural hybridity features strongly in contemporary British fiction, not just as subject matter but as part of the creative act of writing itself. Contemporary writers are aware of a range of British identities and cultural contexts. Post-colonial critics think of hybridity as the 'creation of new transcultural forms within the contact zone produced by colonization'.[1] As Salman Rushdie's work shows, the contact zone is both an actual and metaphorical space, a place between worlds and constitutive of new worlds. Hybridity is not without problems, as Rushdie's work (and the *fatwa* against him) has shown, as life merges with work, fact and fiction blur, and secular redefinitions of sacred texts meet strong resistance. Rushdie's novels interrogate the stability of discursive fields and, once more, this relates to the ways in which history is placed under scrutiny in contemporary British fiction. As Ato Quayson argues in *Postcolonialism: Theory, Practice or Process?*, Rushdie simultaneously refracts 'representations of history beyond the texts themselves and [manages] to parody them, instituting an equivalence between the discourses of official history and those of fiction and myth'.[2]

Hybridity is not simply an issue of migration but of plural cultural identities. Kelman and Welsh approach a fragmented notion of 'Britishness' to re-invoke Scottish identity as a dynamic and counter-cultural force. Both in the drug worlds of Welsh and with the economic and cultural dispossession of Kelman's characters, narratives are centred on an uncertainty of the status and stability of individual selfhood (the self literally attacked by life and abuses of different kinds), but in both a strong sense of dynamic contrariety persists, with both regional and ethnic implications. In other words, beneath the surface negativity of the text can be found a cultural affirmation. For, as Marcuse argues, narrative and fiction operate in a fashion so as to inform readers that they might interrogate the underlying assumptions embedded into habitual readings of culture. 'As fictitious world, as illusion (*Schein*), it contains more truth than does everyday reality. For the latter is mystified in its institutions and relationships, which make necessity into choice, and alienation into self-realization. Only in the "illusory world" do things appear as what they are and what they can be.'[3]

In the world of a variable culture and many sources of identity, books written in this vein are undertaking what might be seen as an interrogation of culture. They combine the real, the illusory and the often fantastic. Thereby, they offer new viewpoints. Such texts question prejudices, often playfully. A variety of cultural elements are refashioned by their very inclusion in such kinds of texts, aware of the potential within hybrid forms. Each one becomes a space of new possibilities, supporting marginal cultures by admitting their presence and questioning the very factors that make them marginal or neglected.

Notes

1   Bill Ashcroft, Gareth Griffiths, and Helen Tiffin, *Key Concepts in Post-Colonial Studies* (London: Routledge, 1999), p. 118.
2   Ato Quayson, *Postcolonialism: Theory, Practice or Process?* (Cambridge: Polity, 2000), p. 83.
3   Herbert Marcuse, *The Aesthetic Dimension: Toward a Critique of Marxist Aesthetics* (London: Macmillan, 1978), p. 54.

9 Salman Rushdie: History, Self and the Fiction of Truth

Stephen Baker

In his memoir *Experience* Martin Amis recounts the following 'exchange' he once had with Salman Rushdie:

> – So you *like* Beckett's prose, do you? You *like* Beckett's prose.
> Having established earlier that he did like Beckett's prose, Salman neglected to answer.
> – Okay. Quote me some. Oh I see. You can't.
> No answer: only the extreme hooded-eye treatment...Nobody spoke. Not even Christopher Hitchens. And I really do hate Beckett's prose: every sentence is an assault on my ear. So I said,
> – Well, I'll do it for you. All you need is maximum ugliness and a lot of negatives. 'Nor is the nothing never is.' 'Neither nowhere the nothing is not.' 'Non-nothing the never –'
> Feeling my father in me now (as well as the couple of hundred glasses of wine consumed at the party we had all come on from), I settled down for a concerted goad and wheedle. By this stage Salman looked like a falcon staring through a venetian blind.
> – 'No neither nor never none not no –'
> – Do you want to come outside?
> End of evening.[1]

Reading Salman Rushdie's fiction, it often seems that this is no isolated incident; Rushdie, it can hardly be denied, is a bit of a repeat offender when it comes to asking other writers 'outside'. There he is, in *Midnight's Children*, having his fun with Rudyard Kipling, E. M. Forster, Proust, Sterne and Günter Grass; in *Shame*, he introduces the figure of Omar Khayyam, only to make him a 'peripheral' figure, marginal even to the story of which he is supposed to be the hero.

Throughout *The Satanic Verses* and *The Moor's Last Sigh*, Rushdie appears to view literary and cultural history as a field of endless competitive conflict (a point particularly true of the European references in his fiction): Dante, Cervantes and Samuel Richardson are all gently invited 'outside'. And who could forget the comically portentous and eroticized bloodlust of D. H. Lawrence, replayed through the aesthetic of Hammer Horror Productions in the opening page of *The Ground Beneath Her Feet*: 'Baretorsoed men resembling the actor Christopher Plummer had been gripping her by the wrists and ankles. Her body was splayed out, naked and writhing, over a polished stone bearing the graven image of the snakebird Quetzalcoatl.'[2] Long after the incident with Amis, Rushdie is still, incorrigible to the last, inviting the manly Lawrence outside.

It will be the purpose of this chapter to suggest that Salman Rushdie's writing is based on endless conflict and revision, particularly in its engagement with cultural, literary and socio-political history. There is little or nothing in this writing that is fixed, settled or secure. It is as though Rushdie's novels were meant to recreate for their readers the disquieting, if exhilarating, semblance of an outside world in constant flux and redefinition, that world of capitalist modernity described by Marx and Engels: 'All that is solid melts into air, all that is holy is profaned.'[3]

It is, then, in the light of Rushdie's thematic recreation and reworking of different strands of history – the national, the cultural, and the personal (that pertaining to the self) – that I shall be looking at Rushdie's work. Rather than offer a close analysis of any one novel, this chapter will develop certain questions which Rushdie's fiction generates. These questions will come, for the most part, from looking at what is probably still seen as Rushdie's most important novel, his Booker-of-Bookers-winning *Midnight's Children*; but they will also open up aspects of Rushdie's other novels and engage with issues that relate in a wider sense to contemporary British and post-colonial writing.

In order to grasp the significance in Rushdie's writing of questions of 'the nation', and of the construction of national consciousness, it is worth calling to mind briefly what is probably the most influential and perhaps the most important book of 'post-colonial literature': that is Frantz Fanon's *The Wretched of the Earth*. Published in 1961, the year of Fanon's death, *The Wretched of the Earth* is a book inspired by the Algerian struggle for independence. In it Fanon argues for the importance of 'national culture' to anti-imperialist struggle, suggesting that the recognition of the worth of national, pre-colonial cultures can serve as a powerful impetus to the taking-up of anti-imperial conflict. The remembering of a national culture from before colonial oppression becomes in itself a potentially political act. Rushdie, however, writes from a quite different context. He is writing about states that have already achieved independence; but the way in which he attempts to represent and to reconstruct the history of a post-Independence Indian subcontinent remains a useful way into looking at, and talking about, Rushdie's fiction. Early in *Midnight's Children* the narrator introduces us to his grandfather (who is not, of course, his grandfather – but for now that isn't too important):

> One Kashmiri morning in the early spring of 1915, my grandfather Aadam Aziz hit his nose against a frost-hardened tussock of earth while attempting to pray. Three drops of blood plopped out of his left nostril, hardened instantly in the brittle air and lay before his eyes on the prayer-mat, transformed into rubies. Lurching back until he knelt with his head once more upright, he found that the tears which had sprung to his eyes had solidified, too; and at that moment, as he brushed diamonds contemptuously from his lashes, he resolved never again to kiss earth for any god or man. This decision, however, made a hole in him, a vacancy in a vital inner chamber, leaving him vulnerable to women and history. Unaware of this at first, despite his recently completed medical training, he stood up, rolled the prayer-mat into a thick cheroot, and holding it under his right arm surveyed the valley through clear, diamond-free eyes.[4]

Later I shall come back to this passage and look at it more closely. For the moment, though, we only have to note the way in which this family history – which is to run parallel to a national history – begins with a loss of faith. The close relationship between religious belief and certain historical forces – here (in *Midnight's Children*) nationalism – is presented to us at the very start of the novel. That this should take place in Kashmir, a disputed territory to the north of the Indian subcontinent, where issues of religion and nationalism have been most explosive since partition in 1947, is itself significant. In fact, much of what *Midnight's Children* charts is the decay of that vision of a secular India so strongly promoted by Jawarharlal Nehru, India's first post-Independence prime minister; the attack upon that idea by sectarian (or communalist) conflict. (The importance of this theme, and this threat, is such that it is re-explored in a slightly different historical context in Rushdie's later *The Moor's Last Sigh*.)

Benedict Anderson, in *Imagined Communities*, writes of the development of nationalism in Western Europe and describes the way in which, though in certain aspects quite distinct from religion,

nationalism is nonetheless constructed in part to satisfy similar appe-
tites, similar needs, to those of religious faith. He writes:

> ...in Western Europe the eighteenth century marks not only the dawn
> of the age of nationalism but the dusk of religious modes of thought.
> The century of the Enlightenment, of rationalist secularism, brought
> with it its own modern darkness. With the ebbing of religious belief,
> the suffering which belief in part composed did not disappear. Disinte-
> gration of paradise: nothing makes fatality more arbitrary. Absurdity
> of salvation: nothing makes another style of continuity more necessary.
> What then was required was a secular transformation of fatality into
> continuity, contingency into meaning. As we shall see, few things were
> (are) better suited to this end than an idea of nation. If nation-states are
> widely conceded to be 'new' and 'historical', the nations to which they
> give political expression always loom out of an immemorial past, and,
> still more important, glide into a limitless future. It is the magic of
> nationalism to turn chance into destiny.[5]

In his fiction, Rushdie demonstrates a quite subtly different relationship, where the idea of the nation does not really replace religious
belief, as it does, according to Anderson, in much of eighteenth-
century Europe, but can either be moulded to a secular form (as,
initially, in Nehru's India) or can be viewed as almost inseparable
from a national faith (as in the foundation of Pakistan). Rushdie's
own preference is quite clear: the 'grandfather' of his narrator must
lose his faith. In other words, this family history has to begin with
scepticism; just as, Rushdie argues elsewhere, it was vital for the
Indian people to choose (in political terms) Nehru's secularism over
Gandhi's mysticism.

However, the expression of this preference for doubt remains itself
in some sense ambivalent. The 'grandfather' who loses his faith is
called Dr Aziz, a name borrowed from E. M. Forster's *A Passage to
India* (1924). Rushdie's representations lean quite heavily on the
literature of imperialism, on Western, imperial representations of
India. The religious doubt that Aadam Aziz experiences is, then,
also associated with the forces of Empire and European Enlightenment. (Think of his scientific training, his stay in Europe and his
European friends.) This of course leads to the whole question of
migrancy, of the construction of Rushdie's own subject position, and
of his extended use of literary allusion – and these are points I shall go
on to discuss in more detail later.

It seems useful to view Rushdie's fiction (and particularly *Midnight's Children*) in relation to the 'Historical Novel', first fully developed by Sir Walter Scott in the early nineteenth century. The

Hungarian, Marxist critic Georg Lukács, in his study *The Historical Novel*, argues that this form of writing can only appear when a 'rational' (i.e. historical) understanding of society (society seen as the product of human agency) has displaced the 'irrational' view of society as divinely ordered. In Lukács's reading, the historians of the mid to late eighteenth century laid the ideological goundwork for the French Revolution; and the experience of the French Revolution in turn paved the way for the historical novels of Scott. Another example of this kind of change would be the title of Balzac's *Comédie Humaine* (*The Human Comedy*). In its revision of Dante's *Divine Comedy* we can see this too as a nineteenth-century literary secularization which has followed the eighteenth-century ideological secularization that we saw Anderson refer to above. The important aspect here is the substitution of 'the rational' for 'the irrational'.

Rushdie's fiction attempts to absorb that genre, to offer – simultaneously – a critique and a reworked expression of it. This is, in fact, the kind of argument that Linda Hutcheon constructs for contemporary, postmodern fiction in general, using the term 'historiographic metafiction'. These are novels which *are* historical novels and yet make quite overt their differences from the more traditional examples of the genre, particularly in terms of their representation of the irrational, the magical. This, of course, leads to the question: what kind of historical representation does Rushdie give us?

Most obviously, at least in novels such as *Midnight's Children* and *The Moor's Last Sigh*, it is a form of personalized history. In a short essay, ' "Errata": or Unreliable Narration in *Midnight's Children*', Rushdie points out some of the narrator's factual errors (it is unnecessary to work through a list of them; suffice it to say he even gets wrong the date of Gandhi's assassination). 'Saleem Sinai,' writes Rushdie, 'is not an oracle; he's only adopting a kind of oracular language. His story is not history, but it plays with historical shapes.'[6] Moraes Zogoiby (known as 'Moor'), the narrator of *The Moor's Last Sigh*, claims, in a manner not dissimilar to Saleem: 'On the run, I have turned the world into my own pirate map, complete with clues, leading X-marks-the-spottily to the treasure of myself.'[7]

This technique, the use of an idiosyncratic narrator through whom all information must be refracted and who is constantly 'play[ing] with historical shapes', or leading us 'X-marks-the-spottily' to the treasure of themselves, has been the focus of some of the most sustained critiques of Rushdie's writing. Aijaz Ahmad (*In Theory: Classes, Nations, Literatures*) reflects on the reliance of the history of an allegorical Pakistan in *Shame* on the personality and selectiveness of its narrator. The implications of that history's dependence upon the person of the narrator are sketched out by Rushdie's narrator himself:

> Although I have known Pakistan for a long time, I have never lived there for longer than six months at a stretch . . . I have learned Pakistan by slices . . . [H]owever I choose to write about over there, I am forced to reflect that in fragments of broken mirrors . . . I must reconcile myself to the inevitability of the missing bits.[8]

Ahmad takes issue with the nature of the *political* vision that results from this narrative perspective. His main problem is the ease with which Rushdie's narrator (whom Ahmad takes to be Rushdie himself) ignores those 'missing bits':

> If one has 'known Pakistan for a long time' and yet, because of circumstance, 'learned' it only 'by slices', the question naturally arises: *which* 'slices' has one chosen to 'learn'? For, if we do not *choose* our own 'bits' of reality, those 'bits' will be chosen for us by our class origin, our jobs, the circuits of our friendships and desires, our ways of spending our leisure time, our literary predilections, our political affiliations – or lack of them. There are no neutral 'bits', not even of not knowing.[9]

Ahmad's argument rests on similar premises to earlier Marxist critiques of modernism. The association of a fragmented narrative structure, and particularly one whose fragmentation is an effect of the narrative's reliance on an individual consciousness, with a *conservative* political stance – an insistence on the primacy of the alienated individual – is something particularly recognizable from Georg Lukács's writings on modernism. Like Ahmad, Lukács criticizes the disavowal of any attempt to represent a whole, a totality. For him, only realist fiction, which maps the interrelations of separate parts of a society, can have any progressive social import. Social critique and the credible narrative representation of historical forces are, for Lukács, dependent upon the work's depiction of this social totality – and this is precisely what seems to be discarded in texts such as Rushdie's.

Criticisms such as those of Ahmad point almost inadvertently, it seems to me, to what is an important feature of Rushdie's writing: namely, the exploration of how narrative authority is constructed. It is not simply that the narrative of India's history is subordinate to Saleem's consciousness, but that that very subordination becomes the subject of the novel: the construction of Saleem's (or, in *The Moor's Last Sigh*, Moor's) identity is constantly held to be as significant a theme as the construction of post-Independence Indian society.

Something similar is going on in *The Satanic Verses* too. There the narrator teases us as to his identity: sometimes suggesting that his narrative is satanic, at others that it is divine. And what this is pointing to, of course, is the manufacturedness and the historical contingency of these terms: who decides what is divine and what is satanic? Moreover, within this narrative structure we find a series of stories focusing on themes of demonization and how that demonization is expressed through racial and sexual representations.

To return to *Midnight's Children*: there Rushdie portrays Saleem's storytelling as an attempt to keep hold of some unified self, a method of survival (and early on Saleem compares himself to Sheherazade who, in the framing story to the *Thousand and One Nights*, tells unfinished stories each night so she'll be able to survive until the next day). In *The Moor's Last Sigh*, too, Moor's survival in Vasco Miranda's fortress is to last the precise duration of the time he takes to write the story of his life. At the same time that self, which survives only by the construction of successive fictions, is seen as inextricably and intimately tied to a *national* destiny. Saleem Sinai's physical fragmentation is offered as a reflection of the fragmentation of the Indian subcontinent: the initial partition of India and Pakistan; and the subsequent division of East and West Pakistan, after the Indo-Pakistan War of 1971, into Bangladesh and Pakistan. We find something very similar in *The Moor's Last Sigh*. Moraes Zogoiby is living his life at twice the speed he should; when he ought to be in his prime, he is already old and weakened: like post-Independence Indian democracy, he has aged far too quickly.

In *Midnight's Children* the survival of Saleem, then, is linked to the survival of the Indian state, based on an imperilled secularism. This makes interesting the unmasking of his family history as a façade, thereby undermining that same illusion of continuity that Benedict Anderson associates with the 'nation', the nation which 'loom[s] out of an immemorial past'. But perhaps it also has a more specific reference. Saleem asks:

> Was my lifelong belief in the equation between the State and myself transmuted, in 'the Madam's' mind, into that in-those-days-famous phrase: *India is Indira and Indira is India*? Were we competitors for centrality – was she gripped by a lust for meaning as profound as my own – and was that, was that why...? (p. 420)

Indira Gandhi, daughter of Nehru and no relation at all to Mahatma Gandhi (the latter, despite the almost constant suggestion in Congress electioneering of the 1960s and 70s, is not her grandfather, just as

Saleem's grandfather is not really his), is Saleem's nemesis: the Widow. The two Indias they claim to embody are quite different. *Midnight's Children* was begun during the Emergency (1975), when Indira Gandhi suspended political opposition and allegedly pushed through social policies such as enforced sterilizations and the compulsory 'relocation' of minority communities of Muslims, the same communities her father had persuaded to stay in India rather than move to Pakistan after partition. This, then, was very much a movement away from a *secular* India.

A history of the Emergency offered by 'the Widow' (or Indira Gandhi) would of course be quite different. And in the juxtaposition of these two different versions of India, Rushdie is not only foregrounding the constructedness of these representations (these Indias), but is also asking us to be capable of investigating what agenda, what particular slant lies behind each construction. In other words, *Midnight's Children* (like *The Satanic Verses* and *The Moor's Last Sigh*, though this is less overtly true of *Shame*) is a novel which, through its dramatization of narrative authority, is investigating the construction of authority in a wider sense, using the construction of narrative authority as an analogy for the construction of social and political authority itself. Here Edward Said suggests why such a step might be significant:

> ...such domestic cultural enterprises as narrative fiction and history ...are premised on the recording, ordering, observing powers of the central authorizing subject or ego. To say of this subject, in a quasi-tautological manner, that it writes because it *can* write is to refer not only to domestic society but also to the outlying world. The capacity to represent, portray, characterize, and depict is not easily available to just any member of just any society; moreover, the 'what', and 'how' in the representation of 'things', while allowing for considerable individual freedom, are circumscribed and socially regulated.[10]

Authority and its construction are being dissected in *Midnight's Children*. Thinking back to the point made by Aijaz Ahmad and these more general comments of Edward Said, it might be useful to think of *Midnight's Children* as a novel about holes. Dr Aziz first sees his wife through a perforated sheet, gradually attempting to build up a picture of her, bit by bit; Saleem Sinai introduces his narrative as viewed through that same perforated sheet, fragmentary and controlled by him. So this is one hole; and the issue of who is to control what fragments we see through the hole is exactly that raised by Ahmad and Said above. We shall now look at that social circumscription and regulation of individual consciousness Said mentions.

Returning to the introduction of Dr Aziz (quoted above), we see that the person who positions the hole in the sheet has a hole inside. With his religion questioned, Aziz becomes a site of conflict; and so what we are witnessing (as we do with Saleem Sinai) is the social and personal formation of an authority figure. The list of social aspects that Ahmad says contribute to individual consciousness includes precisely the sort of things in relation to which we see Saleem: class origin, jobs, friends. The way that all of these things circulate and come into conflict in the 'hole inside' shows us that Rushdie's novels perhaps already pre-empt criticisms such as those of Ahmad.

The question of authority is also, of course, closely connected to the historical subject matter. I've already mentioned the Emergency, which clearly raises questions of authority and was begun as an attempt by Indira Gandhi to evade conviction for electoral fraud. The other major tragic event to hit the Indian subcontinent at around that time was the Indo-Pakistan war of 1971, which led to the foundation of Bangladesh. In Pakistani elections of 1970, East and West Pakistan voted entirely for different parties. The Awami League (East) won the election but Zulfiqar Ali Bhutto refused to accept the result. The civil unrest that this provoked in East Pakistan led to the Pakistani army – made up almost exclusively of citizens of West Pakistan – being sent in to quell the population. The formal, narrative preoccupation with questions of authority is used by Rushdie to reflect in some way key events in the history which is Saleem's raw material for his storytelling. Inevitably, though, there is the question of Saleem's narrative: what political and ideological forces have gone into the making of that?

In fact the narrative is formed by a mish-mash of influences: some Indian, some European. While the open, free-ranging structure is intended to reflect an Indian oral tradition of epic storytelling and Rushdie's writing is stylistically indebted to G. V. Desani, the novel also mimics certain European literary models: the significance of Saleem's nose and birth date point to *Tristram Shandy*; I have already mentioned *A Passage to India*; Günter Grass's *The Tin Drum* is another influence. And while Saleem's pickles recall Oskar Mazerath's drum-playing in Grass's novel, they also point to Marcel's madeleine in *A la recherche*... Rushdie's representations advertise the extent to which they borrow European models to construct an account of post-Independence India. In other words, Rushdie is constantly flirting with Orientalist discourse, the modes of representation used by Western, imperial powers to 'represent' an 'exotic' Eastern Orient, whose people cannot (and cannot be allowed to) represent themselves. By way of digression, it might be noted that this mimicry is something that is particularly pronounced in *The Satanic Verses*.

The mish-mash of influences, the juxtaposition of the European and the Indian can, therefore, be said to represent a playful celebration of cultural hybridity, absorbing the historical and cultural influences of West European literary culture on colonized societies. In this sense it can be defended as quite an accurate portrayal of the contruction of a post-colonial society. On the other hand, it might seem remarkably akin to Jean-François Lyotard's account of a commodified, contemporary, postmodern culture:

> Eclecticism is the degree zero of contemporary general culture: one listens to reggae, watches a western, eats McDonald's food for lunch and local cuisine for dinner, wears Paris perfume in Tokyo and 'retro' clothes in Hong Kong; knowledge is a matter for TV games. It is easy to find a public for eclectic works. . . . Artists, gallery owners, critics, and public wallow together in the 'anything goes', and the epoch is one of slackening.[11]

In connecting both Rushdie and Edward Said (who has also been known to elevate the perpective of the migrant, the figure who straddles various cultures) with this playful contemporary eclecticism, Aijaz Ahmad attempts to identify such a stance as a marker of *class* privilege. Rushdie and Said, writes Ahmad, are 'cosmopolitan intellectuals' and we should not be fooled into accepting their notions of cultural migrancy and cultural rootlessness as necessarily representative of cultural life in the post-colonial societies which they no longer inhabit. Yet both Rushdie and Said explicitly acknowledge the importance of class and class privilege. Saleem's privileged status is made quite clear, as is that of Saladin Chamcha in *The Satanic Verses*. Said, too, writes of the need to recognize the maintenance of oppressive power structures in newly independent, formerly colonial countries:

> Where it got people out on the streets to march against the white master, nationalism was often led by lawyers, doctors and writers who were partly formed and to some degree produced by the colonial power. The national bourgeoisies and their specialized élites, of which Fanon speaks so ominously, in effect tended to replace the colonial force with a new class-based and ultimately exploitative one, which replicated the old colonial structures in new terms. There are states all across the formerly colonized world that have bred pathologies of power, as Eqbal Ahmad has called them.[12]

What we see is neither continuity nor discontinuity. The old order may have gone, but there is no reason to suppose that the new one will necessarily be better. Yet, as Rushdie writes, when commenting on Günter Grass, '...while there is life, there must be analysis, struggle, persuasion, argument, polemic, rethinking, and all the other longish words that add up to one very short word: hope.'[13]

Rushdie's fiction is a determined engagement with the process of constructing hope from such argument, polemic, rethinking; *The Satanic Verses*, after all, begins with the words '"To be born again," sang Gibreel Farishta tumbling from the heavens, "first you have to die."'[14] In fact, it may even be true to say that Rushdie's elevation of the power of art, in these 'degraded', postmodern times, could almost be such as to make a High Modernist blush. Invoking Jean-François Lyotard's description of the postmodern condition, Rushdie associates the writing of fiction with the search for some notion of truth, however ironic and qualified:

> This rejection of totalized explanations is the modern condition. And this is where the novel, the form created to discuss the fragmentation of truth, comes in...The elevation of the quest for the Grail over the Grail itself, the acceptance that all that is solid *has* melted into air, that reality and morality are not givens but imperfect human constructs, is the point from which fiction begins. This is what J.-F. Lyotard called, in 1979, *La Condition Postmoderne*. The challenge of literature is to start from this point, and still find a way of fulfilling our unaltered spiritual requirements.[15]

In this sense, Rushdie's artistic project might be compared to that of Aurora Zogoiby in *The Moor's Last Sigh*, who declares, '"I am getting interested in making religious pictures for people who have no god"'. (p. 220).

The contingency of all truths, selves and histories is both cause for lament – as we witness, for example, the destruction of Saleem Sinai or, in *The Satanic Verses*, the mental disintegration of Gibreel Farishta – and a precondition of art's ability to show us the truth; this time a truth about truths, and the tricks they perform with mirrors. Umeed Merchant, the narrator of *The Ground Beneath Her Feet*, speculates on the relationship between art and the real, true, illusionless world:

> Why do we care about singers? Wherein lies the power of songs? ...Our lives are not what we deserve; they are, let us agree, in many painful ways deficient. Song turns them into something else. Song shows us a world that is worthy of our yearning, it shows us ourselves as they might be, if we were worthy of the world. (pp. 19–20)

While the music of Vina Aspara and Ormus Cama soars, Vina herself is swallowed up in a Mexican earthquake. There is, in truth, no ground beneath her feet, nothing that can be accepted as secure or constant. Celebrating art's capacity to rethink, recreate, reimagine, Rushdie's fiction insists on the transience and historicity of all that seems presently true; our fears, our anxieties, our truths: despite their oppressive reality and concreteness, these are what art reveals as simply and gloriously *groundless*.

Notes

1   Martin Amis, *Experience* (London: Jonathan Cape, 2000), pp. 81–2.
2   Salman Rushdie, *The Ground Beneath Her Feet* (London: Jonathan Cape, 1999), p. 3. Further references in the text are to this edition.
3   Karl Marx and Friedrich Engels, *The Communist Manifesto*, trans. Samuel Moore (Harmondsworth: Penguin, 1985), p. 83.
4   Salman Rushdie, *Midnight's Children* (London: Picador, 1982), p. 10. Further references in the text are to this edition.
5   Benedict Anderson, *Imagined Communities* (London: Verso, 1991), p. 11.
6   Salman Rushdie, *Imaginary Homelands: Essays and criticism, 1981–1991* (London: Granta, 1992), p. 25.
7   Salman Rushdie, *The Moor's Last Sigh* (London: Jonathan Cape, 1995), p. 3. Further references in the text are to this edition.
8   Salman Rushdie, *Shame* (London: Picador, 1984), p. 61.
9   Aijaz Ahmad, *In Theory: Classes, Nations, Literatures* (London: Verso, 1992), p. 138.
10   Edward Said, *Culture and Imperialism* (London: Vintage, 1994), p. 95.
11   Jean-François Lyotard, 'Answering the Question: What is Postmodernism?' in *Postmodernism: A Reader*, ed. Thomas Docherty (London: Harvester, 1993), p. 42.
12   Said, *Culture and Imperialism*, p. 269.
13   Rushdie, *Imaginary Homelands*, p. 281.
14   Salman Rushdie, *The Satanic Verses* (London: Viking, 1988), p. 3.
15   Rushdie, *Imaginary Homelands*, p. 422.

Primary texts

Fiction

Grimus (London: Victor Gollancz, 1975)
Midnight's Children (London: Jonathan Cape, 1981)
Shame (London: Jonathan Cape, 1983)
The Satanic Verses (London: Viking, 1988)
Haroun and the Sea of Stories (London: Penguin/Granta, 1990)
East, West (London: Jonathan Cape, 1994)

The Moor's Last Sigh (London: Jonathan Cape, 1995)
The Ground Beneath Her Feet (London: Jonathan Cape, 1999)
Fury (London: Jonathan Cape, 2001)

Non-fiction

The Jaguar Smile: A Nicaraguan Journey (London: Pan, 1987)
Imaginary Homelands: Essays and criticism, 1981–1991 (London: Granta Books, 1992)

Selected critical texts

Timothy Brennan, *Salman Rushdie and the Third World: Myths of the Nation* (London: Macmillan, 1989)
Catherine Cundy, *Salman Rushdie* (Manchester: Manchester UP, 1996)
Daniel Easterman, *New Jerusalems: Reflections on Islam, Fundamentalism and the Rushdie Affair* (London: Grafton, 1992)
D. C. R. A. Goonetilleke, *Salman Rushdie* (New York: St Martin's, 1998)
James Harrison, *Salman Rushdie,* (New York: Twayne, 1992)
Joel Kuortti, *The Salman Rushdie Bibliography: A Bibliography of Salman Rushdie's Work and Rushdie Criticism* (Frankfurt: Peter Lang, 1997)
Alastair Niven, 'Salman Rushdie', *Wasafiri.* 26 (1997) Autumn, 52–7
Ziauddin Sardar and Merryl Wyn Davies, *Distorted Imagination: Lessons from the Rushdie Affair* (London & Kuala Lumpur: Grey Seal and Berita, 1990)
Geoffrey Wheatcroft, 'Writers and Comparisons: Salman Rushdie and Shiva Naipaul', *Encounter* 75(2) (Sept 1990), 38–40.
Mark Wormald, 'The Uses of Impurity: Fiction and Fundamentalism in Salman Rushdie and Jeanette Winterson', in, Rod Mengham (ed.), *An Introduction to Contemporary Fiction: International Writing in English since 1970* (Cambridge: Polity, 1999)

10 The Fiction of James Kelman and Irvine Welsh: Accents, Speech and Writing

Drew Milne

Differences in the writing of James Kelman and Irvine Welsh run deep. Kelman was born in Glasgow in 1946 and has lived most of his life there, with brief spells in America, London and other parts of Britain.[1] With significant exceptions, his writing is rooted in Glasgow. Welsh was born in Edinburgh in 1961. He has lived elsewhere, notably in London and Amsterdam, but the bulk of his fiction is rooted in Edinburgh. The differences in the two writers' Glasgow and Edinburgh origins are significant, as are their age differences, not least because Kelman's work created some of the critical context for Welsh's work. This essay argues that more important differences in their literary commitments can be understood through an analysis of the politics of accent.

Kelman's first book of stories, *An Old Pub near the Angel* (1973), was published by Puckerbush Press in the US. It was some years before his first novels, *The Busconductor Hines* (1984) and *A Chancer* (1985), were published by Polgyon, Edinburgh University's then student-run publishing house and also the publisher of the journal *Edinburgh Review*. His collection of stories, *Greyhound for Breakast* (1987), marked Kelman's shift into more mainstream capitalist publishing. His next novel, *A Disaffection* (1989), was shortlisted for the Booker Prize and gave Kelman a more national British profile. It was not, however, until he won the Booker Prize in 1994 for his novel *How late it was, how late* (1994) that he earned a measure of financial independence. Having been a Professor of Creative Writing at the University of Texas from 1998–2001, Kelman was appointed a joint Professor of Creative Writing at the University of Glasgow in 2001, along with Tom Leonard and Alasdair Gray. Although Kelman is widely considered the most important contemporary Scottish writer, he continues to need the support of university publishing and teaching to secure a living. His most recent novel, *Translated Accounts* (2001), is an ambitious and challenging book, which seeks to provoke political discussion rather than easy literary consumption.

Kelman's sustained and relatively uncommercial trajectory contrasts with the rapid commercial success of Welsh's first book *Trainspotting* (1993), whose 'bestseller' status was enriched by the success of the subsequent film. Welsh has also published collections of stories, *The Acid House* (1994) and *Ecstasy* (1996), along with three further novels, *Maribou Stork Nightmares* (1995), *Filth* (1998) and *Glue* (2001). *Glue* introduced a new, more self-critical dimension to his work, but his reception continues to be dominated by *Trainspotting*.

Both Kelman and Welsh have attracted considerable press notoriety, much of it focused on the representation of language, but their commercial fortunes are markedly different. This reflects Welsh's media-savvy provocations on sex and drugs, but there are deeper differences over the status of so-called 'popular' culture in their work. Welsh's commercial popularity and his availability for cinematic exploitation have disguised the underlying sociological inquiries in his writing. His approach to storytelling, however, is more populist than Kelman's modernist and existentially distinctive representation of life rhythms.[2] The novels of both Welsh and Kelman are constructed through loosely linked short stories rather than through sustained plots, but the resistance to narrative conventions is motivated differently. Kelman's work avoids the fast-moving and almost cinematic storytelling techniques of Welsh. His work deliberately resists the dominant terms of the capitalist media and the culture industry, articulating a politicized critique of trends within literary modernism. Welsh, by contrast, develops a more sensationalist mode of narrative, intimate with genres such as pulp fiction, pornography and popular music. Welsh is not uncritical of the sensation-seeking immediacy he portrays, but much of the critique is left implicit. Put differently, Kelman's work has affinities with the modernist dissidence of Franz Kafka, Samuel Beckett and Albert Camus, whereas Welsh offers something more like a populist postmodern blend of William Burroughs and Quentin Tarantino. There are also historical precedents for Welsh's work in the history of the Scottish novel. *Trainspotting* mixes the drug sensibilities of Alexander Trocchi's *Cain's Book* (1963) with the sensationalist treatment of urban underworlds in

A. McArthur and H. Kingsley Long's bestselling 'Gorbals' novel, *No Mean City* (1935). Beyond superficial resemblances in the work of Kelman and Welsh, their underlying divergences reveal key conflicts facing the future of Scottish culture and writing.

These conflicts can be focused by comparing the way they characterize the assumed authority of the voices represented by standard written English. Both Kelman and Welsh attack the class basis of public discourse, contrasting vernacular wit with the supposedly accent-neutral voices of anglophone authority and academic argument. The tendency to romanticize working-class speech can short-cut the struggle to socialize the resources of literacy, a tendency criticized by T. W. Adorno in the following rebuke to Bertolt Brecht:

> To play off workers' dialects against the written language is reactionary (...) If the written language codifies the estrangement of classes, redress cannot lie in regression to the spoken, but only in consistent exercise of the strictest linguistic objectivity. Only a speaking that transcends writing by absorbing it, can deliver speech from the lie that it is already human.[3]

Class conflict codifies speech and writing such that 'linguistic objectivity' is a site of social and political conflict. This is exemplified by the often crude misunderstandings of Kelman and Welsh. Representing English as it is spoken shifts the class politics of literary language and the relation of writing to readers. Perhaps the most obvious challenge to literary decorum is represented by so-called 'swear' words, the focus of much of the controversy associated with Kelman and Welsh.[4] The supposed scandal of reading what is not heard on broadcast media, but easily heard almost everywhere else, dramatizes conflicts in the standardization of written English across lines of class, region and identity. Contemporary Scottish writers are, almost of necessity, forced to negotiate the relation between English as a literary language and Englishness as a political identity formation. Scottish writing faces problems comparable to Irish and Welsh writing in Britain and, more generally, in relation to English as a global language.[5]

Kelman and Welsh, although recognizably 'un'-English, are critical of Scottish nationalism, offering instead a literary internationalism of the localized voice. If their writing seems addressed in the first instance to a Scottish readership with some familiarity with Glasgow and Edinburgh, their work also has resonances for wider readerships in Britain and internationally. Readers become aware of localized levels of linguistic competence. For the film of *Trainspotting*, for example, there was some demand for sub-titles to translate local idiom into more standardized English. The book's American edition offered a glossary of Scottish terms. The challenge to standardized conceptions of linguistic competence nevertheless relies on contrasts between speech and writing which are constitutive of literary language as such. Who makes up the implied communities of interpretation?

Kelman and Welsh can be read as part of the demand for a renegotiation of British identity, demands helpfully described by Tom Nairn in terms of the importance of voice for reconstituting the Scottish 'nation'. For Nairn, 'The recovery of collective will by an already constituted nation is not at all the same as "nation-building" in the sense made familiar through the annals of ethnic nationalism and decolonization.'[6] Nairn suggests how ethnic nationalism or postcolonial discourse can only with difficulty be applied to Scotland. As Nairn argues, 'Britishness' has been more important in Scotland than in England, working as 'a very crude balance-mechanism for the preservation of multiple identities'.[7] Defence mechanisms are evident in the political commentary that punctuates *Trainspotting*. A section entitled 'Scotland Takes Drugs In Psychic Defence' locates psychic defence in relation to pop culture:

> Ah'm pure jumping aroond at the front of the stage, a few feet away from The Man. They are playing 'Neon Forest'. Somebody slaps me on the back saying, – You are mental, by the way, my man. Ah sing out, a twisting, pogo-ing mass of rubber.
>
> Iggy Pop looks right at me as he sings the line: 'America takes drugs in psychic defence'; only he changes 'America' for 'Scatlin', and defines us mair accurately in a single sentence than all the others have ever done . . .
>
> Ah cease my St Vitus dance and stand looking him in stunned awe.[8]

'Scatlin' suggests the conflict between Iggy Pop's 'American' accent and written Scottishness. The referentiality of this homage is evident in the iconic use of 'The Man', confusing Iggy Pop with the drug dealer of 'I'm Waiting for My Man'. The displaced possessive of 'my man' reappears in the line 'You are mental, by the way, my man'. Here the politics of accent take on a multivocal level of irony. The character narrates this voice to suggest at least two different levels. The back-slapping voice speaks with a 'posh' accent, marked by the unabbreviated 'you are' of 'You are mental, by the way, my man'. Idiomatically this marks the voice of a non-Scots speaker or a Scots speaker adopting a parodied English voice. The word 'mental' shifts

this voice into a different idiom. The aspirant yuppie voice is ironically consumed by its parodied 'other', playing with the various tonal-
ities of 'my man' in song and speech. This suggests ironic linguistic
and physical solidarity rather than a violent confrontation or verbal
antagonism. 'You are' suggests a further contrast between the pro-
noun 'I' as 'Ah' and 'us'. The 'us' defined by Iggy Pop's alteration of
the line appears to identify the 'Scotland' of the passage's title with the
Americanized spelling of 'Scatlin'. The character identifies himself as
part of the Scotland that takes drugs in psychic defence, assuming that
his imaginary interlocutor or reader will sympathize with this rock
concert epiphany. The authorial representation of this character
nevertheless leaves it to the reader to judge whether this is to be
read as a naive celebration of drug dependency or whether the author
shares the critique of drug dependency in America and Scotland. The
reader can infer that the 'others' who have defined 'us' might offer
more acute analyses than the clichés of stadium-specific rock rhetoric.

The difficulty of identifying Welsh's authorial voice is further complicated by the character's narration through the historic present
tense. The character's present tense speech idioms are punctuated as
writing by the use of quotation marks, scare quotes, parentheses and
the dot dot dot which suggests an interrupted articulacy. The implied
audience of the character can read this as an affirmation of the
supposed lucidity of the experience. Alternatively, Welsh leaves open
an ironic reading in which the representation of the spoken voice is
shown to be part of the character's defence mechanism. The already
ironic, self-defensive quality of the central character is folded into the
author's superiority. The audience addressed by the character's speech
conflicts with the writer's readership.

The way Welsh's representation of speech becomes an ironic authorial defence mechanism is more explicit in the following passage
from *Trainspotting*, which articulates the terrain of Nairn's critique of
Scottish identity politics:

> Ah hate cunts like that. Cunts like Begbie. Cunts that are intae base-
> ball-batting every fucker that's different; pakis, poofs, n what huv ye.
> Fuckin failures in a country ay failures. It's nae good blamin it oan the
> English fir colonising us. Ah don't hate the English. They're just
> wankers. We are colonised by wankers. We can't even pick a decent,
> vibrant, healthy culture to be colonised by. No. We're ruled by effete
> arseholes. What does that make us? The lowest of the fuckin low, the
> scum of the earth. The most wretched, servile, miserable, pathetic trash
> that was ever shat intae creation. Ah don't hate the English. They just
> git oan wi the shite thuv goat. Ah hate the Scots. (p. 78)

The passage moves between a directly addressed, spoken polemic against the 'Scots' and the self-defeating rhetoric of nationalist self-loathing. Polemic against the tendency of Scottish culture to demonize its ruling class as 'English' others is nevertheless complicit with verbal violence against other 'others', such as Asians and homosexuals. The character expresses some recognition of the need to decolonize Scottish identity politics, but self-loathing inarticulacy works through a comic rhetoric that falsely embraces self-identification as the lowest of the low. There is a self-defeating logic in the 'we' and 'us' of this passage, and in the mock-false thought that the colonized 'pick' their colonizers. The construction of Scottish identity as one of colonization involves an inverted racism against the English, despite the character's claim not to hate 'the English'. Understanding this bravura display of confusion involves recognizing the irony of hatred turning against itself. Hatred for the misrecognitions involved in Scotland's self-chosen defence mechanisms nevertheless involves a vocabulary that victimizes 'cunts', 'pakis', 'poofs' and 'effete arseholes'.[9] Posing as a critique of anti-Englishness, the passage confirms and affirms this ironically represented self-loathing, ironically reproducing anti-English sentiment as though in the guise of critique.

There is an important connection between not hating 'England' and not hating 'the English'. Welsh's written rhetoric represents an acute portrait of the political confusions of Scottish self-representation. The ironic way in which the passage undermines the limited articulacy of its character's polemic nevertheless celebrates the wit of self-loathing. An ironic loop allows readers to loathe this rhetoric of self-loathing. Evidence that the full irony of this passage's self-destruction might be lost on readers is provided by the fact that the Scottish National Party used this monologue for a recruitment form in September 1996. A Labour Member of Parliament complained to the Commission for Racial Equality. The rhetorical strategy of nationalist recruitment would presumably claim that the passage is not a celebration of Scottish self-loathing but an incitement to politicize it. Welsh's recourse to the violence of what has elsewhere been called 'hate speech'[10] simultaneously represents what it purports to criticize. Such writing is all too easily recruited for the reactionary politics of ironically mocking oneself while reproducing the misrepresentation of demonized 'others'. Peter Kravitz has commented that the 'berating of Scotland from within shows a new self-confidence'.[11] The implied politics suggest that self-destructive irony also constitutes a new kind of racist defence mechanism. The Scottish National Party omitted the opening lines of this passage, presumably because they preferred not to risk offending the 'cunts' they might recruit, and preferred to omit the way Welsh associates paki-bashing and homophobia with anti-English self-loathing.

Elsewhere in *Trainspotting*, Welsh offers an auto-critique of the tendency of his characters to represent rather than articulate the contradictions of multiculturalism:

> Some say that the Irish are the trash ay Europe. That's shite. It's the Scots. The Irish hud the bottle tae win thir country back, or at least maist ay it. Ah remember getting wound up when Nicksy's brar, down in London, described the Scots as 'porridge wogs'. Now ah realise that the only thing offensive about that statement was its racism against black people. Otherwise it's spot-on. (p. 190)

Passages such as this nevertheless ironize the flickerings of liberal analysis they deploy. *Trainspotting* folds over the incipient politicization of the narrative voice into a series of localized expressions of inarticulate hostility to politics as such.

> Ah've never felt British, because ah'm not. It's ugly and artificial. Ah've never really felt Scottish either, though. Scotland the brave, ma erse; Scotland the shitein cunt. We'd throttle the life oot ay each other fir the privilege ay rimmin some English aristocrat's piles. Ah've never felt a fuckin thing aboot countries, other than total disgust. (p. 228)

This is characteristic of the reductive affirmation of apolitical cynicism that marks the limit of Welsh's supposed radicalism, exemplifying what Geoff Gilbert refers to as 'the kind of commodified oppositional status that Irvine Welsh occupies so successfully'.[12]

Welsh might claim to represent excluded voices. The rhetoric of writing, however, does not simply record language: it also mediates the political implications of its representations. In 'Eurotrash', for example, Welsh displaces localized Scottish speech by positioning accent politics in Amsterdam. The story begins in what seems like standardized English: 'I was anti-everything and everyone. I didn't want people around me. This aversion was not some big crippling anxiety; merely a mature recognition of my own psychological vulnerability and my lack of suitability as a companion.'[13] The story goes on to dramatize the deluded lucidity of this self-analysis, detailing the confused inarticulacy of anti-social masculinity without articulating alternatives to such 'mature recognition'. Welsh might claim that the story offers an ironic portrait of Scottish psychological vulnerability, in effect dramatizing the delusions of the narrator's self-assessment:

– So where do you come from with an accent like that? (...)
I smiled. – Scotland.
– Yeah? Where about? Glasgow? Edinburgh?
– All over really, I replied, bland and blasé. Did it really matter which indistinct shite-arsed towns and schemes I was dragged through, growing up in that dull and dire little country? (*Acid House*, pp. 12–13)

The character's cynicism affirms and denies the refusal to articulate the accent markers otherwise central to Welsh's fiction. Faced with criticism of the narrator-character as a British oppressor, the narrator-character engages in further cynical self-legitimation:

I was almost tempted to go into a spiel about how I was Scottish, not British, and that the Scots were the last oppressed colony of the British empire. I don't really believe it, though; the Scots oppress themselves by their obsession with the English which breeds the negatives of hatred, fear, servility, contempt and dependency. (p. 17)

The difficulty here is the relation between the report of unspoken thought and the implied readership addressed. Welsh suggests a criticism of the decolonization model elsewhere deployed by his characters, but the character's refusal to speak or argue also exemplifies Scottish self-oppression. Generalized theses about Scottish identity function as staged asides, polemicizing against Scottish self-delusion, with half an eye on a more generalized English-speaking audience who need to have Scots identity explained. The levels of irony at work leave open the possibility that Welsh has more sympathy with the way this character thinks and speaks than with the liberal analysis his authorial irony protects itself with. In 'Eurotrash' the voice of the central character is closer to a written representation of standard English than the characters for which Welsh is perhaps best known. The apparent analysis of the delusions of Scottish psychology suggests the difficulty of moving beyond the rhetorical fantasies liberated by a non-standard register into a more sustained analysis of Welsh's written voice.

Welsh's representation of non-standard accents achieves a number of significant local and polemical effects, but the pleasure in local scandals does not extend to an articulation of the difficulties of localized self-defensiveness. The extent to which his writing achieves a distinctive tension between spoken and written voices nevertheless leaves an unarticulated gulf between the lived reality of particular speech-energies and their status within a more sustained realist aesthetic. What emerges is a series of dramatically self-deconstructing narrator-characters. Welsh's authorial voice ironically deploys literary wit to deflect attention from its own responsibility for producing a relentlessly sour and self-destructive cynicism. If the use of rhetorical irony is reactionary, the problems involved are perhaps most evident when Welsh extends the representation of accent beyond representations of Scottish voices into a more generalized representation of the politics of English accents. In 'Fortune's Always Hiding: A Corporate Drug Romance' in *Ecstasy*, for example, Welsh even dramatizes characters who use accents as part of their disguise. Although there is some literary irony in the deliberate cheapness of the effects involved, the confusion between the social use of adopted accents and the literary artifice of almost explicitly racist representation pushes irony to a level of cynical banality. The problem of voice as a marker of local identity is played with by the character's own narration but the effect is to trivialize the estrangement of classes embodied in the politics of accents.

If this analysis begins to confirm Adorno's claim that it is reactionary to play off workers' dialect against written language, Kelman's writing is harder to dismiss, not least because Kelman is more aware of the political consequences of local literary effects. Kelman's understanding of accent politics is more subtle, offering a critique of the socialized and literary tendencies represented by Welsh's staged and commercially cynical dissidence. Consider Kelman's note for the anthology *Three Glasgow Writers*:

> I was born and bred in Glasgow
> I have lived most of my life in Glasgow
> It is the place I know best
> My language is English
> I write
> In my writings the accent is in Glasgow
> I am always from Glasgow and I speak English always
> Always with this Glasgow accent
>
> This is right enough[14]

Strikingly absent is any reference to Scotland or Scottish identity politics. The affirmation 'I write' is located within experience that is hesitantly born and bred in Glasgow and yet asserted in English writing whose accent is 'in' Glasgow. Evading identification as Glaswegian, Scottish or British, Kelman instead affirms a commitment to writing that is existentially, linguistically and geographically located. The deft deflation of 'This is right enough' has a humour which is enhanced if the phrase is heard with a Glasgow accent. This use of self-correcting but knowing understatement marks Kelman's precise disaffection from looser modes of expression. He rejects stage dialect or phonetic deviation from some supposedly standard English, offering an existential poetics of writing which attempts to be true to the articulacy of its origins.

Kelman has eschewed more commercial representations of his literary voice, stressing instead the distinctive sense of what it means to come from Glasgow. Concerned with the representation of language as it is spoken in Scotland, his writing is reticent about the range of already politicized or commodified cultural identities thematized by Welsh. Whereas Welsh's characters speak through a system of reference enmeshed in drug culture, pop cultural reference, television, film and musings on generalized ideas of Scottish identity, Kelman's characters are represented within existential problems of everyday life. Moments of experience and agency are articulated as if immanently, from within experience rather than through the imposed categories of identity. Consider the short story 'Governor of the Situation':

> I HATE this part of the city – the stench of poverty, violence, decay, death; the things you usually discern in suchlike places. I dont mind admitting I despise the poor with an intensity that surprises my superiors. But they concede to me on most matters. I am the acknowledged governor of the situation. I'm in my early thirties. Hardly an ounce of spare flesh hangs on me – I'm always on the go – nervous energy – because my appetite is truly gargantuan. For all that, I've heard it said on more than one occasion that my legs are like hollow pins.[15]

Complete in itself, this story's comedy of precise phrasing and inarticulate self-consciousness presents itself as an allegory. Read in the light of Welsh, this might be read as a critique of the idioms of a deluded psychic defence mechanism, the voice of someone who is anything but the governor of their situation. The false assertion of power echoes through the contempt for poverty and the poor. The tissue of delusions builds up a series of minor clichés, from the curiously redundant 'suchlike' in 'suchlike places' to phrases like 'ounce of spare flesh' and 'truly gargantuan'. Each of these minor infelicities implies a critique of the way this person seems unable to acknowledge how little they can govern their language of self-description, concluding with the strangely suggestive image of legs like 'hollow pins'. This begins to read like an allegory of the way petty-bourgeois resentment can be hostile to poverty and yet linguistically and existentially impoverished. There is also a deliberately Kafkaesque quality of understatement. The precision of the punctuation is unobtrusive and yet quietly dramatic, down to the detail of expressions such as 'dont' which lack apostrophes.

Some of the qualities of this passage are reworked in the short story 'John Devine', also from the collection *Greyhound for Breakfast*:

MY NAME is John Devine and I now discover that for the past while I've been going off my head. I mean that the realization has finally hit me. Before then I sort of thought about it every so often but not in a concrete sense. It was actually getting to the stage where I was joking about it with friends! It's alright I would say on committing some almighty clanger, I'm going off my head.

On umpteen occasions it has happened with my wife. Two nights ago for instance; I'm standing washing the dishes and I drops this big plate that gets used for serving cakes, I drops it onto the floor. It was no careless act. Not really. I had been preoccupied right enough and the thought was to do with the plate and in some way starting to look upon it not as a piece of crockery but as something to be taken care of. This is no metaphor; it hasnt got anything to do with parental responsibility. My wife heard the smash and she came ben to see what was up. Sorry, I said, I'm just going off my head. And I smiled. (p. 204)

The extent to which the voice of the title is reiterated in the first line suggests a curious context for this present-tense narration. What might be the context for stating one's name in such an anecdote? The implied address to someone who doesn't know the character's name nevertheless develops into a suggestive intimacy, one in which a number of localized speech idioms begin to resonate. Working backwards it is possible to identify slight markers of English with a Glasgow accent, perhaps most notably in the use of the word 'ben' for 'in', and also the expression 'right enough', already familiar from Kelman's autobiographical note. This story situates itself in a sceptical position, outside the character's self-consciousness. The speech rhythms suggest a subtle precision of narrative self-consciousness brought to bear in a mode of self-correcting accuracy. This in turn suggests an existential displacement as the implied drama of occasions in which it might be appropriate to say 'I'm just going off my head'. The shift from metaphor to concrete sense emerges as a persistent tension, moving from what is now discovered through hesitant negations. The negation in the expression 'It was no careless act' is doubled over into 'Not really'. Moreover, the truth that this was not really carelessness is extended in the remarkable explanation of the thought-process at work in a moment of absentmindedness. The way the piece of crockery is not thought of as a kitchen utensil becomes a question about concern and what it means to take care of a plate. This could be read as a phenomenological inquiry into the language of concern in everyday life. The risk of appearing too imaginative echoes in the claim that this concern is not metaphorical, and in the denial that what is of concern is the weight of parental responsibility. Denial immediately suggests that absentmindedness is indeed something to do with being a parent in relation to a plate, albeit a plate used for 'serving' cakes. The quality of understatement allows the passage to resonate in ways that locate the subtle twists of idiom within an affectionate comedy of language. This comedy nevertheless manages to imply a shift in perspective appropriate for the otherwise unarticulated relations between action, language and self-consciousness. Anecdote is allowed to speak of more profound burdens.

A short story entitled 'Half an hour before he died' from the same volume suggests a more tragic moment of experience, situated, the title implies, on the verge of death. Developed into free indirect discourse, this passage moves carefully between the third-person narration of Mr Millar and a representation of the linguistically mediated consciousness of his final moments:

> ...For a wee while he became convinced he was losing his sanity altogether, but no, it was not that, not that precisely; what it was, he saw another possibility, and it was to do with crossing the edge into a sort of madness he had to describe as 'proper' – a proper madness. And as soon as he recognized the distinction he began to feel better, definitely. Then came the crashing of a big lorry, articulated by the sound of it. Yes, it always had been a liability this, living right on top of such a busy bloody road. He was resting on his elbows still, considering all of it, how it had been so noisy, at all hours of the day and night. Terrible. He felt like shouting on the wife to come ben so's he could tell her about it, about how he felt about it, but he was feeling far too tired and he had to lie back down. (p. 117)

The expressions 'wee while' and more deftly in 'shouting on the wife to come ben so's he could tell her about it' mark out the lightly sketched idiom of the Glasgow accent. The need to tell 'her' about it motivates a narrative explanation for a possible but unspoken address to Mr Millar's wife, an address which is, accordingly, represented in free indirect. Precision with language suggests an anxiety of delusion which is bestilled by reflection. The possibility of mental disturbance and the risk of pathos in a death-bed narration finds its corrective in the developed recognition – developed as a process of linguistic negation in the movement of 'but no, it was not that, not that precisely' – which allows the distinction between 'proper' madness and lost sanity. The sense of acute recognition is carried across the social context of the noisy street and the 'articulated' lorry. This risky pun on how a lorry might be recognized as 'articulated' by its sound, nevertheless turns to the mild defiance of 'bloody' as the expletive which articulates the 'busy road'. The one-word sentence 'Terrible' earns its ambiguities as a gesture of feeling that lacks the energy for shouting. This is closer to the dynamics of late Beckett than to Kafka, but with an acute sense of the social location and understated relation between experience and language. There is a notable resistance to interpretations keen to overstep the significance of a moment of experience.

These brief stories serve to sketch some of the considered literary techniques that make up the texture of Kelman's longer stories and novels. Consideration of the extended fictional temporality of his novels inevitably brings in a range of other problems. Perhaps enough has been shown to suggest how Kelman's politicized aesthetic of the existential situation of working-class experience is written 'in' a Glasgow accent. In each of Kelman's novels the relation between the protagonist's own speech and the narrative voice is thematic. *The Busconductor Hines* is perhaps the most subtle exploration of an extended oscillation between subjective and objective representations of speech, and between second- and third-person narrative voices. In *A Chancer* the central character's inability to develop metaphors is reflected in a sustained and sympathetic pathology of literalism. The contrast in the literary self-consciousness of the central characters in *A Disaffection* and *How late it was, how late* emphasizes the different conditions of everyday dissidence and self-determination. The centrality of such concerns to Kelman's work is confirmed by his most recent novel, *Translated Accounts*. This novel takes accent politics to a new level by narrating fragments of political violence in voices 'translated' by the pseudo-objectivity of a military bureaucracy.

The significance of Kelman's contribution to the political enfranchisement of Scottish voices is his precise reticence in the face of the journalistic culturalism and 'satanic kailyard' of Welsh's work. This essay has exaggerated the differences between Welsh and Kelman through the choice of particular passages. There are nevertheless similarities in the way their writing represents spoken language with Scottish accents through the rhetoric of extended interior monologue. Kelman's more profound political intelligence stems from his nuanced sense of the politics with which such accents figure as writing. Writing, as Kelman understands it, is a resource which can be socialized. The struggle for a new recognition of existing forms of articulacy is not an ironic strategy for localized scandals and extended apolitical cynicism. Welsh's public notoriety and immediacy reflects a more superficial engagement with politics. Kelman's stories dramatize the unexplored articulacy of language as it is spoken, thought and experienced, suggesting different existential orientations to the priorities of the capitalist media. Peter Kravitz has observed that 'The impossibility of staying and the difficulty of leaving is a constant refrain in Kelman's fiction.'[16] This is part of the general thematics of frustration and the desire for emigration in recent Scottish fiction within what might be called the Scottish diaspora. In Kelman's work the articulation of such problems more often remains at the level of domestic difficulties. Such difficulties may appear insignificant but they make up the lived texture of economic and political estrangement. The novels of both Welsh and Kelman lack narrative directions capable of pointing beyond internalized self-destruction and the associated fantasies of escape, but they approach similar ideological obstacles from very different perspectives. Differences at the experiential and linguistic level of analysis in their work point to divergent analyses of accent politics and of writing's potential to articulate political change.

Notes

1   For more details on Kelman's biographical contexts, see Stephen Bernstein, 'James Kelman', *Review of Contemporary Fiction*, 20:3 (Fall, 2000), 42–80.

2   On Kelman's approaches to narrative, see Cairns Craig, *Out of History: Narrative Paradigms in Scottish and British Culture* (Edinburgh: Polygon, 1996); and 'Resisting Arrest: James Kelman', *The Scottish Novel since the Seventies: New Visions, Old Dreams*, eds Gavin Wallace and Randall Stevenson (Edinburgh: EUP, 1993), pp. 99–114. On Welsh, see Willy Maley, 'Subversion and squirrility in Irvine Welsh's shorter fiction', *Subversion and Scurrility: Popular Discourse in Europe from 1500 to the Present*, eds Dermot Cavanagh and Tim Kirk (London: Ashgate, 2000), pp. 190–204.

3   T. W. Adorno, *Minima Moralia*, trans. E. F. N. Jephcott (London: New Left Books, 1974), p. 103. See also Drew Milne, 'James Kelman: dialectics of urbanity', *Writing, Region and Nation*, eds James A. Davies and Glyn Pursglove, *Swansea Review*, 1994 (Conference proceedings, Fourth International Conference on the Literature of Region and Nation, Swansea, 1992), 393–407.

4   On 'swear words' see Allan Harkness, 'The Ideology of Swearing', *Cencrastus*, 17 (1984), 36–42; and Geoffrey Hughes, *Swearing: A Social History of Foul Language, Oaths and Profanity in English* (Oxford: Blackwell, 1992); and Willy Maley, 'Swearing Blind: Kelman and the Curse of the Working Classes', *Edinburgh Review*, 95 (1996), 105–112.

5   For an overview of related issues, see Siobhán Kilfeather, 'Disunited kingdom: Irish, Scottish and Welsh writing in the postwar period', *British*

Culture of the Postwar: an introduction to literature and society 1945–1999 (London and New York: Routledge, 2000), pp. 9–30.

6 Tom Nairn, *After Britain: New Labour and the Return of Scotland* (London: Granta, 2000), p. 13.

7 Ibid., p. 299.

8 Irvine Welsh, *Trainspotting* (London: Secker & Warburg, 1993), p. 75. Subsequent references in the text are to this edition.

9 On the problem of queering Welsh, see Zoe Strachan, 'Queerspotting', *Spike Magazine*, May 1999, <http://www.spikemagazine.com/0599queerspotting.htm>.

10 On 'hate speech', see Judith Butler, *Excitable Speech: A Politics of the Performative* (New York: Routledge, 1997).

11 Peter Kravitz, 'Introduction' to *The Picador Book of Contemporary Scottish Fiction* (London: Picador, 1997), pp. xi-xxxvi, xxxiii.

12 Geoff Gilbert, 'Can Fiction Swear? James Kelman and the Booker Prize', *An Introduction to Contemporary Fiction*, ed. Rod Mengham (Cambridge: Polity, 1999), pp. 219–34, 220. On the Booker Prize, see Richard Todd, *Consuming Fictions: The Booker Prize and Fiction in Britain Today* (London: Bloomsbury, 1996).

13 Irvine Welsh, 'Eurotrash', *The Acid House* (London: Jonathan Cape, 1994), p. 10. Subsequent references in the text are to this edition.

14 James Kelman (with Alex Hamilton and Tom Leonard), *Three Glasgow Writers* (Glasgow: Molendinar Press, 1976), p. 51.

15 James Kelman, *Greyhound for Breakfast* (London: Secker & Warburg, 1987), p. 90. Subsequent references in the text are to this edition.

16 Kravitz, 'Introduction', p. xxv.

Primary texts

James Kelman

(with Alex Hamilton and Tom Leonard), *Three Glasgow Writers* (Glasgow: Molendinar Press, 1976)
Not Not While The Giro and other stories (Edinburgh: Polygon, 1983)
The Busconductor Hines (Edinburgh: Polygon, 1984)
A Chancer (Edinburgh: Polygon, 1985)
Greyhound For Breakfast (London: Secker & Warburg, 1987)
A Disaffection (London: Secker & Warburg, 1989)
How late it was, how late (London: Secker & Warburg, 1994)
Translated Accounts (London: Secker & Warburg, 2001)

Irvine Welsh

Trainspotting (London: Secker & Warburg, 1993)
The Acid House (London: Jonathan Cape, 1994)

Marabou Stork Nightmares (London: Jonathan Cape, 1995)
Ecstasy: Three tales of chemical romance (London: Jonathan Cape, 1996)
Filth (London: Jonathan Cape, 1998)
Glue (London: Jonathan Cape, 2001)

Selected critical texts

Stephen Bernstein, 'James Kelman', *Review of Contemporary Fiction*, 20:3 (Fall, 2000), 42–80

Cairns Craig, *Out of History: Narrative Paradigms in Scottish and British Culture* (Edinburgh: Polygon, 1996)

Edinburgh Review 108 (2001), special issue on 1Kelman and Commitment', eds Ellen–Raïssa Jackson and Willy Maley

Geoff Gilbert, 'Can Fiction Swear? James Kelman and the Booker Prize', *An Introduction to Contemporary Fiction*, ed. Rod Mengham (Cambridge: Polity, 1999), pp. 219–34

Siobhán Kilfeather, 'Disunited kingdom: Irish, Scottish and Welsh writing in the postwar period', *British Culture of the Postwar: an introduction to literature and society 1945–1999* (London and New York: Routledge, 2000), pp. 9–30

Willy Maley, 'Subversion and squirrility in Irvine Welsh's shorter fiction', *Subversion and Scurrility: Popular Discourse in Europe from 1500 to the Present*, eds Dermot Cavanagh and Tim Kirk (London: Ashgate, 2000), pp. 190–204

Drew Milne, 'James Kelman: dialectics of urbanity', *Writing, Region and Nation*, eds James A. Davies and Glyn Pursglove, *Swansea Review*, 1994 (Conference proceedings, Fourth International Conference on the Literature of Region and Nation, Swansea, 1992), 393–407

Zoe Strachan, 'Queerspotting', *Spike Magazine*, May 1999, http://www.spikemagazine.com/0599queerspotting.htm

Gavin Wallace, and Randall Stevenson (eds) *The Scottish Novel since the Seventies: New Visions, Old Dreams* (Edinburgh: Edinburgh University Press, 1993)

11 Caryl Phillips: Colonialism, Cultural Hybridity and Racial Difference

Brad Buchanan

To understand some of the current widespread interest in the idea of cultural hybridity (and Caryl Phillips's attitude towards it) we should first examine the prehistory of the idea that mixing races or cultures is somehow akin to cross-breeding different species. For most of the nineteenth century, the word 'hybrid' was generally understood to be pejorative when referring to a genetic mixture of European and non-European human beings. As E. D. Cope wrote in 1890, 'the hybrid is not as good a race as the white...The highest race of man cannot afford to lose or even to compromise the advantages it has acquired by hundreds of centuries of toil and hardship, by mingling its blood with the lowest.'[1] Indeed, the very term 'hybrid' in this context implies that a mixture of races was really to be understood as a mixture of species. This was a commonly-held notion in the eighteenth and early nineteenth centuries; in 1774 a Jamaican slave-holder named Edward Long published a book entitled *History of Jamaica* in which he claimed that 'there are extremely potent reasons for believing that the White and Negro are two distinct species'.[2] The offspring of racially mixed parents was viewed as an inhuman monstrosity and said to be sexually infertile.[3] Even once it became clear that a human 'hybrid' was in fact able to breed with anyone, the word was employed to describe the children of interracial couplings, who were still deemed 'the moral marker of contamination, failure, or regression'.[4]

Like many former terms of opprobrium and abuse, 'hybrid' has made a comeback in recent years; in current parlance, as Anthony

Easthope points out, 'hybridity', rather than being a purely biological category, might be understood to mean anyone 'having access to two or more ethnic identities'.[5] The most famous and influential theoretical exponent of this new version of hybridity has been Homi K. Bhabha, who celebrates it as an 'interstitial passage in-between fixed identities' which 'entertains difference without an assumed or imposed hierarchy'.[6] The real power of hybridity, in Bhabha's view, is that it splits open the once-monolithic discourse of authority and imperial identity and shows that discourse to be shot through with ambiguities and contradictions.[7]

Many have objected that Bhabha's notion of cultural hybridity rests (rather dubiously) upon his reading of Bakhtin's famous notion of linguistic hybridity and ignores the necessarily historical and material circumstances of cultural 'hybridization', a process these critics say has been thoroughly conditioned by colonialism. There are serious questions about the usefulness of the notion of hybridity in the post-colonial moment. For Ashis Nandy, hybridity 'seems an insufficient basis on which to consolidate new forms of collectivity that can overcome the embeddedness of prior antagonisms'.[8] Indeed, as Jonathan Friedman points out, 'hybrid ideology has been used to dissipate ... resistance by "creolising" ... from above, by actively criticizing ... ethnic essentialism. This is ... the case in Guatemala, where the Maya are in the majority but where their politics is defused by elite conversion to hybridity.'[9] Marxist critics have argued that for those from disadvantaged or marginalized cultures, who find themselves in positions of cultural authority, 'hybridity' enables them to justify their compromise with the dominant capitalist powers. Once outside a cultural elite sphere, Friedman suggests, hybridity is a less attractive condition.

Perhaps partly because Caryl Phillips's fiction takes us into the world of the commonplace, underprivileged cultural 'hybrid', caught in an unglamorous triangle between England, the United States and the Caribbean, it seems to present a pessimistic vision of the notion of hybridity itself. In Phillips's first published work, a play entitled *Strange Fruit* (1981) we meet Errol, a bitter, cruel and confused twenty-one-year-old, the son of a West Indian family living in Britain. Under the influence of American-style black separatism, Errol tries to organize a boycott against British products and services, refusing to work or ride on buses and the tube and so forth in an effort to prove that, as he puts it, 'I'm my own man' (p. 25). In his distrust of anything resembling 'selling out' Errol pours scorn on black milkmen and newscasters as 'Uncle Toms' and rejects his former heroes, black footballers like Laurie Cunningham and Cyrille Regis.[10] Errol even fulminates against rock bands with black and white members: 'These fuckin' mixed bands are a disgrace...What we want is black bands. Black producers and arrangers' (p. 41). While Phillips shows the ridiculous side of Errol's extremism, he has himself expressed similar views in *The European Tribe*, decrying the fact that in modern Britain 'black people have ended up fighting for top posts in the race relations industry. They are effectively "bought out"' (p. 124).[11] In *Strange Fruit* Errol refuses to accept his place in this process of hybridization-by-commodification and instead idealizes the Black Panthers and dreams of emulating the struggles for independence going on in post-colonial Africa and the West Indies. Errol's brother Alvin, who has spent time in both America and the Caribbean, tries to disillusion Errol about the West Indies; he describes 'all the diseases of decolonization', which eat away at their shared land of origin: 'inflation, unemployment, political violence' (p. 69). He also recalls that 'our own relatives, not just any black people' treated him 'Like a stranger in a very strange land, and that's how I felt. Alone, man' (p. 69).[12] Errol refuses to believe this, blaming Alvin for his cool reception at 'home': 'Seems like you turned into a white man as you crossed the International Dateline' (p. 69).

Although Errol's political convictions are evidently serious, they are recent and conflicted enough that he has not managed to rid himself of his English girlfriend, Shelley, who puts up with his ranting, insults and chauvinism.[13] Errol seems more interested in punishing Shelley for the sins of her race than in sustaining a meaningful relationship with her; he taunts Shelley with the fact that 'Your wonderful parents can't handle the idea of their virginal lily-white maiden possibly falling prey to the lascivious clutches of an old black ram. Othello, page sixty one' (p. 34). Shelley recognizes his indifference, but her own family situation is bad enough that she clings to Errol regardless. It transpires that Shelley is pregnant with Errol's child, but she can't work up the nerve to tell him so until the very end of the play. The news merely adds to Errol's growing anguish and desperation; after planning a bank robbery that would fund more subversive political action, he decides to leave for Africa to join some unspecified 'freedom fighters', and Shelley, tired of her alcoholic father and victimized mother, steals money from them and accompanies him on his unlikely crusade. Loaded down with arms he seems to want to smuggle into Africa, Errol proclaims that 'we're all dead men talking to dead men but...My child shall live. It's a sign...A leader is born in the promised land' (p. 96). Despite his morbid enthusiasm and grandiose rhetoric, Errol clearly can't stand the thought of his own child becoming the leader he has failed to be, and his foolish plans may be the symptom of a suicidal impulse which would prevent him from witnessing the triumph of the biological 'hybrid' (the baby with a mixed racial ancestry), whose cultural correlatives he has so long resisted.

There is less overt resistance to the notion of hybridity in *The Final Passage*, Phillips's first novel, but there are no fewer obstacles for it to overcome on its way to being the positive 'third stage' of non-hierarchical relations that Bhabha and others have celebrated. The novel tells the story of Leila, a young woman of mixed English and Caribbean heritage, who follows her husband Michael to England with their infant son Calvin. Despite being part-English, Leila is unable to make the transition from seeing whites in her native land as 'an endangered species' (p. 195) to seeing them as normal human beings in their own element. Among English people she seems caught in an Orwellian nightmare in which 'the eyes of the white people on the posters never left her no matter what' (p. 121); she also grows paler and less vital as her stay in England goes on, until she looks 'like a yellowing snapshot of an old relative, fading with the years' (p. 205). While searching for an apartment, Michael and Leila encounter widespread and overt hostility against 'coloured' tenants and when they finally sign a lease sight unseen, they soon find that their new place is musty, broken-down and filthy. Leila decides to leave England with Calvin, preferring the 'stern predictability' of the Caribbean (p. 203) to England, though she is convinced that one day her own children will board a ship and come back.

Michael reacts very differently to life in England; despite all the prejudice he encounters, he finds odd jobs without too much difficulty and feels that England 'was more than [he] dared to hope for' (p. 169). For Michael, his wife and son take second place to his inherited wish to 'bring back a piece' (p. 40) of England to the Caribbean. He neglects Leila and Calvin, disappearing for long stretches of time and refusing to help out with the maintenance of their apartment.

Leila does make some contact with the working-class neighbourhood in which she finds herself while in England; she gets a job as a ticket collector on a bus, but her presence is greeted with a 'barrage of whistles and chanting' from the working-class men who ride with her (p. 184). Their openly sexual aggression disorients her and she is unable to finish even one day of work. As if to make up for this setback, a local woman named Mary tries to make friends with her, yet Leila refuses to open up to Mary, and by dint of her suspicion and indifference 'was, without even realizing it, making an enemy in her mind of the only real friend she had in England' (p. 189). The only point on which Mary's behaviour meets with Leila's approval has to do with her attitude towards Michael and other coloured men: 'it was as though she was not interested in them, having long since outgrown seeing them as either something to be attracted to or repulsed from' (p. 190). Mary's indifference reassures Leila, who 'had been led to believe that all white women in England loved coloured men' (p. 190).

Phillips seems to use this rather one-sided friendship to question the viability of any alliance between Caribbean immigrants and English people of the sort celebrated by certain theorists. Part of the problem for Leila is the typically English reserve she encounters, seemingly a defence mechanism, which guards against the display of violent and sexual energies once harnessed and indulged by colonialism. For instance, Leila meets an English doctor who reminds her of the civil servants she had worked for at home, 'the white men, who spoke to her with a smile on their face as if afraid that to release it might be interpreted as sexual aggression, or colonial bullying...the sugary smile became a part of their uniform...behind it a man was frightened, not of her but of himself' (p. 152). The impossibility of ever breaking through this mask of self-mistrustful middle-class civility is exacerbated by Leila's inability to find anything much to like in the working-class English people she comes across. This dislike is clearly mutual, as we see when Leila is greeted by the following bit of local graffiti: 'IF YOU WANT A NIGGER NEIGHBOUR VOTE LABOUR' (p. 122). As Leila notices, the lettering of the slogan on the wall 'got smaller and more hurried, as if the artist was running out of paint and time' (p. 122). This graphological remark implies that racist speech is losing momentum and self-confidence in contemporary Britain, but there is clearly no end in sight to the class oppression that pits new immigrants against lower-class English people. The England Leila leaves behind is a divided and demoralizing space, far from the idealized 'third space' imagined by Bhabha as the locus of carnivalesque hybridity.

As if picking up where *The Final Passage* leaves off, Phillips's next novel, *A State of Independence*, follows a West Indian immigrant named Bertram Francis from Britain, where he has spent the last twenty-odd years, back to the Caribbean, where he hopes to rediscover his roots and start a new yet comfortably familiar life. While Bertram is by no means a 'proper' Englishman, he feels immediately alienated upon his return home; for one thing, he is assailed by feelings of 'liberal guilt' of the very sort that 'he had always despised in some English people' (p. 19). The fact that he no longer belongs where he grew up is also apparent to those he meets, such as the taxi driver who reminds him that 'we don't rush things here...I'm often picking up fellars who been living in England...and they coming back here like we must adjust to their pace' (p. 16–17).[14]

Yet Bertram's predicament is not just the product of his own estrangement from his cultural origins; his country is itself in the process of declaring and celebrating its independence from Great Britain, and is caught up in the many paradoxes attendant on this symbolic moment. For one thing, despite its pride at achieving political and economic autonomy, his native land seems to be turning into a parody of Thatcherite Britain; we hear of 'a woman leader popularly known as the Iron Woman of the Caribbean', who seems destined for power (p. 155). Furthermore, it soon becomes apparent that the possibility of establishing domestic culture is also being undermined by a process of Americanization, which Phillips regards as having worked to suppress left-wing politics in the West Indies.

Despite his secret misgivings about his place in this changed country, Bertram remains outwardly optimistic about both his own prospects and those of his rediscovered home; as he says, 'I feel that the time is right and I must seize the opportunity to help the new nation' (p. 50). Bertram seems to view this opportunity in almost exclusively racial terms: 'The only way the black man is going to progress in the world is to set up his own shops and his own businesses independent of the white man...I don't know as yet what kind of business' (pp. 50–1). As this declaration suggests, Bertram identifies himself with 'the black man' against 'the white man', but Phillips is at pains to imply that during his time in England Bertram's imagination has been colonized by the paranoid white fantasy of the black male body as a powerful and unscrupulous piece of sexual machinery. Thinking of his former friend Jackson Clayton's love affair with Patsy Archibald (the woman he left to go to England on a scholarship) he is tormented by 'recurrent visions of Jackson passing his rough hands across [Patsy's] body, then entering her with the sensitivity of an unoiled piston' (p. 142). Clayton and Patsy seem to represent the country's ruling and working classes, respectively, and the fact that they are no longer a couple when Bertram returns suggests that the nation's social body has become irreconcilably torn apart. Clayton's position as a microcosm of the economic and political elite is obvious enough, since he has become rich, joined the government and even seems to be in line to succeed the current prime minister. Patsy's symbolic status is more subtly implied when Bertram sees a copy of a newspaper called *The Worker's Spokesman* in her house, a local publication notable mainly for its 'parochialism', and for stories which concentrate on petty corruption scandals rather than on any broad-based revolutionary ideal. Bertram's replies to Patsy's enquiries about his love life in Britain are noncommittal but hint of West Indians' ambivalent, ambiguous relationships with working-class English people: 'I have somebody in England who is maybe waiting for me to come back, but I think it's just about finish' (p. 149). Any solidarity between the two groups is nearly gone, as Phillips has already implied in *The Final Passage*. In *A State of Independence* Patsy is remarkably welcoming to Bertram and her demeanour is 'peaceful' and unselfconscious; she still carries a vestige of what Bertram calls 'the childhood girl of his dreams' (p. 90). Bertram and Patsy rekindle their long-dormant affair, but the results are strangely deflating, for Bertram; after their long-anticipated sexual encounter 'all his structural and emotional strength was drained away as if her soft female hand had wrenched out the plug of his masculinity' (p. 147).

Knowing that Patsy can be of only limited assistance, Bertram asks Clayton for help in realizing his rather unfocused sense of 'opportunity' and is rudely rebuffed. Clayton reproaches Bertram for having abandoned his home and for assuming he can contribute something to it after his time away; he asks Bertram rhetorically, 'You never did leave this island, my friend, so how it is you think you can suddenly arrive back' (p. 135) and then advises him to 'go back where you come from . . . England is where you belong now' (p. 136). Clayton's insulting advice is the more galling because of his own status as a kind of cultural hybrid, albeit of a more successful kind. Inspired by American activists rather than British educators (like Bertram), a much younger Clayton had gone through a brief period of militancy during which he called himself 'Jackson X' (p. 132) as if in tribute to the famously uncompromising black leader Malcolm X. Furthermore, even as a so-called nationalist politician, Clayton stakes his political career and his personal economic success on the rising tide of pro-American sentiment, taking credit for bringing 'Hollywood' to his constituents (p. 108) and pointing out that Miami, not London, is the closest major city to the island. The novel ends with an announcement that, thanks to Clayton's efforts, 'That evening the people would receive their first cable television pictures, live and direct from the United States' (p. 158).

Although American culture clearly fascinates Phillips and represents for him the inevitable wave of the future for the inhabitants of former British colonies,[15] he was not ready to turn his back on Europe without first giving it his full critical attention, and the result was a book of essays (published in 1987) entitled *The European Tribe*. In this work Phillips recounts his experiences in Northern Ireland, Germany, Holland and other European countries, but his sharpest and most telling comments are directed at the British. First of all, Phillips attacks the British assumption that a large cultural gap exists between them and the Continent, remarking that 'Britain did not seem that different from the rest of Europe, and I was surprised that I had imagined it would' (p. 119). Interestingly enough, Phillips's most stinging attack on 'Britishness' comes in the context of a short essay on Gibraltar, a place which seems to be making an effort to represent 'Britishness' in its most plastic and xenophobic form, as witnessed in its reassuring appeals to tourists ('like you, we're British'). Phillips suggests that Gibraltar is isolated and paranoid enough to be an interesting caricature of contemporary British mores; its Governor and his family impersonate royalty in an 'interesting commercial performance' that Phillips links to that of the English royal family (p. 25), and its inhabitants' general disdain for all things Spanish mirrors a culture in which, as Phillips points out, television shows such as *Fawlty Towers* present Spaniards as buffoons. Gibraltar's 'schizophrenia' reflects that of Britain in general, since it was originally 'induced by colonialism' and continues to be 'fed by the stubbornness of colonial pride' (p. 27). Phillips ends his essay by reminding us that like Gibraltar, which faces a high unemployment rate and waves of unwanted immigrants, Britain is at 'an impasse' where both her former colonies and domestic population are concerned. The ideal of 'Britishness', cherished by the inhabitants of Gibraltar as a last defence against what they see as barbarism, is under siege at its point of origin.

Not surprisingly, given this view, Phillips emphasizes the increasing presence of visible minorities in England and Europe as a whole; he points out that Europe's 'colonial legacy has returned to haunt her... The former slaves wander freely among the rubble of... formerly all-powerful cities' (p. 120). Phillips calls black immigrants in Europe 'missionaries' whose 'permanence in Europe' no longer relies on 'white... tolerance, or the liberal embrace' but on a 'radical demand' that Europeans reassess their own history and its inescapable relationship to people of African descent. For Phillips, Europeanness, and by extension Britishness, cannot be defined or even imagined without reference to the otherness represented by the inhabitants of former colonies. As he puts it, 'strangers... alone reinforce a sense of self... Europe... knows a "nigger" when she sees one: she should – they were a figment of her imagination' (p. 121). The flip side of this argument is that Europe itself is a hybrid creation of those who, like himself, seek to define themselves against or inside it. As Phillips attests, returning to his native St Kitts made him feel at first 'like a transplanted tree that had failed to take root in foreign soil' (p. 9). Yet he soon recognizes that 'the forces that had shaped [my] development were not to be found in the Caribbean... my Caribbean journey heightened an already burning desire to increase my awareness of

Europe' (p. 9). Phillips's fascination with the recent terrors of European history, especially with Anne Frank and the Holocaust, both stems from and feeds his ambivalence about his marginal position: 'If white people could do that to white people, then what the hell would they do to me?' (p. 67).

The irony of it all, in Phillips's mind, is that immigrants like him were not always made to feel like uninvited guests; as he notes, after the Second World War, Britain welcomed 'guest workers' or 'colonial migrants' from the Caribbean. Of course, since then the situation has changed a good deal and, according to Phillips, 'technology makes labour increasingly obsolete' so bills like the 1962 Immigration Act are passed to discourage immigrants from former colonies (p. 122). Enoch Powell's famous 1968 speech predicting 'rivers of blood' is a kind of negative touchstone for Phillips, a sign that even in times of intense political awareness and progressive activity, something at the core of British culture remains intractably racist and violent. Powell's threat made the 1976 Notting Hill riots inevitable, in Phillips's view,[16] and it also set the tone for the entire 1970s, which he calls 'the worst decade since the Second World War to grow up in' and which set the stage for Thatcherism and 'the industrial decline and depression of the 1980s' (p. 2).[17] Furthermore, as economic hardship set in, immigrants became scapegoats for a broader cultural unease, according to Phillips, which manifests itself in the fact that today 'right-wing extremism is on the rise again all over Europe' (p. 123). While Phillips recognizes that fascism tends to appeal most directly to the lower middle class who fear a return to working-class status, he also mistrusts the right-wing sympathies of the working class itself: 'for the working classes, fascism bestows a sense of worth, makes them feel part of a society that is usually unwilling to grant them anything' (p. 124). Phillips's attitude towards the working classes is deeply mistrustful; indeed, he blames his personal and political 'hangups', as he terms them, on having been raised 'in predominantly white working-class areas' of London (p. 3).

Since the appearance of *The European Tribe*, with its contentious, accusatory tone, Phillips has published a number of works touching obliquely on the vexed question of cultural hybridity.[18] *Higher Ground* (1989) and *Crossing the River* (1995) are both three-part novels following the stories of three related characters living on either side of the Atlantic, unable to communicate with each other and unaware that anyone shares their sense of marginality and placelessness. *The Nature of Blood* (1997) juxtaposes the lives of a Jewish concentration camp survivor and an African general serving in the Venetian army in sixteenth-century Europe. However, none of these works engage with the problem of living in and between two cultures in anything like the depth or detail we see in *Cambridge*, a novel published by Phillips in 1992.

Cambridge is Phillips's most sustained and ambitious fictional examination of the problems of cultural hybridity and incompatibility. Set in the early nineteenth century, *Cambridge* revisits the moment of the birth of 'hybridity' as a human category and tells the related but only briefly intersecting stories of Emily Cartwright, an unmarried Englishwoman, and Cambridge, an African slave educated in England. The first and longest section of the book is narrated by Emily as she sails to the Caribbean to visit her father's sugar plantation after the abolition of slavery in British colonies. Emily begins with what she admits is an 'abstract...belief in the iniquity of slavery' (p. 8), and she does not hide her initial admiration for black people, among them the 'negro pilot' of her ship, whose 'navigational prowess and utmost decorum of deportment' make him seem a good deal more 'polished' than the white seamen on board (pp. 17–18). Yet her abolitionist views have not prepared her for what she terms the 'dark unknown' (p. 22) of the Caribbean; she is disturbed by the physical presence of the black children she sees running 'naked as they were born' (p. 24) and claims to have 'taken' these youngsters 'for monkeys' at first (p. 24).

Emily is equally shocked by the apparent looseness of adult 'negro' morality and deportment. Indeed, her abolitionist views are replaced by a conviction that formalized inequality is not only natural and desirable,[19] but also justified by the seductive 'treachery of the negro' (p. 129):

> untravelled thinkers do not comprehend the base condition of the negro. Nor do they appreciate the helplessness of the white man in his efforts to preserve some scrap of moral decency in the face of so much provocation and temptation. (p. 86)

Despite her evident dislike and contempt for blacks, she is equally if not more disgusted by the 'degraded white people' who live among their former servants. To her, they are 'the offscum...very dregs of English life' and, paradoxically, the most telling sign of their depravity, in Emily's eyes, is the fact that 'It is near impossible...to persuade these white people...that blacks are human beings' (p. 51). By locating Emily at this ambiguous crossroads of racism and humanistic sentiment, Phillips is no doubt critiquing the widespread and hypocritical humanitarian rhetoric of the nineteenth century, and perhaps also implying that the ideal of universal humanity (to which status

Emily, rather reluctantly, admits her black companion Isabella) is an elitist one which only serves to cement the 'differences of class' that Emily is eager to observe among 'white people' themselves.[20]

This is not to say that Emily abandons all her former egalitarian principles the moment she comes into contact with people of African descent. She argues that it is because what she (using the familiar generalizing singular) calls 'the negro father' has been forcibly 'deprived of authority and power over his children' that 'he' is 'least attached to his offspring' and that the English are largely to blame for the fact that 'none of the sacred responsibilities which ennoble the relation of child to parent is present in this world' (p. 39). She recognizes that she is not viewing the Africans in their natural state since they, like her, have been sent to the Caribbean for a purpose not their own:[21] 'The blacks are not, it would appear, considered to be native people. They were ... imported from Africa to help ease our labour problem' (p. 24). Indeed, after spending some time in the colony, she blames the Africans only for having largely accepted the system of values that Europeans have imposed on them, especially the 'belief in their own degradation and inferiority', a belief which, she argues, is 'the greatest impediment to their making progress' (p. 105). Phillips presents Emily as a series of unresolved contradictions, as a disillusioned liberal of sorts, who admires the physician Dr McDonald for being 'a man of impartial mind', who does not pander to 'the unprincipled whites' and their violent prejudices, yet who nevertheless recognizes the 'self-evident inferiority' (p. 35) of the blacks.

Mr McDonald, the apparently disinterested observer who (as Emily's admiration suggests) seems to be the stand-in for nineteenth-century scientific rationality, compares black workers to 'animals of the field' (p. 36) and sympathizes with the plight of colonists whose 'moral fibre' has been debased by 'constant association with an inferior race' (p. 52). Mr McDonald is by far the most articulate and representative theorist of cultural and biological hybridity in Phillips's novel, and his remarks to Emily are a fascinating reconstruction of mainstream European views on the subject. Unlike the infamous 'polygenists', who held that Africans and Europeans were wholly different species (and therefore unable to produce viable offspring), McDonald is under no delusion that the children of blacks and whites are sexually infertile, and he warns against miscegenation as a 'social evil'.

McDonald suggests that the 'hybrid' race born from the coerced union of white men and African women are marked for social opprobrium, partly because of their illegitimacy but also because they are deemed to be freaks or aberrations; they are 'a spurious and degenerate breed, neither fit for the field nor for any work that the true-bred negro would relish' (p. 76). The social anomaly of hybridity not only breaks down the seemingly fixed polarities of race but also endangers the supposedly natural division of labour. After all, if whites are the born administrators and the negroes born fieldworkers, their 'hybrid' children cannot be good for anything, since no occupational middle ground seems to exist.

Given the intense anxieties that surround interracial couplings and the position of 'hybrids', it is little wonder that, as McDonald explains,

'The separation of castes in India...is not more formally observed than the careful division of shades in the tropics caused by...race-mixing. The offspring of a white man and a black woman is a *mulatto*; the mulatto and the black produce a *sambo*; from the mulatto and the white comes the *quadroon*; from the quadroon and the white the *mustee*; the child of a mustee by a white man is called a *musteefino*; while the children of a musteefino are free by law, and rank as white persons...' (p. 53)

This system of fine distinctions (which, as McDonald points out, ends up eliding the legal existence of African blood if enough generations of white descendants intervene) shows how arbitrary the designation of 'white' really is, and how desperate is the need to assert it as the desired norm even in persons of mixed race.[22]

Yet Emily also makes it clear that the Caribbean, inevitably, becomes a place of *de facto* cultural hybridity, although the less threatening word 'creole' is used instead of 'hybrid': 'In England the term *creole* is generally meant to describe those of mongrelized origins, but here the term refers to any, black or white, who is either well-seasoned, and thus deemed to have safely entered this new tropical life, or has been born in this zone' (p. 38). It seems that the overwhelming concern with biological interbreeding has opened up a kind of blind spot in which cultural mixing becomes not only accepted but inevitable; by her own admission, Emily herself clearly becomes culturally 'creolized' to some extent. Yet Phillips's apparent concession to the egalitarian, non-hierarchical nature of the process of creolization should not hearten theorists of hybridity too much. In fact, Emily argues that even creolization is simply one more tool of colonialism whereby the otherness of African culture can be elided and incorporated into a Eurocentric worldview:

'with the passage of time, and inter-breeding among the tribes, the single, indistinguishable *creole* black emerges, who, having been in contact with whites from his birth, and having the great advantage of familiarity with only the English language, is less intractable, more intelligent, and less likely to provoke discord . . . this process of creolisation will soon replace all memories of Africa.' (p. 63)

In Emily's eyes, Cambridge is himself an example (albeit a complex one) of how such a process of assimilation by creolization works. Cambridge is sold into slavery to an Englishman who allows him to be educated and converted to Christianity; deeply impressed by the moral strictures of his new faith, he consciously tries to repress all his formerly pleasant memories of Africa, dismissing his birthplace as a hotbed of sinfulness and ignorance: 'already Africa spoke only to me of a barbarity I had fortunately fled' (p. 143). Emily describes Cambridge almost exclusively in connection with his habits of speech, as if he embodied the contradictions of a 'creole' vernacular language created when an African speaks a European tongue. Emily is ordinarily contemptuous of 'the curious thick utterance of the negro', but she reproaches Cambridge for going to the opposite extreme. She comments on Cambridge's 'highly fanciful English' (p. 93) and describes what she calls 'a lunatic precision in his dealings with our English words' (p. 120). Anything other than the usual 'incoherent slobber of negro speech' (p. 123) is madness in the mouth of an African.

While Cambridge's careful enunciation and decorous diction mark him as an oddity, his Christian convictions make him an especially dangerous and rebellious figure in a colonial context where, as Emily points out, religion is generally a threat: 'spiritually educated negroes would suddenly require themselves to be addressed as Paul, and John, even Jesus, and view themselves as equal with the white man in the eyes of the Lord' (p. 97). Unwilling to compromise his values, Cambridge refuses to accept a promotion to a position in which he would be forced to demoralize his fellow Africans; he is soon accused of stealing meat and ends up killing his overseer in self-defence. Predictably, he is executed and left to rot on a gibbet, a grisly reminder of the dangers of being a self-respecting 'creole' in Phillips's starkly divided world. Furthermore, Cambridge's demise is not the only tragic sign of the hopelessness of hybridity in the novel; his only child, conceived with his English wife, dies on delivery (taking its mother with it), and in an epilogue we learn that Emily's baby, whom she calls 'the little foreigner', has also been delivered lifeless (p. 183).

The idea of 'Englishness', of course, as Phillips himself has suggested, is itself hybrid (as a result of successive waves of invaders and immigrants from the Continent and beyond). It is perhaps this very sense of internal hybridity that drove Britain (a term which, tellingly enough, subsumes different national identities under a single imperial ideal) to colonize other areas and stretch its already composite identity to include newer regions around the world. For Phillips, we might say, both history and hybridity originate in England, although he traces them outwards and backwards in time, finding new ways of approaching the collision of cultures that he lived through both as a child (born in St Kitts and raised in London) and as a writer. That he finds little to celebrate and much to lament in this exploration is perhaps one more sign that 'hybridity' as a concept is still deeply marked with the sign of colonialism.

Notes

1   E. D. Cope, 'Two Perils of the Indo-European' in *The Open Court* 3, 1890, 117.

2   Edward Long, *History of Jamaica*, vol. II (London: Lowndes, 1774), p. 336.

3   Samira Kawash, *Dislocating the Color Line: Identity, Hybridity, and Singularity in African-American Narrative* (Stanford, CA: Stanford University Press, 1997), p. 5. Kawash remarks that the question of hybridity was at the centre of the most contentious debate in nineteenth-century race theory. This debate revolved around the question as to whether different races represented different species (polygenesis) or were the same species developing along different paths (monogenesis). As Kawash remarks, the term *mulatto* is linked to the efforts to prove 'scientifically' a permanent and absolute racial division, and it derives from a reference to the sterile hybridity of the mule.

4   Nikos Papastergiadis, 'Tracing Hybridity in Theory' in *Debating Cultural Hybridity: Multi-Cultural Identities and the Politics of Ant-Racism*, eds Pnina Werbner and Tariq Modood (London: Zed Books, 1997), p. 257.

5   Anthony Easthope, 'Bhabha, hybridity and identity' in *Textual Practice* 12 (2), 1998, 341–2

6   Homi K. Bhabha, *The Location of Culture* (London: Routledge, 1994), p. 4.

7   Bhabha, *Location of Culture*, p. 113. Bhabha writes that 'a colonial difference . . . is the effect of uncertainty that afflicts the discourse of power, an uncertainty that estranges the familiar symbol of English "national" authority and emerges from its colonial appropriation as the sign of its difference'. Hybridity represents 'a disturbing questioning of the images and presences of authority'.

8   Ashis Nandy, *The Intimate Enemy: Loss and Recovery of Self under Colonialism* (Delhi: Oxford University Press, 1983) p. 274.

9   Jonathan Friedman, 'Global Crises, the Struggle for Cultural Identity and Intellectual Porkbarrelling: Cosmopolitans Versus Locals, Ethnics and Nationals in an Era of De-Hegemonization' in *Debating Cultural*

Hybridity: Multi-Cultural Identities and the Politics of Ant-Racism, eds Pnina Werbner and Tariq Modood (London: Zed Books, 1997), p. 82.

10   Caryl Phillips, *Strange Fruit* (Ambergate: Amber Lane Press, 1981), p. 62. Amusingly, Errol takes reluctant pride in the fact that 'England are getting some more black players in the squad'. In many of Phillips's works, sport comes close to offering a space where the English and their former colonial subjects can coexist peacefully.

11   Jonathan Friedman has argued that 'the hybridity celebrated in Cultural Studies has little revolutionary potential, since it is part of the very discourse of bourgeois capitalism and modernity which it claims to displace' (p. 104). This bourgeois discourse would seem to include the 'buying out' strategies of what Phillips calls 'the race relations industry'.

12   Alvin has a gloomy view of cultural hybridity, asking: 'What am I supposed to do'... Live on a raft in the middle of the Atlantic at a point equidistant between Africa, the Caribbean and Britain' (*Strange Fruit*, p. 99).

13   As Shelley says, Errol is 'always on about a woman's place and the man being the "hunter"' (*Strange Fruit*, p. 15).

14   Caryl Phillips, *The European Tribe* (New York: Farrar, Straus, Giroux, 1987), p. 123. He comments elsewhere that 'the first-generation immigrant begins to develop at twice the speed of the country that he has left behind. This virtually ensures that it will be impossible for him to return.'

15   Phillips, *European Tribe*, pp. 120–1. As Phillips says, 'America...the young, arrogant country to which the second-rate Europeans, the crooks, the poor, the starving, the inferior minds and the misfits, escaped...has conquered Europe economically, politically, and culturally'. Phillips also seems to attribute America's ascendancy to the very mixture of races and cultures he depicts as unfruitful in the post-colonial age. No doubt Phillips would wish to distinguish between different kinds of cultural hybridity; he certainly seems to prefer the self-professedly egalitarian 'melting pot' of American life.

16   Phillips, *European Tribe*, p. 127. He argues, 'Rioting is...part of a long tradition of violent response to ignorant rejection.'

17   This decade, however, also saw more positive signs of the acceptance of black Britons into the mainstream; as Phillips notes in *The European Tribe*: 'the mid-1970s were also the years of Bob Marley and the Wailers, the film *Pressure*, and the emergence of black footballers and sportsmen' (p. 3).

18   Recently Phillips edited *Extravagant Strangers* (1997), a book of essays about black writers in English literature and published *The Atlantic Sound* (2000), a non-fictional work on the slave trade.

19   She claims in *Cambridge* that 'the greatest fear of the black is not having a master whom they know they can turn to in times of strife' (p. 37).

20   As she complains in *Cambridge*: 'In this West Indian sphere there is amongst the white people too little attention paid to differences of class.

A white skin would appear passport enough to a life of privilege, without due regard to the grade of individuals within the range of that standing' (p. 72).
21 Emily's widowed father has planned that she should return to England and marry a well-to-do man named Thomas Lockwood, who was to be her 'mode of transportation through life' (*Cambridge*, p. 3).
22 Hence Emily asserts that, 'the more white blood flowing in a person's veins, the less barbarous will be his social tendencies' (p. 25).

Primary texts

Strange Fruit (Ambergate, Derbyshire: Amber Lane Press, 1981)
Where There is Darkness (Ambergate: Amber Lane Press, 1982)
The Shelter (Oxford: Amber Lane Press, 1984)
The Final Passage (London: Faber and Faber, 1985)
A State of Independence (London: Faber and Faber, 1986)
The European Tribe (New York: Farrar, Straus &, Giroux, 1987)
Playing Away (London: Faber and Faber, 1987)
Higher Ground (London: Viking, 1989)
Cambridge (London: Bloomsbury, 1991)
Crossing the River (London: Bloomsbury, 1993)
Extravagant Strangers (London: Faber and Faber, 1997)
The Nature of Blood (London: Faber and Faber, 1997)
The Atlantic Sound (London: Faber and Faber, 2000)

Selected critical texts

Bill Ashcroft, Gareth Griffiths, and Helen Tiffin, *The Empire Writes Back: Theory and Practice in Post-Colonial Literatures* (London: Routledge, 1989)
C. Rosalind Bell, 'Worlds Within: An Interview with Caryl Phillips' in Callaloo 14, 3, Summer 1991
Homi K. Bhabha, *The Location of Culture* (London: Routledge, 1994)
Carol Margaret Davison, 'Crisscrossing the River: An Interview with Caryl Phillips' in *Ariel: A Review of International English Literature* 25, 4, October 1994
Paul Gilroy, *There Ain't no Black in the Union Jack* (Chicago, Ill.: University of Chicago Press, 1991)
Stuart Hall, 'Cultural Identity and Diaspora' in *Identity: Community, Culture, Difference*, ed. Jonathan Rutherford (London: Lawrence & Wishart, 1990)
Claude Julien, 'The Diaspora and the Loss of Self in Caryl Phillip's Fiction: Signposts on the Page' in *Palara* 1, Fall 1997

Ivan Kreilkamp, 'Caryl Phillips: The Trauma of "Broken History"' in *Publishers' Weekly* 244, 17, April 1997

Deborah Madsen, (ed.) *Post-Colonial Literatures: Expanding the Canon* (London: Pluto Press, 1999)

Hanz Okazaki, 'On Dislocation and Connectedness, in Caryl Phillips's Writing' in *The Literary Criterion* 26, 3, 1991

Charles P. Sarvan et al, 'The Fictional Works of Caryl Phillips: An Introduction' in *World Literature Today* 65, 1, Winter 1991

Kay Saunders, 'Caryl Phillips' in *Kunapipi* 9, 1, 1987

Raimund Schaffner, 'Assimilation, Separatism and Multiculturalism in Mustapha Matura's *Welcome Home Jacko* and Caryl Phillips's *Strange Fruit*', *Wasafiri* 29, Spring 1999

Graham Swift, 'Caryl Phillips' in *Kunapipi* 13, 3, 1991

Robert Young, *Colonial Desire: Hybridity in Theory, Culture and Race* (London: Routledge, 1995)

——, *White Mythologies: Writing History and the West* (London: Routledge, 1990)

Part IV

Pathological Subjects

Part IV
Introduction

After 1979, contemporary life came to be regarded as a field of tension and conflict. Writers confronted urban decay, immense wealth and privileges and the stark facts of war and conflict. Thatcherite individualism emerged in a period when a stable sense of social identity was difficult to maintain. Martin Amis's protagonist in *Time's Arrow* (1991) reflects certain aspects perhaps of the author's own British sensibility: 'I puzzle at the local economy, the commerce, the apologetic arrangements of the ignored, of the cooled city. [...] In fact I've had to conclude that I am generally rather slow on the uptake. Possibly even subnormal, or mildly autistic.'[1] Personal pathology and public space combine. The search for identity can be seen to bring the individual into collision with the curious objects that are other subjects. As Geoffrey H. Hartman says in *The Fateful Question of Culture*, 'The search for identity, which never seems to cease, plays its role in this strong and potentially pathological fantasy that others live my life, a life I want to live – fully – myself.'[2]

This captures something of the instability of subjectivity that may be regarded as a common theme and motif in much of contemporary British fiction, while one strand of this broader characteristic might be described effectively as the pathological. The term refers strictly to the disorder of the body or mind. However, in a fuller sense, the pathological can be thought of in relation to the disordered state of the individual within society, often involving an intense sense of dislocation. In this manner, there is something like a contemporary fiction of pathology, in which the individual becomes prone to extravagant, immoral impulses or involved in situations that they often feel strangely detached from. Such characters find themselves at odds with the social norm, drawn to actions that highlight the oddity and falseness both of the political and social environment that they confront and of their own inadequate responses. These are individuals who are marginalized, peculiar, and yet oddly and perversely comic. The contemporary fiction of pathology draws upon a tradition seen in the work of Evelyn Waugh, Anthony Burgess and B. S. Johnson, among others. Their protagonists, and those of their successors, Amis, Carter, Winterson and Ishiguro, operate in a space that is often determined by desire, perversity and sexual abandon in a contest with containment, tradition and self-negation. These writers offer a different way of reading social interaction, the space it inhabits and the subjectivities involved. The pursuit of the bizarre makes the accepted norm something other than the reader may well have assumed. As Pierre Bourdieu says in *In Other Words: Essays Towards a Reflexive Sociology*: 'The interactions, which are accepted at their face value by people of an empiricist disposition – one can observe them, film them, record them, in short they are tangible – conceal the structures that are realized in them. It's one of those cases in which the visible, that which is immediately given, conceals the invisible which determines it. One thus forgets that the truth of the interaction is never entirely to be found in interaction as it is available to observation.'[3] Pathological reflexes can offer a sense of this truth-revealing quality. Satirical, reflective and polemical impulses are at the heart of this mode of fiction with its themes of estrangement. If the modern British social environment after Thatcher is an individualist one, it is one of an ego under threat. The fiction that charts its responses most adequately takes pathology as its central narrative trope.

Notes

1   Martin Amis, *Time's Arrow* (London: Jonathan Cape, 1991), p. 29.
2   Geoffrey H. Hartman, *The Fateful Question of Culture* (New York: Columbia University Press, 1997), p. 21.
3   Pierre Bourdieu, *In Other Words: Essays Towards a Reflexive Sociology*, trans. Matthew Adamson (Cambridge: Polity, 1990), p. 127.

12 The Fiction of Angela Carter: The Woman Who Loved to Retell Stories

Robert Eaglestone

The chances are, the story was put together in the form we have it, more or less, out of all sorts of bits of other stories long ago and far away, and has been tinkered with, had bits added to it, lost other bits, got mixed up with other stories, until our informant herself has tailored the story personally, to suit an audience of, say, children, or drunks at a wedding, or bawdy old ladies, or mourners at a wake – or simply, to suit herself.

Angela Carter, *The Virago Book of Fairy Tales*

I am all for putting new wine in old bottles, especially if the pressure of the new wine makes the old bottles explode.

Angela Carter, *Shaking a Leg*

Angela Carter's novels, short stories, her work of cultural history, and even some of her journalism all work by retelling stories. And retelling a story, with an eye to what has been ignored or left out, is not the same as simply telling it again. She reworks and repatterns the culture of (mainly) the European past in all its forms – literary and non-literary, elitist and popular, opera and pulp fiction, classical epics and movies, comic books and folklore – and, in this process of putting new wine in old bottles, she brings to light the 'old lies on which the new lies have been based',[1] and has a great time doing it.

Actually, she simply can't resist retelling. That's just how she thinks, how she writes ('I write the way I write because that's the way I write').[2] In a review of the cult-horror pulp writer H. P. Lovecraft, a minor piece of her writing, she discusses how he invents scholarly or magical books in his stories (the *Necronomicon* and others) and then bursts into narrative: 'One could write a very Lovecrafty tale about the arrival at his door, late, very late one night of a (preferably) demented student clutching in his hand a copy of the dreaded *Necronomicon*...shocked horror for the master, who never thought the vile thing existed...Opening the pages with trembling fingers, he discovers cryptic marginalia on the time-seared pages, penned what centuries ago in what fearful city yet, *unmistakably, in his own handwriting*'.[3] Here we have a recognizably Carter tale in three paragraphs, using an already established series of devices (the book, the student, the master of horror, Lovecraft), reusing clichés to establish where we are and then reshaping them;[4] the mixture of 'fiction' and 'reality' (twice – a 'fictional' book, a real book; a real writer as a character as a real writer); a twist in which the characters discover that the book – the story – has been in control all along without them knowing, which in turn reveals how Lovecraft is constrained by his own choice of genre, how it comes to haunt and delimit his work (the student comes to the master: 'We hates y'all with the tape recorders', says a character in a later story. 'Reckon us folks thinks you is dancing on our graves)'.[5] The old bottles explode. This is how Carter writes, and because writing is thinking, how she thinks.

Because she thinks, her writing/retelling is always subversive: not following a party line or programme, but upsetting any such programme. Her last novel, *Wise Children*, is an assault on what Fay Weldon in her *Letters to Alice* calls 'Castle Shakespeare'. It doesn't attack Shakespeare himself but the huge institution of Shakespeare which is woven into the British establishment. It is the story of the twin illegitimate daughters of the Melchior Hazard, 'Mr British Theatre himself'.[6] Where he acts in the classics, his daughters are a song and dance act; where his legitimate family lives near Regent's Park in stylish North London, the twins live in down-at-heel Brixton, a part of the city 'the tourist rarely sees'.[7] Throughout the novel, the dark glamour of the serious and the tragic is interrupted by the comic; the abstract and pretentious cut down to size by the practical everyday. What is revealed is not only the joy of singing and dancing – common music hall – but the cruel façades of the great institutions. This practice, this retelling from below, is what almost all Carter's work does – and it does it because of the central importance Carter gives to stories.

What do stories do?

The original painter or the original writer proceeds on the lines of the oculist. The course of treatment they give us by their painting or by their prose is not always pleasant. When it is at an end the practitioner says to us: 'Now look!'. And, lo and behold, the world around us (which was not created once and for all, but is created afresh as often as an original artist is born) appears to us entirely different from the old world but perfectly clear.

Marcel Proust, *The Guermantes Way*

Language is power, life and the instrument of culture, the instrument of domination and liberation.

Angela Carter, *Shaking a Leg*

The world and ourselves as beings in the world are made up through culture, or, more simply, through stories. That is not to say that your existence is simply a story, or your body just words strung together (it clearly isn't: you feel pain, desire and so on): it is to say, though, that how you understand that existence, your sense of yourself, your relationships with others, with the world, with the choices you make, are stories. These stories are in part of your own making and in part forced upon you by others (and 'identity' is the negotiation of these two forces). These stories come in different shapes and sizes. Some are very large indeed, and have in them many smaller stories. (For example, the story called 'Progress' tells us that the human race is improving on all fronts, scientifically, politically and so on, and picks out particular examples: taking men to the moon, civil rights). Some are less global: our sense of our own gender, and how we should behave and regulate ourselves, for example, are put together through the stories and images that present gender in a huge array of forms. We are not simply victims of these stories, however. Stories construct us and are, in turn, something we ourselves construct. We are both the *objects* created by narratives and the *subjects* who, in turn, create them, acting out (or declining to act out) stories and set behaviours. Narratives are both *pedagogical* – taught to us at home, at school, in the community – and *performative*, performed, acted out and 'done' by us in all sorts of ways: shaping and shaped.

Are these stories true or false? A hard question. Some we can check against the stories from our experience: if I tell you (a story) that hammers never fall, you can easily prove me wrong by showing me a falling hammer (if I accept this as proof). If I tell you that you should behave in a certain way, only another story will justify your refusal to do so (if justification is important: it may not be). If the 'central issue of all philosophy' is, as Isaiah Berlin claims, 'the distinction between words (or thoughts) about words and words (or thoughts) that are about things', it is possible to see that each produces different sorts of stories.[8] But the point, in this context at least, is that a true story or a false story are still both stories, still ways of ordering both yourself and the world: the 'story is always real as story' Carter says.[9]

However, what is crucial in this is that not all stories and not all identities are given equal weight: they exist in a world of unequal power relations. Some stories are passed over, or not told, or cannot be told because the resources that enable telling – material and cultural – are not available ('one cannot, in reason, ask a shoeless peasant in the Upper Volta to write songs like Schubert's'[10]). Other stories, more powerful, exclude or ignore, or use part of their power to disempower others, often using abstract terms to do so: Frantz Fanon writes of 'this Europe where they are never done talking of Man, yet murder men everywhere they find them' and clearly states 'with what sufferings humanity has paid for every one of [Europe's] triumphs of the mind'.[11]

In some of Angela Carter's non-fiction writing and journalism, she traces the power of stories. This is the strategy of *The Sadeian Woman*, her essay in 'cultural history', concentrating on pornography and sexuality. The book argues that sexuality 'is never expressed in a vacuum... Sexuality is as much a social fact as it is a human one', stressing how sexuality is a narrative constructed in society 'through social fictions'.[12] She goes on to suggest that, from pornography, especially Sade's pornography, 'we can learn as much about the cultural conditions that help to determine women's sexuality as we can about men's sexuality' (one might add: *heterosexual* women's sexuality).[13] 'Cultural conditions' here means, roughly, the stories and models available. Because, in part, it is one of the first writings in the Western European tradition not 'to see female sexuality in terms of its reproductive function',[14] Sade's work represents important and perhaps founding stories (again, these are stories, neither true nor false) about female sexual behaviour.[15] By examining Sade's thought and his stories, light is cast on how those stories are retold today. Sade's Justine – the 'Good Bad Girl'[16] – becomes, through the movement of cultural processes, the model for Marilyn Monroe, in turn the model for countless other performances of sexuality.

Carter writes, for example, that this model of female sexuality 'does not know how to desire. She is always prey, never the hunter... She must not take her own allure seriously. She must laugh it off'.[17] Juliette, Justine's sister, is the 'profane whore' – Jane Russell, the Bad Bad Girl. Carter aims to show how these stories control and regulate women's behaviour. She wants to show, however, that they are stories – not truths but shapes – and so can be rewritten, reorganized. Where Sade 'goes wrong' is that he is a libertine concerned only with his own arrival into 'the Utopia of desire', the orgasm: she describes this as a 'diabolic solitude', and because the libertine is trying to escape from society where there is only a 'holy terror of love', no love in itself.[18] Her postscript, cited from the revolutionary Emma Goldman (who 'was right about most things')[19] argues that a 'true conception of the relation between the sexes will not admit of conqueror and conquered; it knows of but one great thing: to give of one's self boundlessly, in order to find oneself richer, deeper, better'.[20] But if her non-fiction often traces the condition of the present back through its stories to the past – the 'old lies on which the new lies have been based' – her fiction does something more than this.

What does Angela Carter do with stories?

> Despite its appearance of solidity, realism implies a fundamental unease about self, society and art... Realists take upon themselves a special role as mediator, and assume self-consciously a moral burden that takes a special form: their responsibility is to a reality that increasingly seems 'unnameable'... but it is also to an audience that requires to be weaned or freed from the misnaming literatures past and current. The quest for the world beyond words is deeply moral, suggesting the need to reorganize experience and reinvest it with value for a new audience.
>
> George Levine, *The Realist Imagination; English Fiction from Frankenstein to Lady Chatterley*

Angela Carter is often discussed as a 'magical realist', 'postmodernist' or a 'mannerist', yet she might be equally easily said to be a realist, not least because all these forms or writings claim to be more 'real' than realism. This is because realism is traditionally thought to suggest, implicitly, that there is a real world, with social and cultural norms that can be represented in clear, narrative, mimetic prose. In fact, Carter believed that what we take to be the 'real' world is simply the result of the most powerful stories. Not that there are no bodies or no pain – there clearly are – but that the understanding of these, in what we call the real world, is not in fact real at all but always already mediated through these stories. In order to change the world, either intentionally as part of a programme, or simply by making a voice heard that is usually passed over or ignored, you need to tell stories that challenge these assumptions, to reorganize experience. In *Shaking a Leg* Carter said that she was aiming to create

> a means of expression for an infinitely greater variety of experience than has been possible heretofore, to say things for which no language previously existed ... transforming actual fictional forms to both reflect and to precipitate changes in the way people feel about themselves – putting new wine in old bottles, and, in some cases, old wine in new bottles. (p. 42)

Her work is part of an attempt to offer new worlds and new choices though poesis – artistic making – like the Proustian artist/oculist cited above. As she says herself, of Colette, one of her heroines, 'if you can't win, change the rules of the game' (p. 519), change not just what you see but how you see. One of the paradoxes about the traditions of realism is that it is not really real, only a way of writing that fits a certain understanding of what the real is. Angela Carter believed that this 'real' trampled on the weak and powerless, so she sought to challenge it. This is the reason that she found something (but not much) to be admired in D. H. Lawrence (those 'novels express the vitality and the bewilderment of an emergent class, for whom there were no guidelines laid down, who were engaged in a new way of living. People for whom Lawrence was the Messiah and F. R. Leavis his John the Baptist', p. 534) and the reason she so admired Joyce ('Joyce ... decolonialized English ... and in doing so he made me ... free ... he detached fiction from one particular ideological base', p. 539).

This explains why she tells stories, not why she *retells* them, yet it is the retelling that is central to her work. She retells for a number of reasons. First, this is to do with the nature of cultural forms. How do new cultural forms – pop music, say, or the novel – come about? They are not the invention of isolated individuals. 'Creativity,' Mary Midgely writes, 'is unrealistically thought of as a private process of generation ex nihilo' (*from nothing*).[21] Cultural forms develop from the evolution of cultures (in fact, cultural forms *are* the evolution of those cultures – a culture is its cultural forms, after all). Sometimes these evolutions result in great bursts of creative energy often due to material and intellectual changes (what is called the Renaissance, for example) but more usually 'perhaps' they happen as the result of the mixing of one culture with others (although no culture has ever been hermetically sealed). Salman Rushdie writes that newness enters the world through 'hybridity, impurity, intermingling, the transform-ations that come of new and unexpected combinations of human beings, cultures, ideas, politics, movies, songs...Mélange, hotch-potch, a bit of this and a bit of that'.[22] Newness, then, is retelling, drawing, mosaic-like, on a range of different cultural forms. For Rushdie that mixing comes as a result of the experience of Empire, decolonization, globalization and mass migration.

For Carter, the hybridity comes from mixing those stories usually excluded from the narratives of power (principally for Carter, the stories of women's experience) with the powerful narratives. This means that, while Rushdie has a range spanning (at least) Europe, America and India, Carter's range of reference, despite her time in Japan, is more specifically European and (in her later work) American. She is able to 'loot and rummage' in a European cultural past, and in American culture.[23] Her story 'John Ford's A Pity She's a Whore' draws on both British high culture (John Ford, renaissance playwright) and John Ford (US director, principally of westerns). Of course, she is aware of this: 'I am a pure product of an advanced, industrialized post-imperialistic country in decline' she says[24] and again, 'I write about the condition of my life'.[25] But even her Englishness is 'English in the great tradition of music hall and penny dreadful, seaside pierrot show and pantomime, of radical dissent and continuous questioning, the other side of imperialism, if you like'[26] as she writes of Michael Moorcock. She writes novels and short stories, because these are the forms that she has chosen and are open to her (she could not, for example, compose Balinese dances), and she draws on the cultural resources that come to hand. This is also why she make no distinctions between high and low culture. In this mixing, no one cultural form has dominance: 'If fairy tales are the fiction of the poor, then perhaps *Paradise Lost* is the folklore of the educated'.[27]

Secondly, retelling is the appropriate mode for what she wishes to achieve. If the aim is to transform how people see themselves, to transform narrative and cultural understandings, then it is through the reworking of these cultural understandings that this must take place. Carter is aware, I think, that this is Western, or even European, or even an English understanding: the 'novel, which is my chosen form, has existed as such in *Europe* for only two or three hundred years' she says (my emphasis).[28] But the demand for literature to

'Be Universal! Be Universal!' is part of the power structure that Carter wishes to eschew (thus, for example, the importance of particular locations in her last two novels: south London, specifically, in *Wise Children*, Brixton SW2).[29]

Thirdly, her point is not so much that these voices are new, that these are new stories, but that the stories and experiences have always been there, passed over. It is by going over again the culture that has been inherited that this is seen most clearly. The rewriting is a way of investigating 'the social fictions that regulate our lives – what Blake called the "mind forg'd manacles"', especially, for Carter, those stories about gender. By retelling a story, and taking it over from the inside by drawing attention to its blindnesses and what it passes over, Carter is able not only to create a new story but also to deconstruct the old one. Her stories, at least from the 1970s on, are committed to this deconstruction of other stories.

What does this mean, deconstruction? Surely, deconstruction is a sort of philosophy or a sort of literary criticism? No: deconstruction is not a method of anything, or a philosophy of anything. Deconstruction is a response to a text that bears in mind the 'other' which the text excludes or covers up. An act of deconstruction is always a particular, unique act that is involved with, parasitic upon, another text. It can come in any form that is suitable to the text to which it is responding. Jean Rhys's *Wide Sargasso Sea* rewrites and so deconstructs *Jane Eyre*, using the voice of Bertha Mason, unheard and marginalized in Charlotte Brontë's text.[30] Jacques Derrida deconstructs works of philosophy in a philosophical style: Angela Carter deconstructs stories in a narrative style. ('Oh Hell. What I *really* like doing is writing fiction and trying to work things out that way.')[31] Deconstruction objects to purity and closed-off stories: Angela Carter's narratives are full of odd disjunctures, the bursting of the concrete into fairy tales ('I felt I had the right to retain sufficient funds to start a little music school' says a retold fairy-tale character),[32] of fairy tales into the concrete ('Then she spread out her superb, heavy arms in a backwards gesture of benediction and, as she did so, her wings spread too, a polychromatic unfolding fully six feet across, spread of an eagle, a condor, an albatross') and back again ('"I dye, sir"! "What?" "My feathers, sir! I dye them! Don't think I bore such gaudy colours from puberty. I commenced to dye my feathers at the start of my public career on the trapeze, in order to simulate more perfectly the tropic bird."')[33]

As I have suggested Carter does, deconstruction does not so much create new systems or stories as go back over stories and systems to uncover what has been covered up: Derrida argues that 'the passage

beyond philosophy does not consist in turning the page of philosophy... but in continuing to read philosophy in a certain way'.[34] For
Carter, read: 'retelling stories does not consist in inventing wholly new
stories (even if this were possible) but in continuing to retell stories in
a certain way'. Deconstruction argues that the context is vital for
understanding a text, that the text draws everything into it: Carter's
novels pull on, refract and reflect a huge range of contexts and, in the
later work especially, are clear about their own contexts as novels –
novels that know they are novels. Deconstruction is a way of worrying
about limits and borders between things (the world, philosophy,
fiction, politics, gender), including worrying about its own borders
and practices. And Carter does worry. In an interview she said:

> my fiction is very often a kind of literary criticism, which is something
> I've started to worry about quite a lot. I had spent a long time acquies-
> cing very happily with the Borges idea that books were about books,
> and then I began to think: if all books are about books, what are the
> other books about? Where does it all stop?.... Books about books is
> fun but frivolous.[35]

In fiction, similarly, in *Wise Children*:

> 'Life's a carnival,' he said. He was an illusionist, remember.
> 'The carnival's got to stop, some time, Perry,' I said. 'You listen to the
> news, that'll take the smile off your face.'
> 'News? What news?' (p. 222)

Derrida, as a point of comparison, wrote: 'never before, in absolute
figures, have so many men, women and children been subjugated,
starved, or exterminated on the earth'.[36]

Does this mean that you have to read Derrida to understand or
enjoy Angela Carter? Of course not! It doesn't even mean that Carter
read Derrida or that Derrida read Carter.[37] But it does mean that
there are some affinities between the two, and that, for a label, if you
really wanted one, you could call Angela Carter a deconstructive
writer or, equally fairly (these things go both ways), Derrida a Carter-
esque philosopher.

This deconstruction of previous stories, which simultaneously rewrites them and shows up their blind-spots, is not the work of an
ideologue or a propagandist, however. Contrary to one review/obitu-
ary, Carter's imagination was not 'the obedient handmaid of ideology'[38] and this is the reason why many critics, from many different
positions, had (and still have) profound doubts and worries about her

work. Sarah Bannock, echoing Lorna Sage, writes that for 'feminist and non-feminist alike...who wish to establish political or cultural orthodoxies upon which to build a theory of gender or identity', her work is 'hard to take'.[39] In fact, her work never reached conclusions in a straightforward way and so can't be put simply to the service of any critical approach. This is not only because of her early death at fifty-one, nor because she immersed herself in reading and responding to evolving intellectual debates, although both these are true. It is because her own work and thought are constantly questioning, guided by her realization of the significance of social fictions, and rarely offer answers that last for long before the next question. There are, perhaps, a few guiding principles. As I have suggested, the texts are motivated by a desire to offer a voice to the voiceless, to uncover the stories of those covered over, and to reshape these in new ways. She is always on the side of the less powerful against the powerful, and in her context, as she freely admits, she is mainly concerned with women's experience.

Angela Carter's writing is also guided by what she calls 'an absolute and committed materialism – i.e. that this world is all that there is, and in order to question the nature of reality one must move from a strongly grounded base in what constitutes reality'.[40] While it's true that her work doesn't have transcendental or religious themes, it isn't strictly materialist in a political (say, Marxist) sense. In one of her final stories, *Burning your Boats*, a voice in the first person suddenly emerges (the narrator?) and asks, 'In the beginning was...what? Perhaps in the beginning there was a curious room...crammed with wonders; and now the room and all it contains are forbidden you, although it was made just for you, had been prepared for you since time began, and you will spend all your life trying to remember it' (p. 401). But, if not materialist in an orthodox way, Carter's work is concerned with the needs of the world: to eat, sleep, shag, go to the toilet ('Sleeping Beauty' in *Nights at the Circus* 'evacuates a small, semi-liquid motion into the bedpan Fanny held under her', p. 64), escape pain and fear, earn money (Fevvers banked every penny she earned as an aerialist). A great deal of the humour and pathos comes from precisely the interruption of the abstract with the concrete.

Conclusion: After Carter

Elaine Jordan, perhaps Carter's most acute reader, argues that the sort of 'dymythologizing' that Carter goes in for – stemming not only from her materialism but from her need to retell the story from another point of view – operates 'like a myth itself': whether stories are 'liberatory or oppressive depend on the existing power relations, the company it keeps, the context of its use'.[41] So it's perhaps worth pointing out that Carter's work has not gone unquestioned. Her own 'blind-spots' (over homosexuality, for example, or the links between animals and female sexuality) have been highlighted, explored and argued over. But this is how things should be. Angela Carter's work as a whole is not an orthodoxy, like a political creed, or a firm and final statement of beliefs set as a novel. It is an evolving, moving series of gestures and thoughts, a series of questions asked, answered and asked again in the form of stories. That it is a movement, in turn part of larger stories, is itself a success.

Carter's aim of telling stories usually left untold is one shared by many writers, so it would be hard – if not foolish – to suggest that she had been a specifically powerful influence on particular writers who do this. (The sort of writers who, as Carter remarks pointedly, feature 'your proper old-fashioned char-lady',[42] ignore her work). Her influence is clearer in 'genre fiction' and so-called 'low' cultural forms. In science fiction, the work of Sherri Tepper, concerned with gender, the concrete against the abstract and demythologizing, is clearly influenced by Carter. *Grass* (1989) is an SF version of 'Beauty and the Beast' 'except that the beast not only remains a beast at the end of the tale, it is his very bestiality, his irreducible otherness, that is the reason she falls in love with him'.[43] In the world of comics, Neil Gaiman's much acclaimed *Sandman* not only retold the stories established by DC, the publisher, over generations of comics, but also retold or re-envisioned myths and stories from a huge array of cultures: European, Japanese, African, Australian. His prize-winning issue 'A Midsummer Night's Dream', especially the very sinister characterization of Puck and the interplay between the actors and the 'fairies', is clearly influenced by Carter's reworking of the play in the story 'Overture and Incidental music of *A Midsummer Night's Dream*'. But the most successful writer to have been influenced by Carter is clearly Terry Pratchett. His novels are almost formulaic Carter, with added satire and humour. They retell a range of easily recognized stories (fairy stories, *Macbeth*, *The Phantom of the Opera*) from a perspective that is interested in 'demythologizing' and in the concrete reality of the world. Time and again, characters who rely too much on the abstract are overturned or converted by the interruption of a concrete reality and a dose of liberal humanism. His most popular character, Granny Weatherwax, a witch, usually exercises her power through practical planning, her position in the community and the stories she lets be told about her – 'hedology' – rather than through magic. Pratchett says of Carter that she 'had a way of looking which made you feel that whatever you were going to say next had better be interesting'.[44] He describes Granny Weatherwax in the same terms: perhaps to be turned into a (low) cultural icon, a witch who despises magic and responds to the practicalities and needs of the world, is an appropriate tribute to Angela Carter.

If there is a feminist thinker whose work parallels Carter's, it is perhaps Rosi Braidotti. Her work seeks to bring together the deconstructive motivation which is part of much recent French philosophy (including Foucault, who Carter cites in *The Sadeian Woman*) with a practical and committed feminism. She calls this 'nomadic feminism'. Never at home in orthodoxies or in final statements, it maintains a balance between the need to act to change the world and the need to think through these actions and the world in a open-ended way. This is not to suggest that Carter's fiction is explained or subsumed by Braidotti's thought, but just to notice that negotiating this tension in both, requires, in Braidotti's words, 'the talents of a tight-rope walker, an acrobat'.[45]

Notes

1   Angela Carter, *Shaking a Leg*, ed. Jenny Uglow (London: Chatto & Windus, 1997), p. 41.
2   John Haffenden, *Novelists in Interview* (London: Methuen, 1985), p. 93.
3   Carter, *Shaking a Leg*, p. 445.
4   A technique she used more and more: see, for example, the late short story 'Gun for the Devil'.
5   Angela Carter, *Burning your Boats: Collected Short Stories* (London: Chatto and Windus, 1995), p. 374.
6   Angela Carter, *Wise Children* (London: Chatto and Windus, 1991), p. 41. For more on this, see Kate Chedgzoy, *Shakespeare's Queer Children* (Manchester: Manchester University Press, 1996).
7   Carter, *Wise Children*, p. 1. This is still the case, even for literary tourists: in his *A Reader's Guide to Writer's London* (London: Prion, 2001), Ian Cunningham fails to mention Brixton or any of the writers, poets or fictional characters who have lived there (including, for example, Sam Sevlon, Linton Kwesi Johnson, and Carter's creations).
8   Isaiah Berlin, *The Proper Study of Mankind* (London: Pimlico, 1998), p. 120.
9   Haffenden, *Novelists in Interview*, p. 80.
10   Carter, *Shaking a Leg*, p. 42.

11 Frantz Fanon, *The Wretched of the Earth*, trans. Constance Farrington (Harmondsworth: Penguin, 1990), p. 251.

12 Angela Carter, *The Sadeian Woman: An Exercise in Cultural History* (London: Virago, 1979), pp. 11, 17.

13 Sally Keenan, 'Angela Carter's The Sadeian Woman: Feminsim as Treason', in *The infernal desires of Angela Carter: fiction, femininity, feminism*, eds, Joseph Bristow, and Trev Lynn Broughton (London: Longman, 1997), p. 141.

14 Carter, *The Sadean Woman*, p. 1.

15 These stories are not archetypes, as that would imply that they are timeless: Carter's point is precisely that they are created at particular times, as a result of certain conditions and ideas. It is because of this that they are rewritten. Much confusion about Carter's work comes from her use of myth or folklore, with the implicit assumption that these represent unchanging parts of the human psyche. For Carter they do not.

16 Carter, *The Sadeian Woman*, p. 67.

17 Carter, *The Sadeian Woman*, pp. 67–8.

18 Carter, *The Sadeian Woman*, p. 150.

19 Haffenden, *Novelists in Interview*, p. 93.

20 Cited in Carter, *The Sadeian Woman*, p. 151.

21 Mary Midgley, *Utopias, Dolphins and Computers: Problems of Philosophical Plumbing* (London: Routledge, 1996), p. 44.

22 Salman Rushdie, *In Good Faith* (London: Granta 1990), p. 8.

23 Carter, *Shaking a Leg*, p. 41.

24 Carter, *Shaking a Leg*, p. 40.

25 Haffenden, *Novelists in Interview*, p. 93.

26 Carter, *Shaking a Leg*, p. 603.

27 Haffenden, *Novelists in Interview*, p. 85.

28 Carter, *Shaking a Leg*, p. 42.

29 See Chinweizu, Onwuchekwa Jemie and Ihechukwu Madubuike, *The Decolonization of African Literature* (Washington: Howard University Press, 1983), p. 89.

30 In its 'decolonizing' – both literally, in terms of Empire and more metaphorically in terms of women's experience – and in its method of rewriting a powerful cultural text, it surely is an influential precursor to Carter's work: although she mentions only Rhys's pre-war novels in her critical writing. See also Gayatri Chakravorty Spivak, *A Critique of Postcolonial Reason* (London: Harvard University Press, 1999).

31 Carter, *Shaking a Leg*, p. 43.

32 Carter, *Burning your Boats*, p. 143.

33 Carter, *Nights at the Circus*, pp. 15, 25.

34 Jacques Derrida, *Writing and Difference*, trans. Alan Bass (London: Routledge and Kegan Paul, 1978), p. 288.

35 Haffenden, *Novelists in Interview*, p. 79.

36 Jacques Derrida, *Spectres of Marx*, trans. Peggy Kamuf (London: Routledge, 1994), p. 85.

37   Although Christopher Norris argues that she has in Christopher Norris, *Derrida* (London: Fontana, 1987), p. 51.
38   John Bayley, 'Fighting for the Crown', *New York Review of Books*, 23 April 1992, 9–11, 11.
39   Sarah Bannock, 'Auto/biographical souvenirs in *Nights at the Circus*' in *The infernal desires of Angela Carter: fiction, femininity, feminism*, eds, Joseph Bristow and Trev Lynn Broughton (London: Longman, 1997), p. 201.
40   Carter, *Shaking a Leg*, p. 38.
41   Elaine Jordan, 'Enthralment; Angela Carter's Speculative Fictions' in *Plotting for Change: Contemporary Women's Fiction*, ed., Linda Anderson (London: Edward Arnold, 1990), p. 23.
42   Carter, *Shaking a Leg*, p. 555.
43   Adam Roberts, *Science Fiction* (London: Routledge, 1999), p. 104.
44   Roz Kaveney, 'New New World Deans: Angela Carter and Science Fiction', in *Flesh and the Mirror*, ed. Lorna Sage (London: Chatto & Windus, 1994), p. 171.
45   Rosi Braidotti, *Patterns of Dissonance: A study of women in contemporary philosophy*, trans. Elizabeth Guild (Cambridge: Polity, 1991), p. 14.

Primary texts

Novels

Shadow Dance (London: Heinemann, 1966)
The Magic Toyshop (London: Heinemann, 1967)
Several Perceptions (London: Heinemann, 1968)
Heroes and Villains (London: Heinemann, 1969)
Love (London: Hart-Davis, 1971; Chatto & Windus, 1987)
The Infernal Desire Machines of Dr Hoffman (London: Hart-Davis, 1972)
The Passion of New Eve (London: Victor Gollancz, 1977)
Nights at the Circus (London: Chatto & Windus, 1984)
Wise Children (London: Chatto & Windus, 1991)

Short stories

Fireworks: Nine Profane Pieces (London: Quartet 1974 / Chatto & Windus, 1987)
The Bloody Chamber and Other Stories (London: Gollancz, 1979)
Black Venus's Tale (London: Next Editions/Faber, 1980)
Black Venus (London: Chatto & Windus, 1985)
   (ed.) *The Virago Book of Fairy Tales* (London: Virago, 1990)
American Ghosts & Old World Wonders (London: Chatto & Windus, 1993)
Burning your Boats: Collected Short Stories (London: Chatto & Windus, 1995)

Non-fiction

The Sadeian Woman: An Exercise in Cultural History (London: Virago, 1979)

Shaking a Leg, ed. Jenny Uglow (London: Chatto & Windus, 1997)

Selected critical texts

John Bayley 'Fighting for the Crown', *New York Review of Books* 23 April 1992, 9–11

Joseph Bristow and Trev Lynn Broughton (eds), *The infernal desires of Angela Carter: fiction, femininity, feminism* (London: Longman, 1997)

Robert Clark, 'Angela Carter's desire machine', *Women's Studies* 14 (1987)

Aidan Day, *Angela Carter: the rational glass* (Manchester: Manchester University Press, 1998)

Patricia Dunker, 'Re-Imagining the Fairy Tales: Angela Carter's Bloody Chambers', *Literature and History* 10 (1984)

Patricia Dunker, 'Queer Gothic: Angela Carter and the Lost Narratives of Subversion', *Critical Survey* 8:1 (1996)

Alison Easton (ed.), *Angela Carter; New Casebook* (Basingstoke: Macmillan, 2000)

Sarah Gamble, *Angela Carter: Writing from the Frontline* (Edinburgh: Edinburgh University Press, 1997)

Elaine Jordan, 'Enthralment; Angela Carter's Speculative Fictions' in *Plotting for Change: Contemporary Women's Fiction*, ed. Linda Anderson (London: Edward Arnold, 1990)

John Haffenden, *Novelists in Interview* (London: Methuen, 1985)

Yvonne Martinsson, *Eroticism, ethics and reading: Angela Carter in dialogue with Roland Barthes* (Stockholm: Almqvist & Wiksell, 1996)

Linden Peach, *Angela Carter* (London: Macmillan, 1998)

Sally Robinson, *Engendering the subject: gender and self-representation in contemporary women's fiction* (Albany. State University of New York Press, 1991).

Lorna Sage, *Angela Carter*, Writers and their work series (Plymouth: Northcote House in association with the British Council, 1994)

Lorna Sage (ed.), *The Flesh and the Mirror* (London: Virago, 1994)

Critical Essays on Angela Carter (1998) edited by Lindsey Tucker (London: Prentice Hall, 1998)

13 Jeanette Winterson's Evolving Subject: 'Difficulty into Dream'

Kim Middleton Meyer

Even at the best of times, Jeanette Winterson is something of an enigma. On the one hand, lauded by cultural luminary and notorious highbrow Gore Vidal as 'the most interesting young writer I have read in twenty years',[1] Winterson has received a number of prestigious literary prizes, including the E. M. Forster award and the 1985 Whitbread award for best first novel. At the same time, however, she has been excoriated for her remarkable and unapologetic egotism (referring to herself as a veritable reincarnation of Virginia Woolf[2]), and her negative press includes the critiques 'debased by self-worship' and 'too clever or too perverse'.[3] In fact, like the author herself, each of Winterson's works has inspired contradictory reactions from critics and readers – she appears to be loved and reviled by members of both groups, regardless of the novel in question. How then, does one advance a coherent reading of Jeanette Winterson's writing? How is one to make sense of her work? In this chapter, I suggest that a unitary approach, that explains away contestatory positions *vis-à-vis* Winterson's work, forecloses on the multiplicity that she herself seeks to engender. Thus, we must allow the novels to display the author's developing theory of contradiction in identity.

Varying examples of contradiction within a singular body consistently appear throughout Winterson's fiction. Of the most critically acclaimed and popular, *Oranges Are Not the Only Fruit*, *The Passion*, *Sexing the Cherry*, *Written on the Body*, and finally *Gut Symmetries* explore numerous manifestations of the paradoxical; indeed, this recurs as a central motif in her novels. For example, the texts above move from a figuration of paradox as fantastical intertextuality to one of the grotesque; this, in turn, is eventually discarded in favour of the continued examination of a subjectivity that can only be called *nomadic*. In what follows, I will briefly describe how each novel grapples with the task of narrating multiplicity and contradiction, as well as the benefits and drawbacks of each figuration. In these five representative novels the move to represent the unitary and the fractured, the multiple in the singular, corresponds to the aura of paradox that surrounds the writer and her work, firmly ensconcing her in the emerging canon of contemporary British authors.

Oranges Are Not the Only Fruit

The critically acclaimed *Oranges Are Not the Only Fruit* initiated Winterson's literary career. First published in 1985, this *bildungsroman* charts the early life of a young woman (tellingly named Jeanette), an orphan adopted by a devoutly Christian mother and raised as her spiritual acolyte. Jeanette's particular 'cross to bear' becomes apparent when her emerging lesbianism conflicts with the beliefs of the Church and its constituents. This first novel introduces a number of themes that recur throughout Winterson's work. A fictional/autobiographical technique that continually questions the relationship between literature and life, the written and the real, appears in many of her subsequent writings, but none so dramatically as in this first novel. Given the obvious similarities between Winterson and her protagonist – Winterson too was adopted by evangelicals, trained as an orator by the Church, is vocal about her sexuality – a thematic principle that allows the writer's life to spill over into her work is key to Winterson's literary practice.[4] Rather than creating a *cordon sanitaire* between the two, however, *Oranges* aggressively works to trouble the boundary between fictional and 'real' accounts of the author's experience.

In order to approach the traditionally distinguishable difference between autobiography and fiction, Winterson first establishes a familiar sort of realism. Thus, the primary narrative of *Oranges* chronicles the misadventures of Jeanette: her ostracism from society at large due to her fundamentalist beliefs and later her expulsion from the community that refuses to accept her homosexuality. Reflecting Christianity as an early influence, the novel is structured thematically according to the first eight books of the Bible – Genesis to Ruth. Such a narrative form would apparently indicate an acceptance of biblical authority. In Winterson's hands, however, it acts only as a framework that allows other narratives to intrude. Susan Rubin Suleiman points out that these intrusions continually emphasize rupture and discontinuity: 'Their presence, increasingly unmotivated in realist terms, fragments the text and gives it something like the heterogeneity of collage.'[5] Indeed, biblical thematics give way to vignettes that parallel Jeanette's disenchantment with the Church. Accordingly, stories representing both the 'unholy' literature forbidden by Jeanette's mother, and the promise of escape from a confining and oppressive community continually redirect Jeanette's narrative. A segment of the King Arthur legend – Sir Perceval's search for the Holy Grail – informs Jeanette's search for the remote possibility of acceptance within her Church.[6] A more transparent tale chronicles the adventures of Winnet (which, of course, rhymes with Jeanette), a young heroine adopted by a sorcerer only to be cast out of his domain. Winnet, like Jeanette, wanders beyond the sway of those who would exercise power over her, while at the same time retaining the skills she learned from them (p. 143).

As these stories intersect with – and at points supersede – the guiding principle of each biblical chapter, Winterson calls into question any hierarchy of texts that might provide for the occlusion of others. In so doing, Winterson asserts the power of narratives and counter-narratives to shape life, while at the same time refusing to accept any primary text as guide. Instead, she offers a theory of narratives: 'That is the way with stories; we make them what we will. It's a way of explaining the universe while leaving the universe unexplained ... The only thing for certain is how complicated it all is, like string full of knots. It's all there but hard to find the beginning and impossible to fathom the end' (p. 91). As a citation from 'Deuteronomy: the last book of the Law', Winterson's narrative philosophy insists on a poetics of uncertainty.

Whether autobiography or fiction, Jeanette's story is infused with stories both realistic and fantastic and there is little sense in distinguishing between the two in this narrative world. The orange demon that visits her in her hour of decision sums up the danger of ignoring the plenitude of stories available: 'If you ignore us, you're likely to end up in two pieces, or lots of pieces, it's all part of the paradox' (p. 106). For Jeanette and for Winterson, the paradox of *Oranges* consists of multiple, heterogeneous stories intersecting to empower a young woman to shape her own identity. Whatever the separation between the character and the author, on this point, the two would themselves surely converge.

The Passion

Winterson's third novel,[7] *The Passion*, carries on her fascination with the power of heterogeneity and narrative. In fact, this preoccupation dictates the text's oft-quoted refrain: 'I'm telling you stories. Trust me.' The dual narrators of *The Passion* use the refrain most often after relating a fantastic tale – a young man walks on water, roses grow on a barren rock in the ocean. Like her previous work, *Oranges Are Not the Only Fruit*, however, the stories Winterson adopts here are not solely fantasy. *The Passion* takes up stories of historical import, its episodes revolving around the defeat of Napoleon's army. As the Bible provided the structuring principle for *Oranges*, here the Napoleonic Wars initially direct the narrative. However, unlike the eventual erosion of the Bible's authority in *Oranges*, here the representation of history retains its force. Neither superseding nor rejecting history outright, *The Passion* uses fictional narrative to expand and infuse objective historical fact with the specificity of human responses. In fact, Jan Rosemergy calls the novel a 'cat's cradle of history and fiction...impossible to unknot'.[8] In effect, the two genres depend upon one another to intensify the effects of each. In her analysis, Rosemergy describes the approach: 'Together, the stories...because they intertwine history and fable, are ultimately more trustworthy in their representation of the human condition than either is alone.'[9] Here, two forms often considered oppositional work together to imagine the ways that traditionally neglected historical voices could add depth and texture to flat factual accounts.

The interpenetration of history and fiction in *The Passion* marks a departure in Winterson's exploration of the representation of multiplicity. While *Oranges* used fantasy to upset the boundaries of realism and its favoured texts, *The Passion* seeks a form capable of incorporating two genres simultaneously. In literary parlance, the figure that best characterizes her project is that of the grotesque, an image whose implications are most famously explored by the early twentieth-century critic, Mikhail Bakhtin. In *Rabelais and his World* Bakhtin describes the basic structure of the grotesque: 'One of the fundamental tendencies of the grotesque...is to show two bodies in one; the one giving birth and dying, the other conceived, generated and born...From one body a new body always emerges in some form or other.'[10] *The Passion* exhibits the double in the single, a union of the two giving birth to a new 'grotesque' form. Such a construct places the author in good company; postmodern contemporaries including Martin Amis, Julian Barnes and Angela Carter have all experimented with the incorporation of fiction into history. Helga Quadflieg notes the generic implications for these writers: 'History ...becomes "a playground adventure" and a mine for fragments and anecdotes while central figures of the *grand récit* are pushed into the margins or at least seen from a marginal perspective.'[11] At a formal level, then, *The Passion*'s grotesque formation marks Winterson's entry into a key moment of contemporary postmodern literature: the exploration of historiographic metafiction.[12]

Winterson additionally uses the grotesque to incorporate alternating narratives from Henri and Villanelle. In the beginning, Henri and Villanelle could not be more different. Henri is a naive young man from France, seduced by Napoleon's glamour. He hopes to join the army as a drummer, but his size and strength (or lack thereof) mark him instead for the kitchen.[13] Villanelle, on the other hand, is a Venetian schooled in the mysteries and excesses of her city, who plays at cross-dressing for her own amusement and the fascination/discomfiture of Casino audiences (p. 54). As Napoleon annexes more and more of Europe, Villanelle is sold into the service of the army officers and encounters Henri in the zero winter of Russia. Villanelle's tale of her capture is then relayed in Henri's chapter, just as Villanelle's chapter later must describe Henri's imprisonment and madness. While history and fiction intertwine to tell a more complete story, so do Henri and Villanelle's narratives converge to describe their attached fates.

Like Winterson's earlier work, an air of fantasy pervades the grotesque nature of this novel. Henri retrieves Villanelle's still-beating heart from the Queen of Spades who stole it; Villanelle trusts her webbed feet to walk on water, leading Henri away from the man he murdered. Because it values the imaginary, fantasy in fact comes hand in hand with the grotesque; unfortunately it also strips the genre of much of its power. Critics argue that even the most transgressive work of the grotesque is only an outgrowth of the real itself, which then uses fantasy to channel the revolutionary energy of the people solely into the realm of the imaginary.[14]

True to the limits of this form, Henri ends his tale imagining himself surrounded by his friends who died in the war and designing a fabulous garden on the barren soil of the prison island. Slightly more hopeful, Villanelle abandons her cross-dressing disguises and embraces her identity as a grotesque figure,[15] but consoles herself with the belief that the future will be different. The novel ends with an extant connection between the two protagonists; Henri and Villanelle echo each other's vision of the rewards of the fantastic: 'The cities of the interior are vast and do not lie on any map' (pp. 150, 152). History and fiction, horror and fantasy – the grotesque formations that *The Passion* enacts allow for improbable narrative unions that hold out the promise of multiple interiorities to be explored, but at the same time reassert their inability to impact a world governed by realist notions.

Sexing the Cherry

A key text in the trajectory of her narrative practice, Winterson's fourth novel announced an important turning point in her representation of multiplicity. *Sexing the Cherry* incorporates many of the tropes discussed above. In addition to these elements, however, Winterson begins to aggressively test the limits of the grotesque figurations she has depended on previously. Here the characters consistently search for alternatives to their present circumstances, but they also push their exploration beyond traditional boundaries of time and space. In fact, the novel's epigraphs prefigure the new exigencies that structure this novel:

> The Hopi, an Indian tribe, have a language as sophisticated as ours, but no tenses for past, present and future. The division does not exist. What does this say about time?

> Matter, that thing the most solid and the well-known, which you are holding in your hands and which makes up your body, is now known to be mostly empty space. Empty space and points of light. What does this say about the reality of the world?[16]

Challenging two of the most firmly held beliefs of the nineteenth century – the ultimate rationality of time and space – Winterson delineates the territory she intends to re-survey. The experiences traversed by her dual narrators reflect a world that indeed takes neither conventional time nor solid matter for granted.

Winterson's young hero Jordan is a seventeenth-century adventurer, a boy who dreams of becoming an explorer. In his travels, Jordan tends to come upon places that could not be located on any map: a house whose inhabitants live quite happily suspended over bottomless pits, a town where the population was eradicated three times by a plague of love, a city that abandoned the laws of gravity (pp. 15, 80, 108). He even wanders into the realm of fairy tales, encountering eleven of the twelve dancing princesses each of whom lives out a drastically different fate than 'happily ever after'.[17]

While Jordan is exploring worlds and times, his adoptive mother, known only as Dog-Woman, remains at home in England, challenging the oppressive religious mores of Cromwell's supporters. Dog-Woman's fantastic size empowers her protest: in one carnivalistic scene, she unseats an elephant by acting as a counterweight on a set of scales (pp. 20–1). Dog-Woman additionally enjoys strength proportional to her Rabelaisian size, which allows her to strangle a preacher denouncing the king, using 'only one hand and [holding] him from the ground at arm's length' (p. 24). In a revision of the statutes of matter, Dog-Woman's material excess grants her the power to oppose the restrictive and patriarchal politics of her time.

The odd pairing of these two characters is reminiscent of the intertwined destinies of Henri and Villanelle; separate but repeatedly drawn to one another, Jordan and Dog-Woman alternately narrate the novel, melding fantasy with historical events. In a scene that lends itself to the title of the novel, each character considers the grotesque formation that serves as a metaphoric model for the intricate structure of the text. In the King's gardens, Jordan attempts to create a new botanical yield, a sexed cherry tree that could combine the strengths of more than one species. He explains the science to his mother:

> Grafting is the means whereby a plant, perhaps tender or uncertain, is fused into a hardier member of its strain, and so the two take advantage of each other and produce a third kind...In this way fruits have been made resistant to disease and certain plants have learned to grow where previously they could not. (p. 84)

While Dog-Woman protests that the outcome will be a 'monster', grafting continues to fascinate Jordan and he wonders 'whether it was an art I might apply to myself' (p. 85). On the surface, this allegory evokes images of the grotesque: two strains are fused and produce a third, that in turn allows for new possibilities.

The stakes of this novel, however, are set higher than that of previous works. While the grotesque adequately accounts for the grafting of fantasy and history, of Jordan and Dog-Woman's narratives, it falters with the addition of two new but strangely familiar characters who appear at the end of the novel in a chapter entitled 'Sometime Later'. The first is a modern boy named Nicholas Jordan, who reads history books and dreams of becoming a hero, but must settle for the Navy as there is no uncharted region of the earth in his late twentieth-century context. The second character goes unnamed, but revolts against companies polluting rivers; protesting, she camps on the banks. In her fantasies, however, she appears as an enormous woman able to stuff the leaders of the World Bank and the Pentagon into a sack and subject them to 'compulsory training in feminism and ecology' (p. 139).

With the addition of these new characters, Winterson's novel calls the previous grotesque figurations into question. Its theory of union and synthesis cannot account for the relation between Jordan and Nicholas Jordan, between Dog-Woman and the activist. In *Sexing the*

Cherry, then, Winterson begins to map out a theory of multiplicity specific to subjectivity, one that simultaneously seeks to more fully integrate fantasy into the real, even while erasing the distinction between the two. Christy Burns accounts for Winterson's new deployment of genres thus: 'She incorporates [fantasy] more completely into her critique of contemporary desensitization and alienation, directing attention toward its application to the reader's own "real" political and social context.'[18] In the novel, the 'Sometime Later' characters closely resemble the readers' existences – a world extensively mapped, controlled by multinational companies who care little for ecological devastation. In this world, exploring the unlocatable and possessing immeasurable mass and strength are fantasy at best. Increasingly unclear, however, is which set of narratives is fantasy. Jordan and Dog-Woman's narratives, for example, take up the vast bulk of the novel. Are they then relegated to fantasy simply by the late insertion of a more realistic set of narratives? Susana Gonzalez insists upon the subsumption of fantasy here into the real: 'Fantasy in *Sexing the Cherry* works to show how the binary opposition real/fantastic cannot be established and it does so by levelling reality/unreality to the same category.'[19] Likewise, Susana Onega describes the novel in terms of its 'politics of uncertainty', a status maintained by the continued use of what she calls an 'ontological hesitancy'.[20]

In essence, neither set of narratives can be established as real *vis-à-vis* the other. In fact, Winterson's epigraphs direct us to question what we consider 'real' in the first place. The 'ontological hesitancy' created not only erases the division between fantasy and the real, but also between Jordan and Nicholas Jordan. Far beyond the territory covered by the grotesque, Winterson's text moves towards a notion of an unfixed, mobile representation of selfhood. Rosi Braidotti names this formation 'nomadic subjectivity': 'nomadic consciousness consists in not taking any kind of identity as permanent. The nomad is only passing through; s/he makes those necessarily situated connections that can help her/him survive, but s/he never takes on full the limits of one ... fixed identity.'[21] Nomadism, then, allows the character the necessary and useful facets of multiple homogeneous identities without being cornered by the bounded limits of a solitary one.

More true to a form of nomadism than to the closed duality of the grotesque, Nicholas Jordan and the activist are able to animate the connections to their alternative selves for their own survival in a contemporary context. Focusing on the 'Rabelaisian dimension for rage' (p. 141) that she initially thought did not exist, the activist convinces Nicholas Jordan to help her burn down the polluting factory (p. 165). Whether fantastic or real, characters here are empowered to enact social change, revealing the force contained in a multiple existence. Jordan explains his nomadic subjectivity in terms of exploration: 'Our lives could be stacked together like plates on a waiter's hand. Only the top one is showing, but the rest are there and by mistake we discover them' (p. 100). His travels lead him to the 'mistakes' of discovering other places, other lives. The activist describes hers in terms of spatiality: 'If I have a spirit, a soul, any name will do, then it won't be single, it will be multiple. Its dimension will not be one of confinement, but one of space' (p. 144). Whatever the metaphors that enable an activation of multiple possibilities in simultaneity, *Sexing the Cherry* acts as Winterson's textual move beyond the limits of the grotesque's singularity into the less concrete realm of nomadism.

Written on the Body

In 1993, Winterson published her fifth novel, a crystallization of her preoccupations to date. Equally as concerned with multiplicity and formal innovation as her early works, *Written on the Body* constructs an argument within the philosophical domain of the Self/Other relationship dictated by love. What is desire, *Written on the Body* asks, without the objectification of the beloved?

An admitted 'Lothario', whose past is littered with lovers' broken hearts, the unnamed narrator is rendered helpless by Louise, the woman who quickly becomes the object of affection and obsession. The narrator recounts the effects of an all-consuming love affair, cut short by an ultimatum from Louise's husband, Elgin. Louise has a rare form of cancer, and only if the narrator abandons her will he continue to treat her disease. Elgin is a renowned oncologist; the narrator has no choice but to leave the beloved. The narrator spends the remainder of the novel tortuously debating, and eventually regretting the choice while ruminating on an ethos of love.

In a move most disconcerting to readers, Winterson's unnamed, first-person narrator is unsexed. At no point in the narrative does the speaker definitively identify his/her gender. In addition, the novel is littered with situations that conform most strongly to stereotypes of one gender or another. For example, the narrator has affairs with both men and women, he/she engages in fistfights with Elgin[22] but also compares him/herself to Lauren Bacall (p. 41). This gender play with the reader's expectations sent a number of critics into a frenzy of interpretation. Many, while attempting to retain the critical force of the ambiguity, insisted that the narrator is female.[23] Ute Kauer argued for the female identity in the end, but also declared that the ambiguity serves a definitive, experimental purpose: 'It is one of the aims of the book to deconstruct clichés about love, gender and specific male or female codes of behaviour.'[24] In the process of deconstructing the multiple codes that have traditionally defined and confined gender expression, particularly in the ways that these codes map love between two people, Winterson again employs a version of nomadism that finally allows her narrator to regain the beloved.

A temporal schema of the novel helps to chart the development of the narrator's ideas about love, which condition his/her relationship with Louise. In the beginning, the narrator invokes his/her need for the beloved in terms possession and consumption, terms traditionally coded as masculine.[25] Early on in their relationship, the narrator says: 'I didn't only want Louise's flesh, I wanted her bones, her blood, her tissues, the sinews that bound her together' (p. 51), and 'My lips were sealed and my cheeks must have been swelling out like a gerbil's because my mouth was full of Louise' (p. 51). Both discursive measures map desire in terms that relegate the beloved to the realm of object, something to be possessed completely, or to be consumed. These are clearly methods that the narrator has used previously in failed relationships. In Louise's absence, however, even while he/she notes the difference between those earlier lovers and Louise, he/she continues to explore these objectifying practices. Most notably, the narrator attempts to discover the very truth of Louise's self through the study of anatomy: 'I would go on knowing her, more intimately than the skin, hair and voice that I craved' (p. 111).

The narrator's research backfires, however, as the medical journals he/she investigates lead not to an articulation of the separate other, but instead to a consistent narrative of the deep connections between Louise and him/herself. With each subsequent body part, the medical journals reveal memories of love that mark how deeply Louise has possessed the narrator. She remarks: 'To remember you it's my own body I touch' (p. 130). No longer an object to be controlled, Louise here has agency, and can affect in addition to being affected by the narrator. Realizing Louise as an independent self, the narrator truly begins to grieve over losing Louise the individual: 'To think of Louise in her own right, not as my lover, not as my grief' (p. 153). Having marked the reciprocal relation between Louise and him/her self, the narrator becomes able, through concentration, to conceive of Louise in her own right, materially attached and yet conceptually whole. Remembering Louise in this manner allows the narrator a glimpse at a new type of relation – one that posits a system of desire between two subjects, each whole but connected to the other, neither subordinated or constructed by the other. In effect, neither is Other.

Paulina Palmer notes that a 'fluid interaction between self and Other...characterizes Winterson's treatment of subjectivity'.[26] Indeed, the reciprocity between the narrator and Louise represents Winterson's imagining of the consequences of deployment of a nomadic subjectivity within a love relationship. Here, nomadism would allow the narrator to circulate amongst all terms of the invoked, aligned binarisms: the narrator is neither wholly male nor wholly female, neither definitively subject nor an affectless object. Empowered with the kind of subjective mobility that allowed the activist in *Sexing the Cherry* to activate the most powerful parts of herself, the narrator too can be read as a nomadic subject who inhabits none of these positions to the exclusion of the others. By holding open numerous subject positions, the narrator invokes a new ethics of love that allows him/her to reunite with Louise in a fantastic, but not immaterial, ending.

Gut Symmetries

After the critically panned *Art and Lies*, Winterson returned to the literary scene with *Gut Symmetries*. A complicated novel, dense with an array of opposing discourses, it again embraces a nomadic subjectivity. As in *Written on the Body*, nomadism holds out possibilities for love; at the same time, the novel takes seriously the language of science in a way Winterson refused in the previous novel. In *Gut Symmetries*, science indeed creates the probability of love in a universe that appears to foreclose on dimensions of possibility.

On an elementary level *Gut Symmetries* is about a love triangle – two scientists and a poet, Jove, Alice and Stella, alternatively form 'girl–boy girl–girl'[27] parallel relationships. The triangular model, however, fails to stay within two-dimensional space in Winterson's novel:

> If you want to know how a mistress marriage works, ask a triangle. In Euclidean geometry the angle of a triangle add up to 180 degrees and parallel lines never meet. Everyone knows the score, and the women are held in tension, away from one another...
>
> In curved space, the angles over-add themselves and parallel lines always meet.
>
> His wife, his mistress, met.[28]

True to the dominance of lesbian relations in Winterson's aesthetic, Alice and Stella's love emerges as the defining attraction of the novel. As post-Newtonian physics works to engender their connection, so too it marshals to save it from destruction. Debating the future of his affair with Alice and his marriage to Stella, Jove lures Stella onto a yacht off the Isle of Capri while Alice makes an emergency trip to England to attend her ailing father. Neither Stella nor Jove is an accomplished sailor, and they are soon stranded at sea with dwindling supplies of food and water. Jove, in a fever of hunger, cuts away at and consumes much of Stella's backside. Stella's death seems ineluctable; however, she is miraculously rescued by Alice and a mysterious guide capable of finding the lost boat when no other search party could.

Stella's recovery is nothing short of fantastic. In her own evaluation of the novel, Winterson refuses to problematize this: 'This is a miracle sort of book – the miracles of the universe, revealed through science, and human miracles made possible through love.'[29] The novel works hard to justify the possibility of miracles and to reveal them through science – the exigencies of the ending are foreshadowed throughout by an ongoing discourse on the hidden states of matter. Contemplating the death of her father, Alice tests her scientific training against the reality of her loss: 'Still and still moving matter...If the physics is correct then we are neither alive nor dead as we commonly understand it, but in different states of potentiality' (p. 207). In an earlier chapter on death, Alice applies Winterson's earlier theories on multiplicity to the apparent finality of death: 'According to quantum theory there are not only second chances, but multiple chances...If we knew how to manipulate space-time as space-time manipulates itself the illusion of our single linear lives would collapse. And if our lives here are not the total our death here will not be final' (p. 160). In both of these musings re-evaluations of space and time lend a scientific basis to Winterson's nomadism, previously demarcated by the fantastic. In *Gut Symmetries*, the material that earlier was considered fantastic is now characterized as more real than common perception allows.

In *Gut Symmetries*, any hesitation Winterson's characters previously expressed towards the principles of nomadism are eradicated. Both the activist of *Sexing the Cherry* and the unnamed narrator of *Written on the Body* at some point in their narratives doubted their sanity; *Gut Symmetries* shows the crazy ones are those who doubt that multiple possibilities for a subject exist. Alice and Stella believe, and in her exploration of contemporary scientific thought, Winterson provides them with a set of discourses that work to explain the mechanics behind what previously appeared to be fantasy.

Fantasy and reality, history and fairy tales, love and science – Jeanette Winterson incorporates what seem to be irreducible binary oppositions. Searching for an aesthetics of synthesis that preserves the difference between distinct terms, she passes through intertextuality in favour of the grotesque, and abandons the grotesque for the freedom of a theory of nomadism. Truly, then, Winterson aspires to the articulation of subjectivity's paradoxes: 'What is unwritten draws me on, the difficulty, the dream' (p. 206).

Notes

1   Winterson's American publisher, Vintage Books, in fact includes this quotation on each trade paperback edition of her work.
2   See Andrea L. Harris, *Other Sexes: Rewriting Difference from Woolf to Winterson* (Albany: State University of New York Press, 2000), p. xii. In the introduction to her criticism, Harris remarks that the 'infamy' of such a statement led her (as well as others) to examine Woolf's influence on Winterson.
3   See Christy Burns, 'Fantastic Language: Jeanette Winterson's Recovery of the Postmodern Word', *Contemporary Literature*, 37.2 (Madison: University of Wisconsin Press, 1996), 278–306. Burns's excellent article provides these and other examples of the vast scope of reviews of the novels.
4   In the 1991 preface to the novel, Winterson insists upon the ambiguity of the novel's information: 'Is Oranges an autobiographical novel? No not at all and yes of course' (p. xiv).
5   Susan Rubin Suleiman, 'Mothers and the Avant-Garde: A Case of Mistaken Identity?' *Avant Garde Interdisciplinary and International Review: Femmes, Frauen, Women*, ed. Francoise van Rossum Guyon (Amsterdam: Rodopi, 1990), pp. 135–46, 137.
6   Jeanette Winterson, *Oranges Are Not the Only Fruit* (London: Vintage, 1991), p. 132. Subsequent page references in the text are to this edition.
7   Winterson's second novel, *Boating for Beginners*, has been almost completely disavowed by her since its publication. In fact, despite the probable income that it could generate, the publisher's listings of Winterson's other works continually fail to include the novel.
8   Jan Rosemergy, 'Navigating the Interior Journey: The Fiction of Jeanette Winterson', *British Women Writing Fiction*, ed. Abby H. P. Werlock (Tuscaloosa: University of Alabama Press, 2000), pp. 248–69, 263.
9   Ibid.
10 Mikhail Bakhtin, *Rabelais and his World*, trans. Helene Iswolsky (Bloomington: Indiana UP, 1984), p. 26.

11 Helga Quadflieg, 'Feminist Stories Told on Waste Waters: Jeanette Winterson's Novels', *Anglistik & Englischunterricht* 60 (1997) (Trier: WTV Wissenschaftlicher Verlag), 97–111, 105.

12 For a summary of the phenomenon, see Linda Hutcheon, '"The past-time of past time": Fiction, History, Historiographic Metafiction', *Genre: Forms of Discourse and Culture* (Norman, Oklahoma) no. 3–4 (1987 Fall-Winter), 285–305.

13 Jeanette Winterson, *The Passion* (New York: Vintage Books, 1989), p. 5.

14 See in particular the feminist critic Juliet Mitchell, *Women, the Longest Revolution: Essays in Feminism, Literature and Psycho-analysis* (New York: Pantheon Books, 1984).

15 Del Mar Asensio connects Villanelle's webbed feet to the variety of her gender choices: 'The questioning of sexual identity as traditionally understood is taken to an extreme in the person of Villanelle, a bisexual woman who cross-dresses as a man for money and for fun and who, in the story, shares with Venetian boatmen one of their exclusive male features, their webbed feet' (p. 268). Palmer more strongly asserts the queer significa-tion behind the feet: 'This grotesque feature, as well as acting as a signifier of her sexual difference, parodically reworks the representation of the lesbian as animalistic which . . . frequently occurs in homophobic culture' (p. 81). See Maria del Mar Asensio, 'Subversion of Sexual Identity in Jeanette Winterson's *The Passion*', *Gender, I-Deology: Essays on Theory, Fiction and Film*, ed. Chantal Cornut-Gentille D'Arcy and Jose Angel Garcia Landa (Amsterdam: Rodopi, 1996), p. 268. And Paulina Palmer, *Lesbian Gothic: Trangressive Fictions* (London: Cassell, 1999).

16 Jeanette Winterson, *Sexing the Cherry* (New York: Vintage Books, 1991). Subsequent references in the text are to this edition.

17 The revision of fairy tales is a feminist tool for critiquing patriarchy and heterosexual ideology. See Susana Gonzalez, 'Winterson's *Sexing the Cherry*: Rewriting "Woman" Through Fantasy', *Gender, I-Deology: Essays on Theory, Fiction and Film*, ed. Chantal Cornut-Gentille D'Arcy and Jose Angel Garcia Landa (Amsterdam: Rodopi, 1996), pp. 281–95. Gonzalez concisely describes the implicit message of the original tale: 'twelve princesses manage for a while to face, trick and escape patri-archal oppression represented in the figure of their father; they are kept incarcerated but escape every night to go dancing till they are brought back under patriarchal rule when a prince succeeds in finding out how they escape and where they escape to. The tale ends and the twelve princesses are again under male rule, their husbands, with whom they are said to live happily ever after' (p. 289). Winterson's tales, however, neatly provide the princesses with alternative endings.

18 Burns, 'Fantastic Language . . .', 292.

19 Gonzalez, 'Winterson's *Sexing the Cherry* . . .', p. 293.

20 Susana Onega, 'Jeanette Winterson's Politics of Uncertainty in *Sexing the Cherry*', *Gender, I-Deology: Essays on Theory, Fiction and Film*, ed.

Chantal Cornut-Gentille D'Arcy and Jose Angel Garcia Landa (Amsterdam: Rodopi, 1996), pp. 297–313, 303.

21   Rosi Braidotti, *Nomadic Subjects: Embodiment and Sexual Difference in Contemporary Feminist Theory* (New York: Columbia UP, 1994), p. 33.

22   Jeanette Winterson, *Written On the Body* (New York: Alfred A. Knopf, 1993), p. 172.

23   See Ute Kauer, 'Narration and Gender: The Role of the First-Person Narrator in Jeanette Winterson's Written on the Body', *'I'm Telling You Stories': Jeanette Winterson and the Politics of Reading*, ed. Helena Grice and Tim Woods (Amsterdam: Rodopi, 1998). Also Cath Stowers, 'The Erupting Lesbian Body: Reading *Written On The Body* as a Lesbian Text', *'I'm Telling You Stories': Jeanette Winterson and the Politics of Reading*, ed. Helena Grice and Tim Woods (Amsterdam: Rodopi, 1998), pp. 89–101. Kauer and Stowers both argue for the ultimate reading of the narrator as female for narratalogical and lesbian agendas, respectively. Additionally, see Harris's *Other Sexes* (note 2) which posits the female narrator as an inscription of a feminist ethics of love *à la* Irigaray.

24   Kauer, 'Narration and Gender...', p. 45.

25   Stowers, 'The Erupting Lesbian Body...', p. 90 also notes the preponderance of penetration metaphors in the novel.

26   Palmer, *Lesbian Gothic*, p. 50.

27   Ginny Dougary, 'Truth or Dare' as quoted in Helena Grice and Tim Woods, 'Grand (Dis)Unified Theories?: Dislocated Discourses in *Gut Symmetries*', *'I'm Telling You Stories': Jeanette Winterson and the Politics of Reading*, ed. Helena Grice and Tim Woods (Amsterdam: Rodopi, 1998), pp. 117–126.

28   Jeanette Winterson, *Gut Symmetries* (London: Granta Books, 1997) pp. 16–17. Subsequent page references in the text are to this edition.

29   Jeanette Winterson, *Jeanette Winterson – The Official Site*. www.jeanettewinterson.net/books/gutsymmetries.htm. Wednesday, 25 April 2001.

Primary texts

Oranges Are Not the Only Fruit (London: Pandora, 1985)

Boating for Beginners (London: Methuen, 1985)

The Passion (London: Bloomsbury, 1987)

Sexing the Cherry (London: Bloomsbury, 1989)

Written On the Body (London: Jonathan Cape, 1992)

Art & Lies: A Piece for Three Voices and a Bawd (London: Jonathan Cape, 1994)

Art Objects: Essays on Ecstasy and Effrontery (London: Jonathan Cape, 1995)

Gut Symmetries (London: Granta Books, 1997)

The World and Other Places (London: Jonathan Cape, 1998)

The PowerBook (London: Jonathan Cape, 2000)
Jeanette Winterson – The Official Site. www.jeanettewinterson.net

Selected critical texts

Maria del Mar Asensio, 'Subversion of Sexual Identity in Jeanette Winterson's *The Passion*' *Gender, I-Deology: Essays on Theory, Fiction and Film*, ed. Chantal Cornut-Gentille D'Arcy and Jose Angel Gakia Landa (Amsterdam: Rodopi, 1996), pp. 265–79

Christy Burns, 'Fantastic Language: Jeanette Winterson's Recovery of the Postmodern Word' in *Contemporary Literature*, 37.2 (Madison: University of Wisconsin Press, 1996), 278–306

Susana Gonzalez, 'Winterson's *Sexing the Cherry*: Rewriting "Woman" Through Fantasy', *Gender, I-Deology: Essays on Theory, Fiction and Film*, ed. Chantal Cornut-Gentille D'Arcy and Jose Angel Garcia Landa (Amsterdam: Rodopi, 1996), pp. 281–95

Helena Grice and Tim Woods, 'Grand (Dis)Unified Theories?: Dislocated Discourses in *Gut Symmetries*', in *'I'm Telling You Stories': Jeanette Winterson and the Politics of Reading*, ed. Helena Grice and Tim Woods (Amsterdam: Rodopi, 1998)

Andrea L. Harris, *Other-Sexes: Rewriting Difference from Woolf to Winterson* (Albany: State University of New York Press, 2000)

Ute Kauer, 'Narration and Gender: The Role of the First-Person Narrator in Jeanette Winterson's *Written on the Body*' in *'I'm Telling You Stories': Jeanette Winterson and the Politics of Reading*, ed. Helena Grice and Tim Woods (Amsterdam: Rodopi, 1998) pp. 42–51

Mark Marvel, 'Winterson: Trust Me. I'm Telling You Stories', *Interview* 20. (1990), 165–8

Susana Onega, 'Jeanette Winterson's Politics of Uncertainty in *Sexing the Cherry*', *Gender, I-Deology: Essays on Theory, Fiction and Film*, ed. Chantal Cornut-Gentille D'Arcy and Jose Angel Garcia Landa (Amsterdam: Rodopi, 1996), pp. 297–313

Paulina Palmer, *Lesbian Gothic: Trangressive Fictions* (London: Cassell, 1999)

Helga Quadflieg, 'Feminist Stories Told on Waste Waters: Jeanette Winterson's Novels', *Anglistik & Englischunterricht* 60 (1997) (Trier: WTV Wissenschaftlicher Verlag), 97–111

Jan Rosemergy, 'Navigating the Interior Journey: The Fiction of Jeanette Winterson', *British Women Writing Fiction*, ed. Abby H. P. Werlock (Tuscaloosa: University of Alabama Press, 2000), pp. 248–69.

Cath Stowers, 'The Erupting Lesbian Body: Reading *Written On the Body* as a Lesbian Text', in *'I'm Telling You Stories': Jeanette Winterson and the Politics of Reading*, ed. Helena Grice and Tim Woods (Amsterdam: Rodopi, 1998), pp. 89–101

14 Kazuo Ishiguro and the Work of Art: Reading Distances

Mark Wormald

By most reckonings, Kazuo Ishiguro is among the most successful of contemporary literary novelists writing in Britain. The biographical notes to the Faber and Faber paperback editions of his five novels tell an enviable story, and one that usefully represents a number of trends in the culture of contemporary fiction. The judges of British and European prizes have acclaimed each of his works, which have been widely translated – into twenty-eight languages at the last count. The best-known of these novels, *The Remains of the Day* (1989), also became a successful film.

As the growing body of criticism devoted to him attests, Ishiguro also represents some large cultural trends. For he seems to inform another large story about the rise of the sceptical, politically dissident, novel of post-colonialism. This ironic analyst of Englishness only became a British citizen in 1982, the year he published his first novel. For many readers of Anglophone fiction at the turn of the millennium, the work of writers born in and reacting against the British Empire reveals energies within the English language that white Anglo-Saxon writers can only admire from the hollow of their own culture's attitude of material wealth and imaginative apathy. Ishiguro's career has closely followed that of one of these writers, Salman Rushdie: the attention paid to *A Pale View of Hills* on its publication in 1982 owed much to the phenomenon of *Midnight's Children*, which had appeared the year before. The two writers have gone on, in their turn, to exploit some of the same distinctive tropes of meta- and post-colonial fiction, among them the aspiration to create through the power of art compensatory 'imaginary homelands' (in Rushdie's phrase) for their exiled and deracinated characters. Their fiction seems to respond to a historical narrative of past losses and traumas by overwriting that experience in knowing but confessedly partial commentary.

While these general perspectives are broadly helpful, they overlook some awkward details. Japan has never been a European colony, and Ishiguro himself, as the child of an oceanographer, who brought his family to Britain in 1960 when Kazuo was five, has had only the indirect access of imagination and research to the historical periods and political situations which four of his five novels describe. Ishiguro's internationalism is less earned, arguably less authentic, than Rushdie's; his engagement with international political realities has been mercifully less personal. As will become apparent, Ishiguro's prose is also much quieter, much more evasive in its formality than Rushdie's exuberant syntax and diction.

There is instead a case for thinking of Ishiguro in terms of other contemporary trends in and impulses to fiction. The one I want to develop here is the recent fascination in literary fiction with aesthetics that resist or complicate reading. A cluster of novelists, few of them 'post-colonial', have turned to literature's sister arts, music and painting, to explore how history permits or impedes the transmission of aesthetic values to its survivors and students. Meditations on the composition, history, authentication, loss, restoration, performance, and sometimes faking of great art have proved popular occasions for fiction in the past few years. These include, in the field of music, Bernard MacLaverty's *Grace Notes*, Ian McEwan's *Amsterdam*, Vikram Seth's *An Equal Music* and Rose Tremain's *Music and Silence*. Novels about the fine arts have been more popular; a reading list might include John Banville's *The Book of Evidence* and *Athena*, J. G. Carr's *A Month in the Country*, *The Forger* by Paul Watkins, *Headlong* by Michael Frayn and a clutch, almost a sub-genre in its own right, of novels inspired by Vermeer: Tracy Chevalier's *Girl with a Pearl Earring*, Katherine Weber's *The Music Lesson*, Susan Vreeland's *Girl in Hyacinth Blue*, and John Bayley's *The Red Hat*.

The variousness of these texts suggests a general context for what follows, a discussion of Ishiguro's representations of perspective, art and the artist in three novels. If I do not pursue that context in detail here, that is because of my sense of the distance from them that Ishiguro manages to achieve in the distinctive idiom and approach of his work. Two novels, *An Artist of the Floating World* (1986), and his fourth novel, *The Unconsoled* (1995), have eminent artists as their narrators – a Japanese wood-block painter and a British concert pianist respectively; *A Pale View of Hills* (1982) explains where and why the preoccupation with distance in these two later works originated. The narrators of all three texts at once confront and evade issues of distance in such a way that they prompt larger questions for the reader. These questions are about the function, the work, of art that Ishiguro's narrators describe, defend, sometimes displace and pervasively disguise; but they are also about the art which raises these questions, and which often seems designed to avoid giving a satisfying answer to them. They are, that is, about the manner of Ishiguro's fiction as a whole as well as about their narrators, about the strategies employed in composing his apparently transparent but often purposely obscuring prose as well as the portraits of the artists that this prose reveals.

If Ishiguro's distance from his contemporaries is an issue, it is an issue generated from within, by the complexities of distance and distances in his fiction. The oriental setting of much of the action in three works, *A Pale View*, *An Artist* and *When We Were Orphans* (2000), might have permitted a different writer to settle for exercises in stable, carefully researched realism. Instead, in *A Pale View of Hills* the premises of realism are evoked in order to be challenged. Ishiguro presents a first-person narrative that seems to mediate between East and West, actually beginning long after the events they are set in motion to understand, and in a specifically English setting. But the structure and tone of the narrative swiftly entangle these places distant from each other. The text draws attention to the temporal as well as physical distance between its own multiple but discontinuous acts of retrospection and the somewhat hazy memories these acts of retrospection seemed designed to contain. To contain here means to hold in check as well as to clarify. The impulses to reveal and to suppress compete for dominance in a disturbing dynamic, a calm eye for some long remembered detail and a calmer turn of phrase often standing in for some crucial but suppressed circumstance in the story's present. A compulsion to confess competes, in tone, with a casual but devastating tendency to disguise.

But *A Pale View of Hills* also exhibits Ishiguro's tendency to provide the reader with aids to keep pace with, even to enjoy, this process. These take the form of motifs and episodes unusual enough within the body of the text to strike us as individually aberrant. But they build towards a collective significance; indicating an instability of perception on the narrator's part, and a relish for that instability on her creator's.

In *A Pale View of Hills* our narrator is Etsuko, a Japanese mother resident in England and recently widowed following the death of her English husband. Etsuko has also lost, to suicide, Keiko, her elder daughter by her first marriage to a Japanese electronics worker, Jiro. Etsuko is no artist at all. Instead, it emerges during the course of the novel – an account of a Japanese summer in Nagasaki, composed during her younger daughter Niki's visit to her home in rural England – that she is about to become the subject of a poem to be written by one of Niki's student friends. At the end of the novel, Etsuko responds to this friend's wish to know more of her life before her emigration from Japan. The friend, Niki reports, 'wanted me to bring back a photo or something...Just an old postcard, anything like that. So that she can see what everything was like.'[1] Etsuko responds with a caution, a reticence, that by this stage of the novel seems characteristically guarded:

> 'Well, Niki, I'm not so sure. It has to show what *every*thing was like, does it?'
> 'You know what I mean.'
> I laughed again. 'I'll have a look for you later.' (p. 178)

What she finds disorientates the reader. We may have expected Etsuko to find, and give, precisely what Niki's friend asks for. Earlier in the novel we have read her account of acquiring just such a postcard, of what 'everything was like' in post-war Nagasaki, on a visit she and her father-in-law Ogata-san had paid to the city's peace park and the peace memorial. But the postcard purchased then, of the memorial, a statue which 'resembled some muscular Greek god, seated with both arms outstretched', his right hand pointing 'to the sky from where the bomb had fallen; with the other arm – stretched out to his left – the figure was supposedly holding back the forces of evil' (p. 137) – both this postcard and its subject have been oddly displaced from their expected seriousness. 'Seen from a distance,' Etsuko had told us, 'the figure looked almost comical, resembling a policeman conducting traffic' (p. 138).

What Etsuko offers up instead bewilders in a rather different way. She produces a calendar with 'a view of the harbour in Nagasaki', telling Niki that 'This morning I was remembering the time we went here once, on a day-trip. Those hills over the harbour are very beautiful.' Beyond this observation about the landscape, she is reticent about what made it 'special', or representative.

> 'Oh, there was nothing special about it. I was just remembering it, that's all. Keiko was happy that day. We rode on the cable-cars.' (p. 182)

The difficulty with this quiet revelation is that it is no revelation at all. A trip to Nagasaki harbour, and beyond the hills that Etsuko stared at from the kitchen window in the cramped new concrete apartment block where she used to live in her first marriage, has indeed formed a part of her account. But it formed a much earlier part of the novel – eighty or so pages since. And it had, even in the telling, contained a number of unsettling manoeuvres that prove only their distance from the quiet surface of Etsuko's calm memories of Japan. She had made the day trip, but not, ostensibly, or actually, in Keiko's company at all. Instead, she went with her friend Sachiko and her daughter Mariko. These figures come to dominate Etsuko's memories of Japan, largely for the pressures that their relationship reveals about a sad child and a woman proving an inadequate, haunted mother, split between a restrictive Japanese post-war culture and the prospect of new freedom with an American man. As readers, we are prepared for that account of the day trip by a characteristically dense, if in the context of Ishiguro's fiction not unusually complex, sentence of introduction; this indicates the composite pressures working together throughout the scene. 'I remember I looked forward to it for days; it is, I suppose, one of the better memories I have from those times' (p. 103). Here is the pressure of memory working off, distorting, the pressure of anticipation; the qualifying construction 'it is . . .', that formal syntactical signal that what is being introduced is already controlled, is qualified by that counter-weight of enduringly qualifying doubt: 'I suppose'.

This careful, guarded framing of the episode anticipates its curious central motifs. These miniature enactments of the novel's tricks with perspectives reveal Ishiguro's concern with probing away at the perceptual foundations of the real. Crossing the harbour to Inasa, 'we sat on a bench in the forecourt of the cable-car station', waiting for the cable cars that would take them up into the hills. As they waited, Etsuko recalls:

> For some moments we sat mesmerized by the sight of the cable-cars climbing and falling; one car would go rising away into the trees, gradually turning into a small dot against the sky, while its companion came lower, growing larger, until it heaved itself to a halt at the platform. (p. 104)

As they wait for their turn to turn into that dot, to enter that distance, Etsuko next reveals a tendency to contrive such visual tricks for herself. She braves the heat to wander over to a stall selling sweets; she will, she thinks, buy candy for Mariko. Waiting in the queue, two children before her are 'arguing what to buy':

> . . . I noticed among the toys a pair of plastic binoculars. The children continued to quarrel, and I glanced back across the forecourt. Sachiko

and Mariko were still standing by the turnstiles; Sachiko seemed to be in conversation with two women.

'Can I be of service, madam?'

The children had gone. Behind the stall was a young man in a neat summer uniform.

'May I try these?' I pointed to the binoculars.

'Certainly, madam. It's just a toy, but quite effective.' (p. 104)

Notice, here, the curious failures of perspective, the disjunctions, the continuities suppressed. Some are in response to Etsuko's own rest-lessly wandering gaze, which would account for her surprise and ours, as readers, at the replacement of the reported children's voices with the stall holder's. But at least one is not, as 'these' binoculars get reduced and singularized by the stall holder as 'it . . . a toy'.

Much of the day is devoted to quarrels which break out between the two children, first over the binoculars, then over some sketches that Mariko completes at the top of the hill. The tubby boy claims, predictably, that he has a much better pair of binoculars. And though his mother praises two pictures, one of a butterfly, the other a harbour scene, that Mariko completes from memory, up on the hill – 'I think it's very commendable for a child to use her memory and imagination' – the boy claims that Mariko's sense of perspective is all wrong. 'Those ships are too big,' he said. 'If that's supposed to be a tree, then the ships would be much smaller' (pp. 114–15). But readers have already been given enough of a steer to be alert to Ishiguro's sympa-thies for Mariko and Etsuko's way with perspective. This is a scene, and a medium, in which the significant and the insignificant will be revealed, oddly and suddenly, as either containing or collapsing into each other – even the reflex one of the other. Late in the scene on the hill-top, while the boy is bent on pursuing the agile Mariko up a tree, and Sachiko and her American woman are again 'conversing in English',

The plump-faced woman turned away from the trees.

'Please don't think me impertinent,' she said, putting a hand on my arm, 'but I couldn't help noticing. Will this be your first time?'

'Yes,' I said, with a laugh. 'We're expecting it in the autumn.' (p. 118)

'It', we realize, is Keiko, who, Etsuko will tell her surviving daughter, 'was happy that day'. So what does this say about happiness? And about the motivations contained – revealed, held in check – in Etsuko's presentation of events? As the plump-faced woman goes on talking earnestly to Etsuko, the narrator is the only one to see what is happening in the tree, the boy hanging nervously well below the girl:

Although only a few centimetres off the ground, he seemed in a state of high tension. It was hard to say if she did so deliberately, but as she lowered herself, the little girl trod firmly on the boy's fingers. The boy gave a shriek, falling clumsily.

The mother turned in alarm. Sachiko and the American woman, neither of whom had seen the incident, also turned towards the fallen boy...

'She kicked me,' the boy sobbed. 'She kicked me off the tree. She tried to kill me.'

[...] 'The little girl kicked you?'

'Your son just slipped,' I interrupted quickly. 'I saw it all. He hardly fell any distance.' (p. 119)

In this scene on the hill, with the binoculars, we glimpse through the quietly distorting medium of Etsuko's prose childhood and adult passions looming and losing themselves in each other with primitive passion. Ishiguro is, of course, using those binoculars too, to contrive a brilliant, eerie moment, in a novel that proved merely the first layer in a palimpsest composed of similarly sliding perceptions and perspectives.

For exactly these techniques and complicating perspectives have, since that unnerving, quiet debut in 1982, continued to mark Ishiguro's fictions. They certainly marked his transition to his other Japanese novel, *An Artist of the Floating World*. Here, once more, the first-person narrative, a distinctive and omnipresent presentational strategy of Ishiguro's, is used both to reveal and to suppress slightly different terrain. Now the perspective is male, not female; the tone and attitudes are closer to Etsuko's militarist father-in-law than to Etsuko herself. But resonances and reversals abound disquietingly between the two works. The artist in question, Masuji Ono, is a cultured but compromised spokesman for Japanese militarism, and for a way of life and art that the post-war generation are coming to discredit. He has a daughter called, curiously, Setsuko; the negotiation of a marriage for his other daughter Noriko, entirely suppressed in the first book, here becomes the occasion for Ono's slow self-revelation. Ono reveals himself largely through a series of repetitions and reversals of perspective, staged both between the two novels and within this second text. What his narrative becomes is a gradual, artful, self-conscious but also self-haunted meditation on an art that conceals and overlays, that mixes image and text – an art that celebrates, or used to celebrate, a world of fugitive impressions all now past. He reveals both himself, that is, and the principles on which he is, as a creation, himself founded.

We see Masuji Ono, first, directing us, as if we were visitors to the city in which he lives, in August 1948, to stand on 'the little wooden

bridge still referred to around here as "The Bridge of Hesitation"'.[2]
He points out that 'you will not have to walk far before the roof of my
house becomes visible between the tops of two gingko trees'.

We only ever get a slightly more sustained view of it, and of the
damage which it has suffered in the war. For Ono and Ishiguro are
between them bent instead on revealing, through a number of displaced and often seemingly digressive observations, the power of the
turning glimpse. This power is both stronger and safer when directed
elsewhere than one's own life, but it produces a curious combination
of exaggeration and defensiveness when directed at that frail text. For
instance, we learn that, as a boy, Masuji was often excluded from his
father's reception room in their village house:

> My respect for reception rooms may well appear exaggerated, but then
> you must realize that in the house I grew up in – in Tsuruoka Village, a
> half-day's train journey from here – I was forbidden even to enter the
> reception room until the age of twelve. That room being in many senses
> the centre of the house, curiosity compelled me to construct an image
> of its interior from the occasional glimpses I managed to catch of it.
> Later in my life I was often to surprise colleagues with my ability to
> realize a scene on canvas based only on the briefest of passing glances;
> it is possible I have my father to thank for this skill, and the inadvertent
> training he gave my artist's eye during those formative years. (p. 41)

Not that Ono presents us with much of his own work. Part of it was
burnt, we later learn, in that same room, by his father; none of it is on
display in his own house, he tells his own grandson Ijiro, who gaily
and then savagely covers sheet after sheet of paper with his own
childish sketches. We learn, instead, of his views through how he
views others, his art by his commentary on others' art.

The book's second section, dated April 1949, opens with an observation whose syntax depends on a number of veiled displacements
and shifts in perspective, from participation in the memories being
shared to distanced reticence, and back again:

> On three or four evenings a week I still find myself taking that path
> down to the river and the little wooden bridge still known to some who
> lived here before the war as 'the Bridge of Hesitation'. We called it that
> because until not so long ago, crossing it would have taken you into our
> pleasure district, and conscience-troubled men – so it was said – were
> to be seen hovering there, caught between seeking an evening's enter-
> tainment and returning home to their wives. But if sometimes I am to
> be seen up on that bridge, leaning thoughtfully against the rail, it is not
> that I am hesitating. It is simply that I enjoy standing there as the sun

sets, surveying my surroundings and the changes taking place around me. (p. 99)

By this point in the novel, the degree of Ono's participation in the creation of that pleasure district, and beyond that his responsibility for its rise and fall, a progress produced by a 'new spirit of Japan', a militant patriotism whose image he has claimed to be instrumental in constructing, have become the text's central concerns. Dissatisfied with the art he and his other students were producing in the studio of one artist, he has already recalled them 'battling together against time to preserve the hard-edged reputation of the firm', while on the other hand they were 'also quite aware that the essential point about the sort of things we were commissioned to paint – geishas, cherry trees, swimming carps, temples – was that they look "Japanese" to the foreigners to whom they were shipped out' (p. 69). Ono's response insists on the coincidence, the superimposition, of such popular stereotyping and images of martial confidence. He fondly recollects, with a pride that at this point feels no need to claim possession, a wall hanging at the back of a club he had helped to renovate: 'that enormous illuminated banner suspended from the ridge-pole bearing the new name of the premises against a background of army boots marching in formation' (p. 64). He avoids mentioning its artist's name at this point. It is only towards the end of the novel, when the workings of his own 'conscience', and his attitude to his 'environment' and to 'changes going on around me' have become crystallized through a series of painful meetings with representatives of the post-war generation, that he feels the need to reveal his hand.

It is the uneasy fusion of the political with the aesthetic that preoccupies *The Unconsoled*, which seems like a departure for Ishiguro, an exercise in Kafkaesque surrealism. The narrator, Ryder, flies into a more or less contemporary central European city to give a concert, but then finds himself embroiled in bewildering responsibilities and memories. Ryder significantly never gets round to performing, though he does manage one strange rehearsal. Instead, hailed as the representative of high art, and as such as a potential saviour of the city's culture, he is forced to mix abstruse and sometimes comically exaggerated discussions of contemporary music theory with groping forays into the cultural politics of the place, all the while encountering palpably real figures and memories displaced from his own English childhood. Through these memories, and through the experiences of the local artists and others – from the staff of his hotel to a young boy who may or may not be Ryder's son – to which the narrative's mysterious logic grants him access, Ryder repeatedly confronts the power of art to console individuals and communities for losses and wounds, whether real or imagined.

The Unconsoled is a difficult book to summarize. But it does knowingly revisit and exaggerate the problems of perspective and of distance, of leitmotif and ambiguity of tone, that mark Ishiguro's earlier work. In doing so, it breaks through into a wild but unpredictable emotional hinterland of distorted echoes and resonances. The functional and the theatrical coincide. Thus Gustav, the extraordinarily hyper-dignified hotel porter in the novel, rehearses and pushes to a tragi-comic conclusion that commitment to his profession that Stevens had communicated merely through his wooden prose in *The Remains of the Day*. At one point he turns in a brilliant performance of dancing on a table top while laden down with implausibly heavy bags.

Ryder, too, comes to carry the baggage of all Ishiguro's earlier probings into questions of art's obligation and ability to evoke or to penetrate the surface of ordinary people's lives. Ryder is accorded the status of a hero in the city – 'Many people here believe you to be not only the world's finest living pianist, but perhaps the very greatest of the century,' he is told[3] – just as, we discover, two now largely discredited champions of art in the city, the cellist Christoff and the conductor Brodsky, had once been. Like them, Ryder is credited with the artist's mysterious power of resolving the city's crisis in its cultural and social identity. Like them, he unquestioningly believes in these powers: 'Look,' he says impatiently at one point, 'the fact is, people need me. I arrive in a place and more often than not find terrible problems. Deep-seated, seemingly intractable problems, and people are so grateful I've come' (p. 37).

But like them, and Ono, he is riding for an aesthetically qualified fall. Ryder's name may be designed to suggest this; so is the novel's glancing but insistent way with the music for which Ryder and Brodsky are both renowned. This music punctuates the increasingly dreamlike wanderings across the city and the countryside beyond, to which Ryder agrees in the days before his concert. Arriving at the hotel, Ryder is told of Brodsky's preparations for the concert at which they are both scheduled to perform: 'listen to him now!' the desk clerk tells him. 'Still hard at it, working things out by himself.'

> He indicated the rear of the lobby. Only then did I become aware that a piano was being played somewhere in the building, just audible above the muffled noise of the traffic outside. I raised my head and listened more closely. Someone was playing a single short phrase – it was from the second movement of Mullery's *Verticality* – over and over in a slow, preoccupied manner.(p. 4)

This passage condenses the movement of the novel, and points towards the dynamic of immersion in social affairs (that 'traffic outside') yielding to intense, repetitive introspection that Ryder and reader both experience through this work. It also identifies the emphases of the prose that carries this experience. During one exchange about the difficulty of 'the modern forms' in music, Christoff complains what he confirms: that they might be just too tough, too abstract, for most ordinary people. 'They can't distinguish a crushed cadence from a struck motif. Or a fractured time signature from a sequence of vented rests'(p. 186). There is, to be sure, a delicious play being had here with the jargon of 'modern forms' in art; and yet for much of the novel Ryder's mission seems, with Ishiguro's, to pursue this fleeting private music and the emotions that had been driving Brodsky to 'work things out by himself'. Ryder insists that this music can and should be performed, by suitably distinguished players, because such performance rises to the challenge posed to the music by misunderstanding, and helps to combat those 'failures of nerve', and other 'unattractive traits', in those who misrepresent it. These are:

> A hostility towards the introspective tone, most often characterized by the crushed cadence. A fondness for pointlessly matching fragmented passages with one another. And at the more personal level, a megalomania masquerading behind a modest and kindly manner. (p. 202)

Oddly, however, throughout the book, and especially at the concert at the novel's climax, to which Ryder himself never manages to contribute, we encounter passages which seem to reward just such a matching of these teasing fragments. What is revealed, simultaneously ironized and celebrated, is the function of these arcane, minutely interrogated forms of art; in prose which invites both assent and scepticism about the experience that its own 'crushed cadences' seem to be offering. Brodsky is now conducting Mullery's *Verticality*. He is on stage despite having been found drunk, and despite having just lost a prosthetic leg in a bizarre cycling accident on the way to the concert hall. He is using a folding ironing board as a crutch – an absurd touch that we know will nevertheless produce the performance's final collapse, its own 'crushed cadence'. And yet for all this, the forms revealed in the meantime by the old man's strangely frenetic, absurdly framed performance seem to release some genuine sense of 'mystery' from this musical landscape which surprises even Ryder.

> Brodsky took advantages of the looser form of the second movement to push into ever stranger territories, and I too – accustomed though I was

to every sort of angle on Mullery – grew fascinated. He was almost perversely ignoring the outer structure of the music – the composer's nods towards tonality and melody that decorated the surface of the work – to focus instead on the peculiar life-forms hiding just under the shell. There was a slightly sordid quality about it all, something close to exhibitionism, that suggested Brodsky was himself profoundly embarrassed by the nature of what he was uncovering, but could not resist the compulsion to go yet further. The effect was unnerving, but compelling. (p. 492)

But it is transient too. Soon, Ryder senses that Brodsky 'had taken things too far'; he notices a 'tentativeness of technique' marking the moment just before 'the music veered dangerously towards the realms of perversity' (p. 494). By the time Ryder has nursed him through the inevitable physical and emotional collapse, the audience has dispersed; Ryder knows that his own projected performance cannot now take place. It is of some comfort to him that, with the arrival of dawn, and breakfast, and a rousing speech from one of its own political leaders, the community seems to be feeling good about itself without his help. A simpler, sensory level of pleasure seems possible after all, to be shared with ordinary people. But even this is undercut by ambivalence. Slumped in the office of the woman who had helped organize this chaotic tour, 'a number of doubts had passed through my mind and suddenly I felt something inside me beginning to collapse. To conceal my discomfort, I turned away and looked out at the dawn' (p. 511). As she comforts him, he notices 'her eyes still on the distance' (pp. 512–13). It is a distance which, I suspect, even when offering its own form of consolation, Kazuo Ishiguro's strangely unsettling fiction will never be content to close.

Notes

1   Kazuo Ishiguro, *A Pale View of Hills* (London: Faber and Faber, 1982), p. 177. Subsequent page references in the text are to this edition.
2   Kazuo Ishiguro, *An Artist of the Floating World* (London: Faber and Faber, 1986), p. 7. Subsequent page references in the text are to this edition.
3   Kazuo Ishiguro, *The Unconsoled* (London: Faber and Faber, 1995), p. 11. Subsequent page references in the text are to this edition.

Primary texts

A Pale View of Hills (London: Faber and Faber, 1982)
An Artist of the Floating World (London: Faber and Faber, 1986)

The Remains of the Day (London: Faber and Faber, 1989)
The Unconsoled (London: Faber and Faber, 1995)
When We Were Orphans (London: Faber and Faber, 2000)
with Oe, Kenzaburo, 'Wave Patterns: a dialogue', *Grand Street* 10.2 (1991), 75–91.

Selected critical texts

Andrew Teverson, 'Acts of Reading in Kazuo Ishiguro's *The Remains of the Day*', *QWERTY* 9 (October 1999), 251–8
Kathleen Wall, '*The Remains of the Day* and its Challenges to Theories of Unreliable Narration', *Journal of Narrative Technique* 24.1 (1994), 18–42
Ben Winsworth, 'Communicating and Not Communicating: the True and False Self in *The Remains of the Day*', *QWERTY* 9 (October 1999), 259–66
Cynthia F. Wong, *Kazuo Ishiguro* (Tavistock: Northcote House, 2000)

15 The Fiction of Martin Amis: Patriarchy and its Discontents

James Diedrick

Soon, Father will have her all to himself . . . He will come in and kill me with his body.

Martin Amis, *Time's Arrow*

Among the many uncanny effects wrought by the reverse chronology of *Time's Arrow*, Martin Amis's 1991 novel about the Holocaust, none is more chilling than the novel's final paragraphs, where the marriage bed becomes a place of murder as the narrator's father extinguishes his son's embryonic life with his penis.[1] The fact that the contemporary novelist most often accused of misogyny has created this and so many other unforgettable representations of phallocentric power is one of the many great ironies of Amis's career, a career marked by a profoundly conflicted relationship to the patriarchy itself. It is no exaggeration to claim that every aspect of Amis's career, his early rivalry with his novelist father, his stylistic virtuosity, his satirical impulse, his devotion to the work of Vladimir Nabokov and Saul Bellow, is grounded in a profound struggle with the world of his literal and symbolic fathers. This chapter begins by exploring the autobiographical sources and literary dimensions of Amis's gender politics and then moves on to analyse the Oedipal dynamics of *The Rachel Papers* (1974), *Money: A Suicide Note* (1984), *Einstein's Monsters* (1987), and *The Information* (1995). It ends by suggesting some of the ways Amis's outlook and writing have changed in the wake of his father's death in 1995.

Given the Freudian connotations of my title, a preliminary word about method is necessary. Although my reading of Amis's fiction relies on fundamental psychoanalytic concepts, I am deeply sceptical of classical psychoanalysis, especially its phallocentrism and its tendency to isolate individuals from their social and historical milieu.[2] The work of Jacques Lacan, Michel Foucault, and Juliet Mitchell is thus more important than that of Sigmund Freud in the analysis that follows, especially Lacan's insistence that language structures the human subject, mediating all relations to the other and the real as well as defining it. Not only is 1anguage central to Amis's aesthetic, 'style is morality', he has insisted,[3] but his first-person narratives virtually dramatize the ways in which language systems and the cultural ideologies that shape them in turn shape consciousness. Consider Charles Highway's account of his initial intimacy with Rachel Noyes in *The Rachel Papers*:

> Only her little brown head was visible. I kissed that for a while, knowing from a variety of sources that this will do more for you than any occult caress. The result was satisfactory. My hands, however, were still behaving like prototype hands, marketed before certain snags had been dealt with. So when I introduced one beneath the blankets, I gave it time to warm and settle before sending it down her stomach. Panties? Panties. I threw back the top sheet, my head a whirlpool of notes, directives, memos, hints, pointers, random scribblings. (p. 158)

In addition to the performance anxiety inscribed here, Charles's manner of speech and thought radiate beyond his single consciousness. His 'prototype hands' reference, like his subsequent use of 'memos' and 'directives', and 'marketed', derives from the larger discourse of commodity capitalism. Henri Bergson's theory of comedy posits that human beings laugh at the spectacle of other humans reduced to automatons, which is one obvious source of the humour here.[4] There is something chilling about this comedy, however, since the dehumanization it captures has its source in a social and economic system. Charles's most intimate thoughts and actions are never wholly his own, shaped as they are by a cultural logic that penetrates even the unconscious. In the description above, Charles and Rachel are reduced to body parts, Charles's hands to defective products, his consciousness to an implementation plan. All of Amis's novels emphasize the degree to which cultural conditions condition character, especially the characters of males living within what Frederic Jameson has called 'the cultural logic of late capitalism'.

Approaching Amis's novels as texts that dramatize the interrelationship of language, ideology and gender offers a way of directly addressing the two most persistent charges levelled against his work:

that he has never discovered a subject equal to his stylistic virtuosity, and that he harbours a deep (if unconscious) animus towards women.[5] Whatever Amis's weaknesses in the rendering of female characters, his novels have always come to query masculinity, not to praise it. It is no accident that the first piece in *The War Against Cliché: Essays and Reviews, 1971–2000* (2001), in a section titled 'On Masculinity and Related Questions', is an hilariously scathing review of the poet Robert Bly's book *Iron John: A Book About Men*, which accuses Bly of wanting 'to establish, or re-establish, a world where men are so great that women *like* being lorded over' (p. 7). Amis concludes this review with a reminder, if any were needed, that his own evolving views of gender both derive and depart from those of his father: 'Feminists have often claimed a moral equivalence for sexual and racial prejudice. There are certain affinities; and one or two of these affinities are mildly, and paradoxically, encouraging. Sexism is like racism: we all feel such impulses. Our parents feel them more strongly than we feel them. Our children, we hope, will feel them less strongly than we feel them. People don't change or improve much, but they do evolve' (p. 9).

I   Father(s) and Son

From the first, Martin Amis's literary sensibility was shaped by his father's career, his father's waywardness, and his contact with other literary father-figures. He was born (on 25 August 1949) to the novelist Kingsley Amis just five years before *Lucky Jim* brought transatlantic fame to its author and transatlantic travel to his family. During the almost ten years he lived in South Wales, his father's friend, the poet Philip Larkin, made frequent visits to the Amis household (and served as godfather to Martin's brother Philip). When Martin was thirteen, his father abandoned his wife Hilly and his family for Elizabeth Jane Howard (whom he married in 1962).[6] From 1968 to 1971 Martin attended Exeter College at Oxford University, where his tutor was Jonathan Wordsworth, a direct descendant of the poet, William Wordsworth. Graduating with a formal first in literature, he reviewed books for the distinguished weekly, the *Observer*, where his byline appeared alongside those of Anthony Burgess, Stephen Spender, W. H. Auden, and Kingsley Amis. During the 1970s he also wrote (and edited) for the *Times Literary Supplement* and the *New Statesman*.

Combined with his remarkable verbal gifts and his early devotion to the writer's art ('from a very early age, the one thing I wanted to be was a writer, and that was long before I had any real sense of what kind of a writer my father was'),[7] these experiences and connections laid the groundwork for a rich and productive career. In 1979, having published three novels and sold one screenplay, he resigned as an editor of the *New Statesman* to write full-time, although continuing to date to publish non-fiction journalism in England and America.[8] His rapid rise to prominence made him the target of attacks in the popular press: the satirical journal *Private Eye* took to calling him 'Smarty Anus', and some attributed his early success to nepotism. Amis himself later acknowledged that his family name guaranteed that he would get at least one novel in print: 'Any London house would have published my first novel out of vulgar curiosity' (*Experience*, p. 25).

The parallels between the careers of Amis *père et fils* suggest one source of all the 'doubles' that haunt the younger Amis's fiction. Both attained formal firsts at Oxford; both won the prestigious Somerset Maugham prize for their first novels; both are known for comic fictions that satirize prevailing social conditions; both have been alternately labelled voices of their generations and pornographers. Even the significant aesthetic and political differences between the two should not obscure two larger ideological affinities: to differing degrees, bourgeois and patriarchal assumptions inform (and often diminish) all their writings.

The tensions and conflicts masked by such a summary, however, have been most influential in shaping Martin Amis's outlook and career. Indeed, the complex question of Amis's 'anxiety of influence' in relation to his father, and his father's generation, is central to an understanding of his fiction and to his particular brand of 'postmodernism'. The phrase 'anxiety of influence' derives from the writing of literary theorist Harold Bloom, who places the Oedipal struggle between literary 'fathers' and 'sons' at the symbolic centre of all relations between writers, texts and their predecessors. In Bloom's view (which, like Freud's theorizing, is unrepentantly and reductively phallocentric), a writer unconsciously perceives his most significant precursors as potentially castrating father-figures, and thus employs strategies intended to disarm them. These characteristically involve taking up the literary forms of the precursors and revising, recasting and displacing them.[9]

In Martin Amis's case, of course, this symbolic conflict assumes a literal dimension. It even comes complete with primal scenes of rivalry in which texts substitute for other extensions of the male self, their concealment and display all part of the filial competition. Kingsley Amis reported that when his son was still living at home,

'whenever I walked into a room where he was writing, he immediately put his hand over the paper in the typewriter'.[10] This account
implies a father's interest turned back by a son's suspicion, but the
son's way of representing the situation shifts the emphasis radically:
'My father, I think, aided by a natural indolence, didn't really take
much notice of my early efforts to write until I plonked the proof of
my first novel on his desk.'[11]

The sounds of psychic warfare can be heard in these descriptions,
and the skirmishes continued even after Kingsley's death in 1995. In
the *Kingsley Amis Letters*, published in 2000, Kingsley resentfully
reports to Philip Larkin (in 1979) that Martin is spending a year in
America as a tax exile because of his considerable earnings. He
follows this statement with this economical fragment: 'Little shit.'[12]
It is worth noting that Kingsley Amis fired most of the public shots in
this lengthy conflict. Complaining to one interviewer of a 'terrible
compulsive *vividness* in his style', he complained that he couldn't
finish his son's novels. 'It goes back to one of Martin's heroes –
Nabokov. I lay it all at his door – that constant demonstrating of his
command of English.'[13] Julian Barnes has called Kingsley Amis's
public attacks 'scandalous', adding 'it's a hurt that will never go
away'.[14] One result of this disapproval has been a search for substitute literary 'fathers'. Beyond their considerable intrinsic merit, the
pieces Martin Amis has written on such writers as J. G. Ballard, Saul
Bellow, Norman Mailer, Vladimir Nabokov, V. S. Pritchett, Philip
Roth, John Updike and Angus Wilson reveal a writer obsessed with
(male) precursors. With a few exceptions (Jane Austen, Iris Murdoch,
Fay Weldon, Joan Didion) Amis's considerable body of literary criticism concerns male writers. In terms of Bloom's theory, the proximity
and intensity of his father's influence have led him to seek a series of
father substitutes, whose influence he can acknowledge without filial
conflict.

The aesthetic allegiances of most of these writers are clearly opposed to those of Kingsley Amis, whose fiction conforms to the mode
of 'classic' (as opposed to modernist) realism as David Lodge defines
it. In this sense, the rivalry of the two novelists has implications that
reach far beyond individual psychology. 'Classic realism, with its
concern for coherence and causality in narrative structure, for the
autonomy of the individual self in the presentation of character, for a
readable homogeneity and urbanity of style, is equated with liberal
humanism, common sense and the presentation of bourgeois culture
as a kind of norm.'[15] Among other things, classic realism strives for
verisimilitude, the artfully constructed illusion of reality, achieved in
part by a balanced, unified combination of authorial speech and

represented speech. The author seeks to fade into the background as the reader is immersed in narrative detail.

By contrast, postmodern texts typically call attention to their status as fictions, as verbal artifices. The language of such texts calls attention to itself, and the author or an author surrogate is often present as a character in the narrative. Consider the opening of Martin Amis's *Money* (1984): 'As my cab pulled off FDR Drive, somewhere in the early Hundreds, a low-slung Tomahawk full of black guys came sharking out of lane and sloped in fast right across our bows. We banked, and hit a deep welt or grapple-ridge in the road: to the sound of a rifle shot the cab roof ducked down and smacked me on the core of my head. I really didn't need that, I tell you, with my head and face and back and heart hurting a lot all the time anyway, and still drunk and crazed and ghosted from the plane' (p. 7). Amis's language becomes a kind of character here (and in his other novels) – self-conscious, virtuosic, vying for attention with the plot and the other characters. Amis transforms nouns into verbs ('sharking', 'ghosted'), invents a new model of car ('Tomahawk'), and describes its encounter with a cab in a way that evokes America's violent past and present ('across our bows', 'Tomahawk', 'rifle shot'). The inanimate world itself comes vividly to life in Amis's reifying prose: the very roof of the cab is called into action during America's assault on the narrator (who has just arrived in New York from London). This opening paragraph also represents an implicit assault on the fictional practice of Kingsley Amis.

These formal and stylistic differences between father and son reflect significant ideological oppositions as well. Explaining why Kingsley Amis, once a member of the Communist party, became so outspokenly conservative in the 1970s and 1980s, Martin Amis positions himself far to his father's left:

> The thing about him and his contemporaries – these former Angry Young Men, all of whom tend to be right-wing now – is that while they weren't born into poverty, they didn't have much money. Then they made some money, and they wanted to hang on to it. And they lived through a time when the left was very aggressive and when union power made life unpleasant. There are many aspects of the left that I find unappealing, but what I am never going to be is right-wing in my heart. Before I was even the slightest bit politicized, it was always the poor I looked at. That seemed to be the basic fact about society – that there are poor people, the plagued, the unadvantaged. And that is somewhere near the root of what I write about.[16]

Amis reminds the reader here that history has played a part along with Oedipus in determining the differences between his outlook and his father's. Seeking a source for the fury that fuels much of Amis's cruellest comedy, for the large number of orphans and absent, absent-minded, or downright abusive fathers that populate his fiction, the reader might consider the unresolved anger he feels towards a father who never extended full approval to his son's writing. And this would reveal part of the truth. But historical developments have also influenced his outlook, and they continue to inform his work.

II   Totem and Taboo: *The Rachel Papers*

Charles Highway's preternatural self-consciousness as he composes his one and only narrative (*The Rachel Papers*) is analogous to Martin Amis's own as he wrote his first novel in the shadow of his famous novelist father.[17] How to put oneself on the map, place enough distance between oneself and one's most significant precursor? Charles's conflicts with his father, his provisional reconciliation with him, and his success in fashioning his own narrative voice suggest some answers. Significantly, and despite the novel's focus on his pursuit of Rachel Noyes, Charles's relationship with his father forms the emotional centre of the novel. This is made clear in the first chapter, when Charles notes that it is 'strange' that 'although my father is probably the most fully documented character in my files, he doesn't merit a note-pad to himself, let alone a folder' (p. 8). He is present even (especially) in his formal absence, in other words. Like Kingsley Amis, Gordon Highway has spent some time lecturing at Cambridge, and he is also in the writing profession (he is the editor of a prestigious business journal). Charles subsequently informs the reader that he was thirteen when he discovered that his father had a mistress; that he has begun a 'Letter to My Father' (Kafka wrote a famous letter of the same title), documenting his grievances against him; that his father is becoming a political reactionary – sources of familial tension familiar to Martin Amis, in other words. Charles's 'rebellion' takes complex forms, including equal measures of moral disapproval, presumed superiority and exaggerated difference on the one hand, and parody which sometimes turns into outright imitation on the other.

This is not unlike the relationship between *The Rachel Papers* and *Lucky Jim*. Both are first novels by gifted comic writers, and bear many family resemblances, from mastery of dialect and dialogue to delight in comic incongruities. But *The Rachel Papers* is clearly, defiantly different from *Lucky Jim*. At first glance, the earlier novel might seem the more subversive: Jim Dixon is lower middle-class, anti-establishment and anti-pretension, a would-be radical lecturer in history who calls into question certain class-bound pieties of British intellectual culture. It was written when its author was a member of the Communist party, and it won him the label 'Angry Young Man', applied to a handful of British writers who railed against the status quo in the 1950s. Charles, by contrast, seldom meets a pretence he doesn't want to adopt, and he is all too eager to join the (intellectual) establishment. The genuinely radical student movements of the 1960s have merely provided him with another pose to assume (that of the drug-savvy hippie) when the right social opportunity arises.

Yet for all his supposed subversiveness, Jim Dixon never questions the patriarchal, materialistic, even homophobic assumptions that inform his sensibility. Nor does his author. *Lucky Jim* conforms to the traditional comic paradigm (definitively outlined by Northrop Frye in his *Anatomy of Criticism*) in which a well-suited couple, attracted to one another but separated by various social barriers, overcome all obstacles to their union and end up in each other's arms. *Lucky Jim* is more comic romance than comic satire: Jim Dixon is treated with authorial sympathy throughout. His favourite maxim is 'nice things are nicer than nasty ones'[18] and the nicest thing in his world is the conventionally attractive Christine Callaghan. He is rewarded with her at the novel's end, along with a job working in her uncle's office.

Charles Highway has clearly read *Lucky Jim*, because midway through the novel he explicitly rejects Jim Dixon's maxim and replaces it with his own down-and-dirty comic aesthetic: 'surely, nice things are dull, and nasty things are funny. The nastier a thing is, the funnier it gets' (p. 87). Expressed so crudely, this may sound like little more than an adolescent male's malicious sense of humour – and Martin Amis's way of tweaking his father. But it is in fact consistent with Charles's earlier aesthetic announcement: 'I had begun to explore the literary grotesque, in particular the writings of Charles Dickens and Franz Kafka, to find a world full of bizarre surfaces and sneaky tensions with which I was always trying to invest my life' (p. 62). The fictions of Dickens and Kafka often combine cruelty and laughter, of course. So do the satires of Jonathan Swift. What is emerging here is Martin Amis's own literary manifesto, one part exorcism of his father's precedent, one part declaration that his own province is the comedy of the grotesque. While *The Rachel Papers* can be read as a (male) adolescent coming of age story, it can just as easily be taken as a *parody* of the genre, not to mention a parody of the kind of comic romance Kingsley Amis produced in *Lucky Jim*.

III 'Taking over the family pub': *Money*

Money: A Suicide Note (1984) represents a high-water mark in Amis's career, building on the strengths of his earlier novels but far exceeding them in scope, depth of characterization, and organic unity.[19] It also stands as one of the indispensable novels of and about its decade. Its eponymous protagonist and narrator John Self, a producer of intentionally crass television commercials, is a one-man carnival of junk taste and junk morality, who has relinquished most of his free will by embracing commodity culture in all its pornographic excess. The fact that most of Self's pleasures are solitary and onanistic reinforces the sense that he is a prisoner of his own addictions. Amis's public statements about Self sanction this reading: 'he has no resistance, because he has no sustenance, no structure'.[20] The spectacle of Self's 'private culture', by turns appalling, savagely hilarious, touching, and contemptible, represents a *tour de force* of satiric representation. Self's narrative, written in 1981, is like an extended hangover following the orgy of the 'Me' decade, as well as a prescient commentary on unabashed entrepreneurial greed that characterized Anglo-America in the 1980s.

At the same time, *Money* constitutes a serio-comic commentary on the relationship between literal and figurative fathers and sons. Self's own (largely unconscious) Oedipal preoccupations even spill over into his advertisements. Although he has always turned a deaf ear to literature itself, he appreciates its commercial currency. One of his best-known TV commercials was an ad 'for a new kind of flash-friable pork-and-egg bap or roll or hero called a Hamlette. We used some theatre and shot the whole thing on stage. There was the actor, dressed in black, with his skull and globe, being henpecked by that mad chick he's got in trouble. When suddenly a big bimbo wearing cool pants and bra strolls on, carrying a tray with two steaming Hamlettes on it. She gives him the wink – and Bob's your uncle. All my commercials featured a big bim in cool pants and bra. It was sort of my trademark' (p. 70). This is the first of many Shakespearean allusions in *Money*, all of which echo with serio-comic relevance to Self's situation. Like Hamlet's relationship to his stepfather, Self has a troubled, violent relationship with his father. In fact, Barry Self has recently taken out a contract on him, Laertes' employment of Rosencrantz and Guildenstern echoed in a pulp fiction mode. In addition, the revised script for the autobiographical film Self is attempting to make echoes the Oedipal dynamics of *Hamlet*: the son kills his father hoping to protect his mother. Beyond these plot parallels, Self's existential soliloquies, which often seem slightly crazed, crackle with a skewed insight that recalls Hamlet's own high-pitched dramatic monologues.

Throughout the novel, Self's personal life and moral squalor are refracted through the filter of his film project. The project itself is one of Self's many attempts to double himself in the novel. The most extensive of these doublings involves Self's relationship with the character Martin Amis, hired to rewrite the film script (which is also of course Self's story). All four of Amis's previous novels have contained self-reflexive elements; in *Money* he makes this explicit. He does so with a blunt honesty worthy of Self's narrative voice. He creates a protagonist named Self whose life parallels his own to a surprising degree; he embodies himself in the novel as a recurring character; and he doubles this character through the American Martina Twain ('twain' literally means two). He even has Self voice the theme: 'people are doubling also, dividing, splitting' (p. 64). The reader is virtually invited to consider Self, Amis and Martina as aspects of a single consciousness.

The presence of Amis's persona in *Money* has generated much criticism and critical misunderstanding. John Bayley has called the strategy 'tiresome' and an 'artistic trick'.[21] Laura L. Doan, following the lead of earlier critics, claims its sole function is to maintain a satirical distance between Self and his creator: 'Amis takes exceptional care to ensure that the narrator-protagonist, so disgusting in his values and lifestyle, cannot be mistaken for the writer by literally putting himself into the text. Martin Amis, the character, is a suave, intelligent, highly educated, comfortably middle-class writer who quite obviously finds Self, and what he represents, unsavoury.'[22] Yet Self and the Amis character are secret sharers more than antagonists. Many of Self's experiences are in fact those of his creator viewed through the distorting lens of an unlikely double. During their first conversation, Self tells Amis he heard that his father is also a writer, adding, 'Bet that made it easier.' Amis's sarcastic reply is: 'Oh, sure. It's just like taking over the family pub' (p. 85). This of course alludes to the difficulties inherent in the actual Amis's struggle to establish his own identity and voice in the shadow of his famous literary father, mirrored in Self's relationship to his father (who owns a pub named after the ultimate literary father: The Shakespeare). Barry Self's inter-actions with his son in the novel range from cavalier to callous to cruel. Their most emotional encounter is a grotesque parody of famil-ial intimacy, in which Self is invited to share the joy of his step-mother's appearance in a pornographic magazine (this occurs after Self's father has sent him a bill for his upbringing). Under ordinary circumstances, Self might have assumed that he would eventually inherit his father's pub. By the end of the novel, however, his father has denied paternity and disowned him. In this case, life did not imitate art: *Money* earned Martin Amis a degree of critical and popular acclaim that eclipsed the fame of his father.

IV   Figuring Fathers: From *Einstein's Monsters* to *The Information*

Published after the births of Amis's two sons, *Einstein's Monsters* is a collection of science fiction stories (and an essay) on the nuclear threat that hums with patriarchal anxiety.[23] It coincides with and embodies a decisive shift of sensibility and public persona on the part of its author. As John Lanchester has written, 'the stories in *Einstein's Monsters* are haunted, as is the introduction, by the imagined deaths of children. Often, this death (these deaths) is where the real imaginative weight of the story seems to be placed: the emotional balance is, as in "The Immortals," slightly off-centre.'[24] The murder of Bujak's granddaughter, the suicide of Dan, the near-deaths of Hattie and Andromeda, the death of all children, all future children, and childhood itself in 'The Immortals', these are the central stories of *Einstein's Monsters*.

But the central argument, captured in Amis's polemical introduction 'Thinkability', is with his father. In the debate about nuclear weapons, Amis claims, 'we are all arguing with our fathers' (p. 13). 'They got it hugely wrong' he claims, adding 'perhaps there will be no hope until they are gone' (p. 13). This critique would seem to call for radical rethinking, but aside from his rhetorically extremist tone, Amis's ideas in 'Thinkability' are surprisingly traditional. Amis presumptuously assumes that he will become the reluctant executioner of his wife and children if London suffers a nuclear attack. Writing in an apartment a mile from his home, he imagines what will happen if he survives the first blasts. 'I shall be obliged (and it's the last thing I'll feel like doing) to retrace that long mile home, through the firestorm, the remains of the thousand-mile-an-hour winds, the warped atoms, the grovelling dead. Then – God willing, if I still have the strength, and, of course, if they are still alive – I must find my wife and children and I must kill them' (p. 4). After recovering from the shock of this vision of violent patriarchal authoritarianism, many readers will be moved to ask: shouldn't his wife have some say in this?

A similar patriarchal anxiety pervades *The Information*, written while Amis was in the midst of a painful divorce from his first wife. Of all the author surrogates in this most autobiographical of Amis's novels, Richard's son Marco is the most haunting. Like the rival authors Richard Tull and Gwyn Barry, Marco and his brother Marius were born one day apart (they are twins, but emerged on either side of a midnight divide). From the first Marco is identified with Richard and with novelists generally. His learning disability, for instance, is suspiciously similar to the 'stupefaction by first principles' Richard says all artists are reduced to: 'If you told Marco why the chicken crossed the road, Marco would ask you what the chicken did next. Where did it go? What was its name? Was it a boy or a girl? Did it have a husband – and, perhaps, a brood of chicks? How Many?' (p. 70). As this passage also suggests, Marco loves narrative. He often cries inconsolably in the night when he awakes in the middle of a dream, because 'he never wanted any story to end' (p. 225). Marco bears the emotional brunt of his father's anger at Gwyn's successes and is more sensitive than his brother to the widening rift between his parents. 'All this had made Marco more vigilant, more sensibly watchful, than a six-year-old would normally have need or reason to be' (p. 220). He is losing his innocence, in other words, while developing the mental habits of a novelist.

Amis's rendering of Richard's relationship to his sons is realistically compelling in ways that most of the rest of the novel is not. Compared with the portrayal of Richard's marriage to Gina, for instance, which relies on crude gender stereotypes, it is a marvel of engaging realism. Despite Amis's emphasis on Richard's self-pitying self-absorption, he can't help investing his absurd alter-ego with his own parental love, care and anxiety (*The Information* is dedicated to Amis's two sons and his murdered cousin). The scenes of Richard at home and at play with his sons are the most touching in the novel, vividly capturing the boys' distinct speech patterns, their skewed insights, their love of toys and television, parks and zoos. What's more, Marco and Marius inspire their father's most lyrical language: 'Richard contemplated his sons, their motive bodies reluctantly arrested in sleep, and reef-knotted to their bedware, and he thought, as an artist might: but the young sleep in another country, at once very dangerous and out of harm's way, perennially humid with innocuous libido' (p. 11).

Amis wrote *The Information* during a national uproar in Britain over two brutal child murders.[25] Anxiety about children and childhood itself is central to the novel's plot and painful ending. The depth of Richard's downward spiral ('it seemed to him that all the time he used to spend writing he now spent dying' (p. 446)) is marked by a reversal of parent–child roles. As his miseries mount, he begins telling Marco and Marius 'Twins stories'. He told these stories 'while the boys lay on their backs, clutching their boyhoods, with drugged eyes'. The last story he is reported telling his sons is one 'in which they bravely rescued their daddy – rescued him, and then tended to his wounds' (p. 475). Richard had earlier thought of the day when his wife Gina would ask him to leave, and 'the children will have to come to love us separately' (p. 448); now as he leaves the sleeping boys, they 'looked like figures on a battlefield, arrested, abandoned' (p. 476).

V After Kingsley

Five years after *The Information* was published, readers learned that Martin Amis had experienced such parent-child role reversals first-hand:

> When I was a child I would sometimes hear my father in the night – his horrified gasps, steadily climbing in pitch and power. My mother would lead him to my room. The light came on. My parents approached and sat. I was asked to talk about my day, school, the games I had played. He listened feebly but lovingly, admiringly, his mouth open and tremulous, as if contemplating a smile. In the morning I talked to my mother and she was very straight. 'It calms him down because he knows he can't be frightened in front of you.' 'Frightened of what'? 'He dreams he is leaving his body.' It made me feel important – up late, holding the floor, curing a grown man: my father. It bonded us.[26]

Both the intimate knowledge of masculine compulsion that informs Amis's novels and the paternal anxieties that marked them from the late 1980s through the late 1990s can be traced to primal scenes such as this one. And his willingness to confront and write about them in the wake of his father's death has led to a shift of emphasis and tone in his fiction. Since 1995, Amis has descended from the lofty perch of the satirist, and his fiction has become more soulful as a result. It has also broken free from what I would call the 'prison of patriarchy', that produced so many false notes in *Einstein's Monsters* and such vacillations of tone in *The Information*. The neo-*noir* novella *Night Train* (1997) is the best-known example of this shift, featuring a female protagonist-narrator, whose emotional pain continually leaks through the cracked shell of her hard-boiled prose. But I want to end this chapter by considering the story 'What Happened to Me on My Holiday', published originally in the *New Yorker* in 1997 and reprinted as the final story in *Heavy Water*. Like *Experience*, it inhabits an intimate domestic sphere where relationships are messy, primal and indispensable, where patriarchal authority gives way to existential bewilderment and wonder, where verbal virtuosity is married to emotional vulnerability.

The resonance of this intensely autobiographical tale is deepened by means of a linguistic device that may alienate many readers. 'What Happened to Me on My Holiday' is narrated by an eleven-year-old boy, a fictional version of Amis's son Louis, whose summer holiday on Cape Cod is shattered by the death of his step-brother (Elias Fawcett, the son of Amis's first wife Antonia Philips, who died at seventeen). Amis represents Louis's response to this loss by means of a highly stylized phonetic speech (part American slang, part British phrasings), that is the verbal equivalent of the estrangement and stupefaction death leaves in its wake: 'I dell id thiz way – in zargazdig Ameriganese – begaz I don'd wand id do be glear: do be all grizb and glear. There is thiz zdrange resizdanze. There is thiz zdrange resizdanze.' Reading the story aloud, the reader feels Louis's grief as a physical presence – thick, hard, unyielding.

Wordsworth's 'still, sad music of humanity' sounds throughout 'What Happened to Me on My Holiday', preserved in a meticulously crafted fugue-like structure in which the voices of other characters and nature itself contribute to the theme of loss. Louis plays with his younger brother and his four-year-old cousin, catching crabs and minnows, understanding all too well (as his cousin does not) that a dead sprat will never return to life. He sees in the natural world intimations of the mortality he is now struggling to understand, observing the 'gloud of grey' he sees rising from a pond on the day he hears that his step-brother has died back in London: 'nat mizd [mist], nat vag [fog], but the grey haze of ziddies and of zdreeds [cities and streets]... and nothing was glear.' Elias now inhabits the distant land of memory, where Louis imagines him hurrying about 'with bags and bundles...jaggeds and hads [jackets and hats], gayadig, vestive [chaotic, festive]'. Meanwhile, another of Louis's cousins goes into the pool without his arm-floats and has to be rescued. At the end of his holiday, in the car on the way to the airport, the word 'grey' returns again, like a haunting melody – the melody of mortality: 'Greynezz is zeebing ubwards vram the band. And nothing is glear. And then zuddenly the grey brighdens, giving you a deeb thrab in the middle of your zgull.' Now all the notes of the story converge, all the deaths come together, and Louis thinks of his brother: 'one vine day you gan loob ub vram your billow and zee no brother in the dwin bed. You go around the houze, bud your brother is nowhere do be vound' (p. 185).

Like most of Martin Amis's fiction, 'What Happened to Me on My Holiday' exhibits what Kingsley Amis would have called a 'terrible compulsive *vividness*' of style. But in this case, style is feeling as well as morality, the morality of deep imaginative sympathy. Martin Amis's artistic quest is nowhere near its end, but this remarkable story, like *Experience*, demonstrates that he has emerged from the fires of filial conflict with his emotional compass intact.

Notes

1 Following the logic of the reverse chronology, the narrator's life is extinguished when the sperm separates from the egg that created him and re-enters his father's body. Since the narrator represents the residual conscience of Odilo Overdorben, a fictionalized representative of the notorious Nazi doctors, the entire novel can be read as an indictment of the sins of the fathers on a world-historical scale.

2 On phallocentrism, see Heather Jones, 'Phallocentrism', in *An Encyclopedia of Contemporary Literary Criticism*, ed. Irene R. Makaryk (Toronto: University of Toronto Press, 1993), pp. 606–7, and Jane Gallop, *The Daughter's Seduction: Feminism and Psychoanalysis* (Ithaca: Cornell UP, 1982).

3 Review of *The Adventures of Augie March*, *Atlantic*, October 1995, v. 276, 114–127; reprinted in *The War Against Cliché*, 447–469, 467; 126.

4 Henri Bergson, *Laughter: An Essay on the Meaning of the Comic*, trans. Cloudesley Brereton and Fred Rothwell (London: Macmillan, 1911).

5 John Fuller's comment on Amis's treatment of Ursula and Jan in *Success* is a typical example of those critics who confuse Amis's first-person narrators with their creators: 'In keeping with their creator's misogyny, they're discarded once they've served their purpose' ('Yob Action', *Village Voice*, 1 December 1987, 66).

6 This marriage ended in 1980. Both marriages, and both break-ups, are recounted, movingly, in *Experience*. See especially pp. 28, 105–6, 142–7, 214–16.

7 Charles Michener, 'Britain's Brat of Letters', *Esquire*, January 1987, 111.

8 Work has appeared in the *Observer, Guardian, London Review of Books, New York Times Book Review, Atlantic, Esquire, Vanity Fair, New Yorker*, and *Talk*.

9 See especially *The Anxiety of Influence: Theory of Poetry* and *A Map of Misreading*.

10 Michener, 'Britain's Brat...', 110.

11 'Martin Amis', *1990 Current Biography Yearbook*, ed. Charles Moritz (New York: H. W. Wilson, 1990), p. 20.

12 'Did I tell you that Martin is spending a year abroad as a TAX EXILE? Last year he earned £38,000. Little shit. 29, he is. Little shit.' (letter to Philip Larkin, 10 May 1979, *Letters of Kingsley Amis*, ed. Zachary Leader (New York: Harper Collins, 2000), p. 216.

13 Michener, 'Britain's Brat...', 110.

14 Ibid.

15 David Lodge, *After Bakhtin: Essays on Fiction and Criticism* (London: Routledge, 1990), p. 26.
16 Susan Morrison, 'The Wit and Fury of Martin Amis', *Rolling Stone*, 17 May 1990, 102.
17 Amis acknowledged the autobiographical matrix of *The Rachel Papers* in an interview with Charles Michener. See 'Britain's Brat...', 110.
18 Kingsley Amis, *Lucky Jim* (London: Penguin, 1975), p. 140.
19 Amis says, in effect, that *Money* represented an artistic breakthrough in his career: 'I dispensed with form and trusted entirely to voice, and this released a great deal of energy.' *Independent* 25 April 2001, 7.
20 Patrick McGrath, 'Interview with Martin Amis', *Bomb* 18, Winter 1987, 27; reprinted in *Bomb Interviews*, ed. Betsy Sussler (San Francisco: City Lights Books, 1992), p. 181.
21 John Bayley, 'Being Two Is Half the Fun', *London Review of Books*, 4 July 1985, 13.
22 Laura L. Doan "'Sexy Greedy' *Is* the Late Eighties: Power Systems in Amis's *Money* and Churchill's *Serious Money*"; The Minnesota Review, Spring-Fall 1990, 73.
23 Louis was born in 1985, Jacob in 1987.
24 John Lanchester, 'As a Returning Lord', *London Review of Books*, 9, 7 May 1987, 12.
25 See Martin Amis, 'Blown Away', *New Yorker*, 30 May 1994, 49.
26 Martin Amis, *Experience: A Memoir* (London: Jonathan Cape, 2000), p. 180.

Primary texts

The Rachel Papers (London: Jonathan Cape, 1973)
Money (London: Jonathan Cape, 1984)
Einstein's Monsters (London: Jonathan Cape, 1987)
Time's Arrow (London: Jonathan Cape, 1991)
The Information (London: Flamingo, 1995)
'What Happened To Me on Holiday', *Heavy Water and Other Stories* (London: Jonathan Cape, 1998)
Experience: A Memoir (London: Jonathan Cape, 2000)
The War Against Cliché: Essays and Reviews, 1971–2000 (London: Jonathan Cape, 2001)
'Sex in America', *Talk* (February 2001), 99–103, 133–5

Selected critical texts

Harold Bloom, *The Anxiety of Influence: Theory of Poetry.* (London: Oxford University Press, 1975)

—— *A Map of Misreading* (New York: Oxford University Press, 1975)

Michel Foucault, *The History of Sexuality, I: An Introduction* (Harmondsworth: Penguin, 1981)

Frederic Jameson, *Postmodernism, Or, the Cultural Logic of Late Capitalism* (Durham: Duke University Press, 1992)

Juliet Mitchell, *Psychoanalysis and Feminism: Freud, Reich, Laing, and Women* (New York: Vintage Books, 1975)

Juliet Mitchell and Jacqueline Rose, *Feminine Sexuality: Jacques Lacan and the Ecole Freudienne* (London: Macmillan, 1982)

James Wood, 'Martin Amis: The English Imprisonment', *The Broken Estate: Essays on Literature and Belief* (London: Jonathan Cape, 1999), pp. 186–99.

Glossary of Major Theoretical Sources

Richard J. Lane and Philip Tew

Theodor Wiesengrund Adorno (1903–69) was born in Frankfurt, son of a Jewish wine merchant, taking his mother's maiden name, Adorno, during the first World War. Educated at the University of Frankfurt (Germany), he studied musical composition in Vienna before returning to Frankfurt to teach. Sacked by the Nazis in 1933, he spent three unhappy years at Oxford University before moving to Los Angeles in 1938. During his exile in the United States, Adorno collaborated with Max Horkheimer to produce *Dialectic of the Enlightenment* (1947; trans. 1972), which argued that the Enlightenment concept of reason had led not only to the domination of nature, but also to that of man. After the end of the Second World War, the Frankfurt Institute for Social Research reopened in 1949 with Adorno and Horkheimer as joint directors. In 1972, Adorno wrote *Negative Dialectics*, a systematic and conscious rejection of all theories. In Adorno's view, systems of knowledge must concede that their picture of things and events will always be incomplete, while philosophy should assimilate apparently non-commonsense elements. In 'The Actuality of Philosophy' he states that theory 'must learn to renounce the question of totality'. This involved the conceptualizing of non-identity – of unrealized forms of subjectivity – by means of avant-garde art and aesthetics. In *Sociology of Music*, he famously rejected as banal and vulgar the 'crudely simple' music of the 'screeching retinue of Elvis Presley'. Nevertheless, despite his rejection of youth culture, Adorno's critique was popular with the student revolutionaries of the 1960s, although Adorno himself maintained he was not a Marxist and rejected such violent applications of his system of thought. In due course, many commentators came to think that

Adorno privileged culture over practical politics. His theoretical study *Aesthetic Theory* (1970) is still highly influential.

Georges Bataille (1897–1962), a Roman Catholic who later lost his faith, worked as a medievalist librarian at the École des Chartes. For a brief period, he was a member of the Surrealist group (although Breton would eventually call him an 'excremental philosopher' in the *Second Surrealist Manifesto*). Bataille's writing was obsessed with extreme states of mind and physical existence, as part of a philosophical project to counter the Hegelian dialectic and the massive influence of Hegel's *Phenomenology of Spirit* (1807) upon French intellectual thought in general. He wrote constantly about transgressive sexuality, waste and scatological subjects, as well as pursuing anthropological research into non-European practices such as the potlatch (a ritual system of gift-giving and expenditure, which can be read as contradistinctive to capitalist accumulation and exchange). Bataille's original writings in French were published in a number of reviews and journals, the most important being *Documents*, founded in 1929. The first chapter of his later destroyed novel, *W.C.*, is published in English as *Blue of Noon* (trans. 1978).

Walter Benjamin (1892–1940) was initially well-known in English translation for a single essay, 'The Work of Art in the Age of Mechanical Reproduction', which explores the historical shift from the production of original and unique works of art to that of mass production and reproduction (the world of copies). Benjamin now has a large following in the West within the fields of cultural and literary studies. Other key works are 'On Some Motifs in Baudelaire' and 'The Storyteller', and longer works include *The Origin of German Tragic Drama* (trans. 1977). More recent translations of his work include a multi-volume selection of his writings and the monumental *Arcades Project* (1999), a miscellaneous, fragmentary archival text, composed mainly of quotations and commentary. It could be argued that Benjamin's work falls into two main phases: an early interest in German-Judaic Messianic theological concepts and writings is succeeded by an interest in dialectical materialism and Marxist theory. Benjamin developed further the notion of montage exploited by the Surrealists in relation to a materialist philosophy, in works such as *One Way Street* and the *Arcades Project*. Towards the end of his life, he was supported financially and intellectually by a number of friends, including the Frankfurt School philosopher **Theodor Adorno** and the important Judaic scholar Gershom Scholem.

The French philosopher **Henri Bergson** (1859–1941) won the Nobel Prize for literature and was highly influential around the turn of the century. The son of a Jewish musician and an Englishwoman, he attended the Lycée Condorcet and studied philosophy at the École Normale Supérieure. He was a secondary school teacher from 1881 until 1898, then professor at the École Normale Supérieure and finally chair of philosophy at the Collège de France. His most influential works include *Matter and Memory* (1896; trans. 1911), which concerns perception and the relation between human consciousness and the mechanisms of the brain, and *Creative Evolution* (1907; trans. 1911) which conceives of human existence and the mind as products of the *élan vital*, or vital force, responsible for all organic evolution. Bergson questioned and extended narrow Victorian concepts of rationality, insisting that matter is subject to the operations of time in a condition that is endlessly provisional.

Homi K. Bhabha   (dates unknown) is a post-colonial theorist who is most well-known for a collection of highly theoretical essays called *The Location of Culture* (1994). Bhabha utilizes poststructuralist, postmodernist and psychoanalytic theory to address the complexities of post-colonial cultures and representation in aesthetics. For example, in his essay 'Signs Taken for Wonders', Bhabha looks at the way in which the appearance of the 'English book' within colonial cultures reveals hybridity not just of the indigenous peoples subjugated by colonialism, but also within the subjectivities of those doing the colonizing, whose identities are constituted via the Other. In other words, at the moment of forcing diverse peoples to conform to one standard, the standard itself is constituted through the act of trauma (of colonialism) and the recognition of difference. While Bhabha both adopts and produces complex theory, this is not simply an act of Western intellectual activity or appropriation, since one of his key precursors is **Frantz Fanon**, who in turn drew upon high-level theory and philosophy to write from an indigenous perspective some of the most important books for colonized peoples throughout the world.

Pierre Bourdieu   (1930–2002) was professor of sociology at the Collège de France. Early in his career he shifted from more empirical sociological studies to the application of sociological method to education, culture and art. He argued that people as 'agents' work within overlapping fields of activity, often doing so conventionally in bourgeois society because they are drawn to opt for actions in 'position-takings' that are allowable by what he describes as society's 'space of possibles'. He sees literature as part of a field of cultural production, where time and energy are invested for monetary return or symbolic value in 'the field of the present', which is a site of struggle. He is concerned with what makes art necessary and with its generative principles. His work includes *Language and Symbolic Power* (1991) *The Rules of Art* (1992), and *The Field of Cultural Production* (1993).

Michel de Certeau (1925–86) was a French historian, critic and theorist of the human sciences. He trained in theology, history, comparative religions, psychoanalysis and anthropology. He was Director of Studies of the École des Hautes Études en Sciences Sociales in Paris and shortly before his death also a visiting professor at the University of California at Los Angeles. He wrote much about the relationship of psychoanalysis and the humanities, drawing especially on the works of Freud and Lacan. De Certeau saw discourses as constituting forms of social interaction and practice. His analyses examine social space and subjectivity as the product of a language shared by the human community. *The Practice of Everyday Life* (1974) contends that cultural activity is produced by the specific practices of powerless people who are considered non-producers by traditional analysts. He stresses that fragmentary tactics are the main tool of both writer and theorist. His important works included *The Practice of Everyday Life* (1974) and a collection of essays, *Heterologies: Discourse on the Other* (1986).

Guy Debord (1931–94) was a key French member of the *Internationale Situationniste* or Situationist International, an anarchic grouping which emerged in the 1950s and 1960s, and whose slogans included 'Never Work!' It was the vehicle of leftists who rejected both capitalism and Stalinist Russian-style Marxism. The Situationists used art as a statement to convey both revolutionary ideas and to reveal the underlying contradictions of Western life. They also championed other schemes such as Unitary urbanism, attempting to make disparate parts of Paris communicate with each other. After frequent expulsions, the core of Parisian Situationists consisted of Debord, Raoul Vaneigem and Michele Bernstein. Debord's writing was derived from the strategy of using the situations of his own life to make works of art intended to subvert the existing state of society. His most notable writing is found in his substantial contribution to the twelve collective issues of *Internationale Situationniste*, and in his book, *Society of the Spectacle* (1967). Debord committed suicide a few weeks before his sixty-third birthday.

Jacques Derrida   (1930–   ) is widely acknowledged as the catalyst for the intellectual movement now known as 'deconstruction', although it must be admitted that the process of deconstruction is also to be found in the earlier work of German philosopher Martin Heidegger (famous for his monumental, yet incomplete work *Being and Time* [1927]). Deconstructive criticism is often represented as a generalized process of critique that bears little relation to the philosophical questions and issues explored by Jacques Derrida himself. When Derrida looks at 'undecidables', or concepts that are both foundational (for a system of thought or argument) and unstable (allowing the system to be subtly taken apart), the process of examination does not result in the total reverse or overthrow of the system concerned. Deconstruction examines many of the myths and illusions of philosophical thinking, to show that there are subtle interrelationships between metaphysics (philosophy) and aesthetics (art, literature, music and so on), even where the former would paradoxically deny, or exclude, the latter. Derrida has been accused of saying many ludicrous things, such as 'there is no meaning', whereas a close study of his texts reveals a preoccupation with the complete opposite: with the play of meaning, difference and contradiction, generating further meaning or signification. Key early texts include *Of Grammatology* (1976), *Writing and Difference* (1978) and *Margins of Philosophy* (1982); the most comprehensive theoretical accounts of Derrida's entire project are Rodolphe Gasché's *The Tain of the Mirror: Derrida and the Philosophy of Reflection* (1986) and Geoffrey Bennington's *Jacques Derrida* (1993).

Frantz Fanon   (1925–61) has been very influential in the field of post-colonial studies (e.g., impacting on the work of **Homi Bhabha**). He was born in Martinique, eventually studying medicine in France before moving to Algeria, where he became involved in the Algerian uprising. Fanon developed an interest in psychiatry, but came to the conclusion that notions of 'normality' and mental health were heavily influenced by the politics and practices of colonialism; in other words, mental health was not just an individual issue, but one that entire societies must contend with. Fanon attempted to recover and explain the underlying subjection and violence upon which colonialism was based, demonstrating that apparent oppressors were tied into such contexts in a limiting fashion. Colonial subjects were encouraged to despise their original identities and identify with these new socio-political conditions. Key texts include *Black Skin, White Masks* (trans. 1967; republished with an introduction by Bhabha in 1986) and *The Wretched of the Earth* (trans. 1965). Fanon draws extensively upon thinkers from a wide range of backgrounds, including Sartrean existentialism and the works of Hegel.

Michel Foucault (1926–84) was a French thinker and writer who contributed to the development of Structuralism, yet who was nevertheless infamous for denying that he was a Structuralist. He came to prominence with the publication of three key texts: *The Order of Things* (trans. 1970), *Madness and Civilization: A History of Insanity in the Age of Reason* (trans. 1973) and *Discipline and Punish: The Birth of the Prison* (trans. 1977). Foucault's work involves studying marginal or marginalized subjects and bringing them centre-stage in relation to their significance for language, philosophy and society. His theoretical approach is set out in complex detail in his book *The Archaeology of Knowledge* (trans. 1974), and a later, much larger project was begun in his unfinished work, *History of Sexuality* (three volumes, trans. 1978, 1986 and 1988). Overall, Foucault's work is a rejection of Jean-Paul Sartre's existentialism, and it indicates a shift in French thought towards the analysis of discourse, language and sign-systems.

Sigmund Freud (1856–1939) was born in Freiburg (now in the Czech Republic) and is credited by many as the creator of psychoanalysis. Freud studied under the famous neurologist Jean-Martin Charcot (1825–93) in Paris; he practised for many years in Vienna, but as a Jew moved to London after Hitler's invasion of Austria. He collaborated with Josef Breuer (1842–1925) in writing *Studies in Hysteria* (1895), and in the therapeutic uses of hypnosis, but later adopted a method of free association with his patients, as demonstrated within his subsequent case studies. His idea was that the unconscious was subject to a process he called 'repression', whereby the causes of mental conditions become buried. He believed that no experience was ever finally eliminated from the unconscious, and placed great importance on the emergence of sexuality in childhood. He used free association on dreams, verbal errors ('parapraxes'), and on the reactions of the patient to the therapist (a process known as 'transference'). This ensemble of methods recovered the repressed pathogenic material. His chief concepts have become known universally and have entered the language as the *id, ego* and *superego*, the *Oedipus complex, projection*, the *death wish*, the *Freudian slip, penis envy*, and *phallic symbolism*. His works include *The Interpretation of Dreams* (1899) and *Totem and Taboo* (1913). Freud used literary examples himself, although often dealing with characters as if they were real, an ongoing underlying problem in much psychological criticism.

György (Georg) Lukács   (1885–1971) was a Hungarian, born in Budapest; the son of a wealthy Jewish banker, he studied philosophy and law at the universities of Berlin and Heidelberg. Following Hitler's rise to power in 1933, Lukács went to Moscow to join the Institute of Philosophy, returning to Hungary in 1945 to be appointed Professor of Aesthetics at the University of Budapest. His most important work is *History and Class Consciousness* (1923; trans. 971), which compared the philosophies of Hegel and the young Marx, but he disowned it after condemnation by Soviet authorities. Two influential works were *The Theory of the Novel* (1916; trans. 1971) and *The Historical Novel* (1955; trans. 1962). Lukács preferred dialectics to materialism in literary analysis and saw historical forces as the dynamic motivation for art. Central to his theories were concepts such as alienation (negating individual self-determination and desire through social structures and stereotypes) and reification (giving a concrete status to a hypothetical construct). In essence, Lukács saw literature as reflecting material conditions in a class-based society.

Early in his career, **Jean-François Lyotard** (b.1924) was a member of the *Socialisme ou barbarie* group, but is now most famous for his 1979 publication, *The Postmodern Condition: A Report on Knowledge*, where he analyses the shift within postmodernity from an emphasis on truth-content to one on performativity. For Lyotard, defining features of the postmodern era include the centrality of modes of knowledge and language-systems (such as computing and cybernetics), but particularly the functioning of such systems in terms of the criterion of performativity or efficiency. The postmodern prizing of usefulness is seen as a counter-Enlightenment notion of how, and what, society values. Controversially, Lyotard stresses the ways in which knowledge, and especially scientific knowledge, is ideologically embedded within narrative. Commentators on Lyotard stress how *The Postmodern Condition* is in fact the least representative of his works taken as a whole; key earlier texts include *Discours, figure* (1971), *Economie libidinale* (1974) and *Le Différend* (1984).

Maurice Merleau-Ponty   (1907–61) was a French phenomenologist and founder with Jean-Paul Sartre of existential philosophy. Merleau-Ponty describes the world as a field of experience in which human consciousness derives from primary access to the world through the body. In *Phenomenology of Perception* (1945) he conceived of the body neither as subject nor object, but as an ambiguous mode of existence through which all knowledge and understanding is channelled. Unlike Sartre, he emphasized intersubjectivity, the under-lying shared basis of human understanding and life. He was chiefly concerned with the raw or primordial contact with the world that systems of knowledge and theories of experience obscured. He saw language and perception as 'enigmatic', and being as a kind of 'invisi-bility' compared to the world's visibility. His further work included *Sense and Non-Sense* (1948; trans. 1964), *The Adventures of the Dialectic* (1955; trans. 1973), and the unfinished *The Visible and the Invisible* (1968).

Vladimir Propp (1895–1970) was a Russian Formalist, whose most influential work was his *Morphology of the Folktale* (1968; originally published in Russian in 1928 as *Morfologija skazki*). Propp's major contribution to Formalism concerned his argument about narrative 'functions' (character 'roles'), whereby every narrative will contain permutations of a set number (31) of functions, usually in a set order of plot development. Propp's analysis provided a structural account of the elements in such tales. His work has been used by many critics as the basis from which to recover archetypal characters and situations in textual and filmic narratives.

The early texts of **Edward Said** (b.1935), including *Beginnings, Inten-tion and Method* (1975) and *The World, the Text and the Critic* (1984), were well received, but the attention paid to them was dwarfed by the reception of his monumental post-colonial study called *Orientalism* (1978). While the latter book has come under a recent, sustained critique (especially from historians in the field of colonial/post-colonial studies), it continues to be highly influential in the world of post-colonial literary criticism. Said's basic premise is that the discursive field known as 'orientalism' is an ideologically generated construction of the Other, based upon the intersection of power and knowledge; as such, Said is heavily influenced by the work of **Michel Foucault**. A more recent post-colonial book, *Culture and Imperialism* (1993), has also made a major impact upon the field of post-colonial studies.

Ludwig Wittgenstein (1889–1951) is recognized as one of the most famous language philosophers of the twentieth century, largely be-cause of two central works: the *Tractatus Logico-Philosophicus* (trans. 1922) and *The Philosophical Investigations* (trans. 1953). Wittgenstein's *Tractatus* is broadly speaking a work of modernism, whereby all philosophical problems are analysed and contained via his system of logic. The book opens famously with the statement 'The world is all that is the case' and continues to break down this world into logical components via a series of propositions. The concluding quotation is equally famous: 'What we cannot speak about we must pass over in silence.' However, Wittgenstein's remarkable text is re-examined, reworked and in many respects rejected by his later work, most forcefully in the methodological approach of the *Philosophical Investigations*, where instead of abstracting meaning from the world by means of logic, Wittgenstein places meaning firmly in the world itself, in speech acts and language-games: the actual uses of meaning in a particular moment. Virtually all of Wittgenstein's later philosophy, sometimes called a philosophy of language, takes such an approach.

Index